"Dear Josie"

"Dear Josie"

Witnessing the Hopes and Failures of Democratic Education

WITHDRAWN

Joseph Featherstone
Liza Featherstone
Caitlin Featherstone

FOREWORD BY HERBERT KOHL

Teachers College
Columbia University
New York and London

19.95

Published by Teachers College Press, 1234 Amsterdam Avenue, New York, NY 10027

The following articles originally appeared in *The New Republic:* "Schools for Children," August 15, 1967; "Teaching Children to Think," September 9, 1967; "Ghetto Classroom," December 1967; "Experiments in Learning," December 14, 1968; "Teaching Teacher: A Utopian Bulletin," December 1968; "Ocean Hill Is Alive, and, Well . . .", March 29, 1969; "The Problem Is More Than Schools," August 30, 1969; "The Real Thing in Teaching," September 27, 1969; "Open Schools II: Tempering a Fad," September 25, 1971; "Busing the Powerless," January 1976; "John Dewey Reconsidered," 1972.

"My Good War" first appeared in *Ploughshares*, Summer 1994, Vol. 20/Nos. 2&3.

"Rousseau and Modernity," reprinted by permission of *Daedalus, Journal of the American Academy of Arts and Sciences*, from the issue entitled "Rousseau for Our Time," Summer 1978, Vol. 107, No. 3.

"Family Matters", *Harvard Educational Review*, Volume 49:1 (February 1979), pp. 20–52. Copyright © 1979 by the President and Fellows of Harvard College. All rights reserved. Reprinted with permission.

"Democratic Vistas," originally appeared in *The Nation*, June 19, 1995.

"To Touch More Life" was originally published in *The New York Times Book Review*, June 8, 1980.

"Foreword to 'The Living Classroom,'" originally published in *The Living Classroom: Writing, Reading and Beyond*, Washington, D.C.: National Association for the Education of Young Children, 1997.

"Letter to a Young Teacher," originally appeared in *To Become a Teacher*, ed. William Ayers, New York: Teachers College Press, 1995.

Library of Congress Cataloging-in-Publication Data

Featherstone, Joseph.
  Dear Josie : witnessing the hopes and failures of democratic education / Joseph Featherstone, Liza Featherstone, Caitlin Featherstone ; foreword by Herbert Kohl.
    p. cm.
  Includes bibliographical references and index.
  ISBN 0-8077-4327-5 (cloth : alk. paper) — ISBN 0-8077-4326-7 (pbk. : alk. paper)
    1. Education—Aims and objectives—United States. 2. Democracy—Study and teaching—United States. I. Title: Witnessing the hopes and failures of democratic education. II. Featherstone, Liza. III. Featherstone, Caitlin. IV. Title.
  LA217.2 .F43 2003
  370.11'5—dc21   2002038430

ISBN 0-8077-4326-7 (paper)
ISBN 0-8077-4327-5 (cloth)

Printed on acid-free paper

Manufactured in the United States of America

10   09   08   07   06   05   04   03   8   7   6   5   4   3   2   1

For the late David Hawkins,
and for Frances Hawkins,
"A child said, what is the grass?"

Contents

Foreword

Jay Featherstone:
An Educator's Educator

Herbert Kohl

EDUCATIONAL THINKING is a form of moral activity. The stance one takes toward children, how they learn, and how they should be absorbed into the adult world is a reflection of one's fundamental values. If there is a science of education, it is a peculiarly value-driven science, balancing careful observation of specific children's behaviors and responses with speculation on how children might behave in different learning contexts. It is tempered by ideas about what children should value and how they should behave. All of this is complicated by the capacity of children to make choices and resist adult formulations of who they are or must become.

Thinking about children and education often involves clarification of one's own childhood and reflection on the choices one made or didn't make. It also involves major leaps of imagination into unfamiliar cultural, economic, geographic, and spiritual milieus; of imagining childhoods one never lived. Finally it requires a respectful humility toward the wonder of childhood and a skeptical regard of adult dreams for children's future lives. Joseph Featherstone is an educational thinker of substance.

Jay, as his friends call him, is not a public rhetorician, but he speaks carefully and well and always bears listening. His steady lifelong commitment to the values of progressive education makes him an educator's educator. It is always useful and refreshing to encounter his latest thinking on the relationship of learning to issues of growth and social justice.

The Romantic poet William Wordsworth wrote (1802/1888):

The child is father of the man;
And I could wish my days to be
Bound each to each by natural piety.

I thought of this poem recently when Jay and I talked about the formation of his ideas and values, after I reread some of the essays in this volume where he talks about balancing Wordsworth's personal romanticism with John Dewey's social romanticism. For Jay, if the child is father of the man, the family, community, and historical time of the child provide the material to work on as she or he grows and begins to determine how to integrate or reject the given and become a unique, acting, responsible adult.

Jay was born in Wilkes-Barre, Pennsylvania, in 1940 and grew up in a Catholic family whose structure was shaped by World War II. The women were home; the younger men were off fighting; and the older men were left behind. His grandfather, the only man left at home, was a supervisor in the railroad yards. He describes his grandfather this way:

> A skeptic about many things, he was a believer in the rights of ordinary working people. The world, he always said, constantly screws up the one workable idea—that everyone should help each other, and be kind.

Jay is a staunch progressive who knows that people screw up all the time and this sense of fallibility, conflict, and contradiction has drawn me to his work over the years. He is a skeptical Romantic and his take on the history of progressive education and ideas about what schools should be is tempered by this playful and persistent commitment to his grandfather's philosophy.

This collection begins with a personal story of childhood guilt and a budding sense of justice that to me is a faded black and white photo of a transforming moment in his life. The ship that has transported his family to Japan is moored at some gray ship dock in Japan. Jay, the young boy of 6 sees his first Japanese person, a man who is wearing "the ruins of a Japanese army uniform." The man, who had one missing leg, was collecting cigarette butts. Jay decided to act; he recalls, "I went down below where everyone else was still asleep and fished quietly in my parents' dresser for cigarettes, and took a full unopened carton up to the deck and threw it down on the pier." The old man picked up the cigarettes and then looked up to Jay and gave him "a formal military salute of thanks."

Jay did not have an imperial response. Even as a young child he "began to sense from that moment that, whatever the intricate balance of sin and virtue surrounding the incomprehensible, monstrous fact of the war, something had messed with my mind, and filled it with lies and hatred and fear."

I have learned over the years to distrust people with missions that override their humanity—their personal, intimate sense that small things matter. And of course that is why Jay's story about that pack of cigarettes is so important.

Pennsylvania coal country and Japan are the silent backdrops for his writings on how to make classrooms serve democratic goals. They are also the explicit themes of the marvelous poetry he is currently writing.

I didn't know any of this when I first met Jay. He seemed like a sophisticated Harvard professor to me; he had also reviewed my first education book, *36 Children*, for *The New Republic*, where he was an editor. That review brought attention to the book and, more important, the pedagogical and political issues it raised. It was clear that everyone at Harvard School of Education respected his intelligence, his commitment to children, and his capacity to take a measured and yet quite radical approach to educational change. What I discovered as we got to know each other was an unshakable commitment to social and economic justice and a properly skeptical approach to quick fixes and easy solutions.

The writings in this book reflect Jay's quest for democratic pedagogy and his discoveries of places where people are trying to make democracy happen in the classroom. He looks for good education everywhere and often finds it before many of us are aware of it. He reflects on tradition and grapples with new modes of thought. Over the years he has written about children and how their thinking works, about his respect for young life, and about his vision of a world in which all children will be honored and privileged. The writings in this book reflect these ideals in ways that remain fresh and are of continuing value for all of us who still honor education's potential to foster social and economic justice. These lines from one of Jay's recent poems (2000) reflect the spirit and toughness of his mind, its combination of intellectual rigor and earthy, gritty love of children and learning:

> *I have tried to be kind like marshgrass*
> *Accepting both the salt and the fresh,*
> *Hoping for one crystal of wisdom left on the skin.*

Acknowledgments

T HE IDEA FOR THIS BOOK came from Herb Kohl—who himself has done so much over the long haul to promote democratic education ambitious for children's minds. Thanks also to Carole Saltz, my editor, and to Catherine Bernard at Teachers College Press.

Other debts need to be summarized, or they would take up too much space. Thanks to the late Perry Miller of Harvard for convincing me that ideas matter, and that the romance of democracy remains a live option—and for pointing to education as a window on the deepest dilemmas and aspirations of American culture. Thanks to the late Richard Titmuss of the London School of Economics, for making the link between democracy and decent social services. Huge thanks to Gilbert Harrison, a great editor of the *New Republic*, for his vision, and for spoiling me shamelessly as a young journalist. Thanks to the Harvard history department for unwittingly warning me away from a career in conventional academics.

To the late David Riesman, for showing how university education could be collegial, passionate, and participatory. To the late Tony Kallet, Marjorie Martus, Maurice Kogan, and a host of teachers and school heads for help in exploring British schools—and to David and Rosemary Armington. To the teachers' groups and the principals' group I've been part of, who have shown me how important conversation is for creating and sustaining a craft of practice. Thanks to Vito Perrone and the members of the North Dakota Study Group for their fellowship and advice over the years. To David Cohen, who found me a berth first at Harvard and then at Michigan State, for friendship and the example over the years of his intelligence applied to the issues of education. Thanks to my colleagues at Harvard for friendship and advice—Sara Lawrence-Lightfoot, Courtney Cazden, Eleanor Duckworth. To the students of the Commonwealth School for the standing ovation. To Ted Sizer and Deborah Meier for the power of ideas and the example of shrewd idealism applied to the problems and politics of daily practice. To Judy Lanier, of Michigan State, for being that incredible rarity, a visionary dean in the field of teacher education. Gratitude and affection for my MSU colleagues on Team One, and especially to my students over the years in TE-301, who have gone from child study to salting the schools they now teach in with new energy and imagination.

Thanks to my son Jody, who taught us so much without words from his wheelchair; to my youngest daughter, Miranda, for keeping her aging parents interesting by refusing to put up with long discussions of teacher education; to my wife Helen, also of MSU, who has shared in every step of all this, more often leading the way; to my two older daughters, Caitlin, a teacher, and Liza, a journalist, for doing such a splendid job of gathering and editing this collection, and for providing that most satisfying of educational experiences, work in the best company.

Joseph Featherstone

Introduction

THE WRITINGS ON EDUCATION in this volume cover far more than the nine lifetimes granted me if I were a cat. Some are selections from my days as a young journalist and editor of the *New Republic*. They include portions of a famous series of articles on British primary schools that played a role in educational reform in that legendary time we now call "the sixties." Others cover school wars in New York and Boston, in the 1970s, another far-off country. I believe they still add to our understanding of the nation's most durable and tragic dilemmas, the shadows cast over classrooms by race and class in an increasingly unequal republic. Other essays include portraits of teachers and classrooms. Still others reflect my own work as a historian and activist interested in the place of childhood and arrangements for kids in our culture. (Sadly, I omit the *New Republic* article with my favorite title: "Kentucky-fried Children.") The historical pieces offer corrections to our bad national habit of living in what I call the United States of Amnesia. Recent pieces focus on good practice and good ideas. The book ends with a letter to a young teacher getting ready for her first classroom.

Together, these essays chronicle the vicissitudes of the idea of democratic education over a turbulent period of more than 30 years. They offer, in portions that each reader will measure out separately, heartbreak as well as hope.

None were written for insiders, experts, or academics. All aim for clear prose that can do justice to the intricate and even mysterious nature of teaching and learning, or such tangled topics as school desegregation. I have struggled over the years to conjure up that necessary, possibly mythical, character, Virginia Woolf's "common reader." Education is a vitally important, rich, and lively topic—perhaps the most important of all for any democracy—surely it deserves sustained coverage and conversation it rarely receives.

Not only are the ends and means of education in dispute in each generation, but anything you say that matches any classroom reality is bound to be complicated and messy. This is why most truths about teaching require more than one sentence to utter. And why recurring simplicities like the reading wars pitting "phonics" against "whole language," or even "traditional" versus "progressive" education, ought to be sternly rationed.

F. Scott Fitzgerald once wrote that the mark of an educated mind is the capacity to hold two contradictory ideas at the same time. Such educated minds are always in need as the terrible American pendulum of educational fashion sweeps mindlessly back and forth.

As a young journalist with some experience working with teachers, I brought some of these ideas to the early writing. I developed them more as time went on and my wife and I became the parents of four wonderful children, one of them severely disabled. As a parent of four incredibly different kids, I felt all the more strongly that we need an education system where teachers are supported in efforts to strike individual balances of rigor and humanity—so kids of all kinds can grow to their full height. The pieces on child-rearing and families included in this volume should insist even more vehemently than they do on the need for a vision of education as the ongoing creation of communities of grown-ups and kids, in which the young can apprentice for adult life through conversation and informal learning as well as formal lessons. These essays argue that progress in education on a large scale will probably not happen without parallel democratic gains in the rest of society—in child care, adequate preschools, full funding for Head Start, medical care for all families, adequate housing, full employment, voting and political and campaign finance reform, human rights, and other vital steps toward a less radically unequal society. With a sense of the true intertwined complexity of the nation's educational and social agenda, a slogan like "Leave No Child Behind" can be our inspiration; without it, or restricted to education alone, the slogan can become a slick politician's joke on all the rest of us.

The frightful parable of the wild 60s, told by conservatives, matches a legend of the heroic 60s liberals and radicals tell their grandchildren. Both are exaggerations. Even as I lived them, I felt I had to write about those times as a profoundly mixed bag. Selected versions of some 60s debates remain contemporary in our consciousness. In education, at least, one reason is that many at that time challenged what the historian David Tyack (1974) has called the One Best System, the organized school bureaucracies, professions and routines and methods codified and standardized somewhere between the 1880s and World War I. For better and for worse, since the 60s, many, many successive mutinies against the One Best System have taken place.

I identify passionately with one strand of revolt against the One Best System in the name of two intertwined ideas, democracy and children's minds. I believe—all these pieces reflect this belief—that a good education helps all children, but especially poor kids, to make themselves intellectually at home in the world. Good teaching is a matter of finding ways for all kids to use their minds well.

I'm especially proud of the portraits of teaching and teachers, and the reviews of books by teachers. Apart from classics—like the sketches the 19th-century Russian novelist, Leo Tolstoy, wrote describing his own efforts to teach peasant children—the genre of teachers' writing was new to a general public in the late 60s; I wanted to give space in the *New Republic* to life in classrooms—to present teachers' voices and the sound of children in the pages of a journal of opinion based a few blocks from the White House and the Capitol. I am also very proud of the pieces promoting children's writing. The least heralded of the curriculum reforms of the 60s and 70s was the spread of this, the most neglected of the 3 Rs across the elementary and secondary curriculum. Too many kids are still not asked to write in schools, but writing has become much more common across the curriculum in the last 30 years. More children are doing more varied writing in our schools today than at any time in the past about which we tend to be so nostalgic. Herb Kohl and the other teachers who made writing central to learning deserve a statue or at least a plaque in the nation's Capitol; some of the essays in this book are at least the beginning of a tribute to them.

The piece included here on Deborah Meier's work may be taken as a representative of some of today's best promise. Her past efforts in New York City (public) high schools and her current practice at the Mission Hill (public) elementary school in Boston are small beacons of sanity, worth keeping in mind as the present education season runs its course. Her work also reminds us that we can have both careful assessment and an emphasis on school community and local decision-making at the grass roots. We must, however, stop the current trends that are transforming tests from the medical equivalent of physical exams into the equivalent of autopsies.

The pages in this volume about Meier's work and that of other teachers like Elwyn Richardson and Vivian Paley and Herb Kohl—and many other testimonies over the years and around the world—show that classrooms can and should be ambitious for the minds of children of color, immigrants, the poor, and the working class. Democratic teaching has happened in the past, is happening in some places today, and can happen on a far greater scale tomorrow.

In the United States of Gridlock, our current school debates pitting "conservatives" against "progressives" have become as stylized and ritualized as Japanese Kabuki plays. They might look different if the debaters were willing to think more broadly about the place of child-rearing generally and new space for children's minds and young imaginations in the culture and in families, in other settings, in sports and the arts and after-school programs, as well as in schools. We might attach less importance to narrow disputes over styles of pedagogy, about which pedagogues and parents and reformers may and will surely differ until the Second Coming. Yes, of course, phonics. Yes, of course, the Great Books and diagnostic skills for teachers, too. But—yes, of course, reading not only as a set of small splintered skills, but as a complex intellectual achievement—the making of culture itself, fed by the hungry, complex thinking children can do when they can respond to worthwhile texts under the guidance of a good teacher. Here is where the lack of passion and imagination really takes its toll. Here is where schools and parents might take a leaf from those excellent master teachers of ambitious literacy, Oprah Winfrey and Harry Potter.

Conservatives, liberals, and radicals might form a coalition on one other commonly neglected point: the importance of good teacher education. On this, a staunch conservative like Diane Ravitch and an old (small d) democrat like myself can agree: Neither intellectual progressivism nor any conservative ideal of sound teaching is likely to take root in the public schools without a teaching staff of well-educated people. I say this with particular feeling; my colleagues and I have been working on a decent version of school-based teacher education at Michigan State University, where I run one of the teams in a huge teacher education program. This is a many-sided enterprise—I'll close with one small example relevant to this volume and its themes. I teach a course in which incoming juniors in our 3-year program tutor and study a real child for 15 weeks. Among many other readings and projects involving children's literature, and much else, these apprentice teachers have to spend time with the kid, and learn how to talk to a child; they learn (not a natural skill) how to pay careful attention to thinking, how to elicit it, and how to create and look for domains where the kid has ideas—the secret gardens and treehouses that nearly every child inhabits, but which classroom teachers often miss. The results are deeply satisfying and instructive.

Vivian Paley, with her precise thinking about young children's thinking and curriculum in literacy, her kids' stories, and her sense of the daily drama of classroom life, becomes a hero. For many of our students, I hope, a fascination with kids is a passport to lifelong pleasure. They may over time begin to understand why Paley insists that Jane Austen is a sovereign guide to life in classrooms. And intellectual pleasure for teachers, as well as children, is, dear Puritans, a big message of my sermon. Teachers need a way to keep renewing what children start with, the sense of wonder Aristotle pointed to as the beginning of all philosophy—they need a practical way to keep alive the romance of teaching.

The very last essay in this collection is a letter to a young teacher I call Josie, after W. E. B. Du Bois's wonderful, tragic student in *The Souls of Black Folk*. Du Bois painted a picture of himself as a young teacher in a rural African-American school—teaching, but being taught, in turn. Du Bois's sense of this kind of exchange lies at the heart of his book—and of this one. His Josie died young, never fulfilling her dream of an education. She stands for all the young lives our system is still wasting. My Josie stands for a new generation of young teachers who can help make a better country and a better world.

This final essay hints at some of the reasons I remain an optimist in the long run. Because of my teaching at MSU, I know firsthand that young teachers like Josie are in the wings, ready to add a fresh chapter to what Abraham Lincoln called the unfinished work of democracy.

Josie and her young colleagues won't have to follow my prescriptions for democratic, progressive teaching in order to make me happy. They will find their own way, working together (I hope) in more solidarity than today's isolated classroom teachers. But I believe that the ideas about teaching and children in this volume help point young teachers and parents toward a vision of classrooms more suited to a world in which adults and kids share thoughts that matter together, and in which education makes room for—and even celebrates—individual children and their difference.

Such a stance sounds soft and sentimental in the current hard-bitten educational climate, but its underlying realism points to the necessary communal complexity of all good schools—places where the moral, intellectual, esthetic, and academic are intertwined. My friends Louisa Cruz-Acosta and Sid Massey, who teach at River East in New York City, one of the many small progressive public schools that are the jewels of the New York system, have told us how teachers and kids at the school dealt with the aftermath of the terrorist attack on 9/11. River East is a school where kids and teachers and parents are used to talking together about things that matter, so that, although 9/11 was not in the curriculum, the capacity to make sense of the horror together was. Contrast such a school with some of the other schools in the city where children and teachers never really talk—where thoughtful conversation is not the mark and goal of a community of learning. Keep River East in mind, Josie. Keep it in mind, American parents. Work to make your school a place where the basics include not only reading and writing but the mutual learning that permits a community of grown-ups and kids to face something unspeakable together. Such a school is not only a good preparation for life, but life itself.

Joseph Featherstone

PART I

Childhood

W E PLACE THESE works first because they provide a framework for the later pieces more directly connected to schools
and classrooms. Understanding whom Featherstone sees
when he looks at the children in classrooms and what he wants them to
learn, we are ready to see progressive education through the eyes of a
practitioner and advocate.

In his work as a historian, Featherstone has spanned intellectual
and cultural history as well as the history of education. In the writings
collected in this section, he explored ideas about childhood. As an
educator, Featherstone drew his ideas from John Dewey and the romantics as well as educators in this country and in Britain building on
traditions of progressive education and developing classrooms
in which learning could be a serious and joyful enterprise.

At the heart of this work is an awareness of children and families—
where they stand historically and socially and what the institutions that
touch them reflect about a society and its educators. This section includes excerpts from several long essays that Featherstone wrote in the
1970s and 1980s. "Family Matters," published at the end of the 1970s in
the *Harvard Educational Review*, takes broad issues—what is changing
about the way we think about families—who is in them, what they
need—and asks what this shift (or imaginary shift) in the way we raise
children tells us about our lives. "Rousseau and Modernity" explores
what education can tell us about modernity but also outlines how we
might take a page from the utopians and struggle toward a complex
picture of human nature and of childhood and the institutions that care
for and shape children and families. "An American Education" rounds
out this this lens into childhood, exploring adolesence, or what an
education that turns a child into an adult might look like. Written for
his high school students at The Commonwealth School, a small private

school where Featherstone was principal, the essay describes just what it is that the school is trying to give students. He uses Mark Twain's account of learning to pilot on the Mississippi River to trace a vision of the development of educated Americans in an imperfect time. We begin with a recollection of his own childhood in which Featherstone conveys a sense of what is important to him for children and in education—a sense of battles worth fighting and alliances worth struggling after.

My Good War

THE OTHER DAY I was wondering how to make onion soup, and my mind served up the bowl I had in Seattle just before we shipped out to Yokohama—my first onion soup, with a slice of toasted french bread and some melted Gruyere cheese. This was the end of 1946. I was 6½, and the restaurant in Seattle was dark and warm, as well as fancy. We were heading for Japan in the morning, where my father had a job as a civilian lawyer with the U.S. Occupation. The good soup took my mind off the strangeness of having a father I did not recognize—he had been in the Pacific during the war—and the misery of leaving Wilkes-Barre, Pennsylvania, and the grandfather and aunt I loved.

The group moving across the country into chosen exile included my mother and my older brother, and a brand-new baby sister. Crossing the Pacific in winter was bad. There was a typhoon, and we were seasick. Worse for me was the fact that the Pacific had just been a war zone. Our gray navy ship was still equipped with guns. I dreaded confronting the Japanese, whom I had thought about and dreamed of every day in a sheltered and lucky childhood rocked by rumors of war.

When the men went off to fight, many families regrouped, like us, into a kind of commune. Ours was a commune of women and children, except for an occasional male cousin home from the merchant marines—and my grandfather. Papa combined a railroad man's cap with an elegant cigarette holder, like FDR's. He was lovely to pets and children, assuring us that pine trees heal, and telling us to always speak well to our cat, Colors. A skeptic about many things, he was a believer in the rights of ordinary working people. The world, he always said, constantly screws up the one workable idea—that everyone should help each other, and be kind.

I noticed that he found kindness toward other grown-ups a difficult spiritual discipline. He could be a hard man to those who worked under him at the railroad yards, and to those at home at 481 South Franklin St. He was not a tyrant in the family commune—all the patriarchs were off, in uniform—more of a dissident, really, a rebel from established ways. I helped him in his long campaign to permit the cat to have her kittens in the linen closet—the first of many good losing causes for me, though another routine defeat for him. When my mother in exasperation gave our heroic cat away—Colors could leap to the garage roof in one jump, and had all the neighborhood dogs cowed—Papa roamed the city and found her, bringing her home on his back in triumph. The cat and my mother glared at each other, enemies.

It was tough for my mother to do business with the likes of Papa and the family commune all the time. The setup gave my brother and me odd-angled, but roomy, tribal space in which to grow with our dogs and adventures. I went off to kindergarten and came home the first afternoon insisting that I had been fired. My Aunt Mary let me stay home for the rest of the year, the sort of ruling you were not likely to get from a parent. We were part of a safe and cozy neighborhood on the Susquehanna River that knew Bing Crosby was a Catholic, too. Everyone understood that the country lost something big when FDR died.

The war was an invisible version of the terrible Susquehanna floods, soaking our lives. It formed a vast pressure system in our heads. There were the missing men, of course, constant presences, though in fact all of our family's hostages came home safe—they had what people called a good war. Each day my grandfather showed me the progress of the various fronts in the maps in the four newspapers he pored through. Even before I could read I always checked the newsstand on the square to see if the headlines were in big Bodoni type, which meant war news, maybe casualties, perhaps with the names of neighbors on the list.

Every Saturday morning, my brother and I walked uptown to see movie matinees, which always included newsreels of combat along with the serials like *Terry and the Pirates*. I don't know if you have ever looked at World War II–era comic books—people collect and sell them now—but the dark, overpainted, claustrophobic colors can still take me back. The Japanese soldiers were inked bright yellow in fierce dark panels, and they had fangs for teeth and they wore glasses with lenses thicker than the bottoms of Coke bottles, magnifying their terrible insect eyes, and they killed babies and tortured women and said stuff like "Aieee, ten thousand purple demons!" when the brave American soldiers overran their jungle foxholes. My father had been near them in New Guinea, where he caught malaria, and I supposed they had been trying to kill him—he once wrote of someone finding a Japanese sniper and wiping him out of a cave with a flamethrower. Now here I was going away to live with beings little better than murderous bugs.

There was something else, which I never told a soul at the time. My thoughts were on making my first communion, and learning to confess my sins. The one sin I could not bear to tell anyone, even Aunt Mary, was a sin inadequately dealt with in the questions and answers in our blue Baltimore

Catechism, which seemed to dwell on puzzling offenses involving sex, or else disobedience toward rightful authority. In a time and place awash in the Catholic homily, no nun or priest or text ever gave us a single piece of advice about how to stay intact in the face of war. "Offer it up," they said of suffering. What did this mean? My big problem was that I sometimes had to be or pretend to be—I wasn't clear on the difference—a Jap or a German. I wondered if my perplexity stemmed from the weakness and confusion that some people located as one source of sin. It was surely a product of a small but systematic injustice. My friend Alan and I were the youngest on the block. All through the years of playing war under the two big cherry trees in our backyard, the bargain was clear: Little kids often had to agree to be the German or the Jap, or the big kids might not let you play. I may have had a choice, but I didn't feel I had one. So I played, risking my soul.

Christ himself, I was sure, had never faced anything so complex, although for him becoming human might, I supposed, have created a similar feeling of shame and betrayal. "Jap" was our word for the Japanese. It conveyed more horror than "German." It's curious that, although my mother's family was political, on the left, and profoundly antifascist, we kids seldom called the Germans Nazis. In the game, you were the German, not the Nazi. I think we hated Japs more than Germans because the Germans were like us—my brother's best friend was named Fritzi, after all—whereas we saw the Japanese as less than human. And there was a summary playground verdict: The Japs had started the war. We took our ideas from the war's weather system, storming along inside our heads on some principle of unfolding chaos. The times made it hard to be good.

So I spent the war in combat for the enemy—always losing, sometimes crying, wounded and dying from gunshot and bayonet damage and bombs and grenades and flamethrowers, haunted by the pictures of Jap insects in the comics, and a kid's version of Japanese and Nazi horrors pressed in the mind by the steady pressure of real and imagined violence. We kids were enacting the war, making a replica we could experiment with, and maybe understand, but the war was a planet on fire, and even the replica burned.

On VE day, my aunt and I were uptown when we heard the news. We stepped inside the nearest church, which had a large German congregation. The choir was singing thanks for peace in German, and I breathed a sigh of relief. The war was not over for those of us assigned to the Imperial Japanese Army, however. We had to soldier on, every day bringing more young lives lost under the cherry trees. On a lucky day we had a furlough. We could join Robin Hood's men, and escape the nightmare of current history.

I got more and more scared as our ship approached Japan. We docked in Yokohama at night. Everybody was sleeping. I got up first and went out on deck in the early light. The fog was lifting. You could start to make out the new piers and those bombed by the Americans in the great raids my grandfather read to me about in the papers, the vast incalculable tonnage of bombs and firebombs we had exulted in, the flaming rivers in which, in the backyard, I had sometimes died along with my fellow insects. Later my brother and I explored in fear the bombed-out buildings, and Yokohama neighborhoods where all the cats and dogs had been eaten in the hungry time. A mind trained in war by my grandfather could begin to guess even from the state of the docks that the city had been twisted by strange hot storms.

I could smell land, a few pine trees, scents of a port city, foreign garbage. In the fog on the pier there was one man stooping over. He was collecting cigarette butts in a large khaki shoulder bag. He had only one leg, and a crutch for the missing leg. He was wearing the ruins of a Japanese army uniform. He was the first Japanese I saw outside of a comic or a newsreel. I went below where everyone else was still asleep and fished quietly in my parents' dresser for cigarettes, and took a full unopened carton up to the deck and threw it down on the pier. At first the Japanese soldier didn't notice the Lucky Strikes. Then he did, staring down, astonished. He looked up at me, caught my eye, grinned, paused a second, and gave a formal military salute of thanks. I felt the first shock of a short life rich in what to that moment I believed were certainties: With his wire-rimmed glasses and his frayed cap and his cigarette holder and his hungry old face, he looked exactly like my grandfather.

It felt as though I was starting to push back against some great coercive pressure, fighting to stay intact. I think I began to sense from that moment that, whatever the intricate balance of sin and virtue surrounding the incomprehensible, monstrous fact of the war, something had messed with my mind, and filled it full of lies and hatred and fear.

I was a winner, looking down on the face of defeat. I hated myself for being the side that took the man's leg, for the bombings, for being a German and a Jap, for letting myself be made a Jap, for the hatefulness of faces staring at other humans and calling them bugs. I feared and hated the Germans and the bug people, too, the Japs most of all. I hated them for losing, and would have hated them even more for winning. Even my bones felt confused. I don't know to this day how I didn't explode, or how I found the beginning of a way out, except that what I did made things start to feel better.

I look at myself looking at the old Japanese man (who may in years have been as old as I am now), my mind awash with the firestorms that ripped apart the world. The war was a civil war, taking place inside all of us, whether we realized it or not. I was trying to mend its tears, and to fit my sense of dislocation and fear and exile to a startling new reality: my hunger for a human web.

The war was history's loudspeaker blaring at us, flooding our thoughts, ordering me and my store of experience to get lost. It was an enemy, too. In fighting back against its flood of words and images, it helped, strangely, sadly, that I was a migrant now, that I had left my own sweet valley—that I was one of all the others who had to make a new, provisional home out where nothing was solid, where everything floated, like my gray ship. Every migrant in the new floating world would have a name and a different story.

My picture of my grandfather and my aunt was next to my migrant's heart; nobody was going to take it away. I was forever a product of America and Wilkes-Barre, but even as one of the new conquerors of Japan, it would be impossible for me from that moment on to believe that truth has only one face.

I wanted, finally—it seems so simple—to meet the world without hatred or coercion. Even a small boy could see that it was time to shed some hard, ancient skin in 1946. How much more so in 1994. Not to see this is to be far more blind than the blind children my brother and I were soon playing with at the famous big school in the bluffs over Yokohama. These Japanese were our neighbors now. They gave us our puppy, Dusty, whose mother was one of the school's Seeing Eye dogs. Some of the children were blind from birth, others from the U.S. firebombings. We started games of hide and seek at night out where the blind knew the terrain—hiding in tall bamboo thickets, our faces lit moony-green by the cool explosions of fireflies. We were young boys, playing together like crickets in the same cage.

I count myself doubly lucky—I grew up easy, and I once found, by an accident of grace, or the fortunes of war, an imaginative moment in which I floated up out of the dark mirror that most of us in this terrible century have been forced to look into. No wonder I feel tender toward myself on the deck of my ship, still afloat, and reaching out. I like to see the sources of my childish bravery in my own small sufferings. I savor the roots of dissent in the love and curious example and teachings of my harsh old grandfather. Lapsed Catholic that I am, I have enjoyed making my confession to you: I was a thief, like my hero, Robin Hood, on behalf of humanity.

I relish the Japanese soldier, too. He and my rebel grandfather are surely two of a kind. His military salute has more than a hint of mockery, at the same time that it manages respect and even affection for the small stranger in the temporary role of the colonial big shot. Man to man, I want to look him in the eye today and laugh. We fought together on the same side in the world's stinking war.

Rousseau and Modernity

T HOSE WHO DOUBT that ideas play an important part in history should take two steps to remedy their mistake. First they should read Jean-Jacques Rousseau's great Enlightenment treatise on human nature and education, *Emile* (1762/1933). Then they should tour the world, looking at families and schools dealing with young children. From Los Angeles to Dar es Salaam, parents and teachers are pursuing "natural" modes of child-rearing, a pursuit as old and as young as modernization itself. Rousseau set the terms of a long conversation on families, education, politics, and modernity that is still going on.

John Locke's radical new portrait of human nature and his revolutionary insistence that experience, not tradition, is the great teacher mark the beginning of the conversation. It is a debate between modernizers and counter-moderns, between the rational Enlightenment and what we call "Romanticism," between "low" and "high" Romantics, and the topics of families, children, and education are at its center. It becomes a true dialogue, however, with Rousseau's dissent from Locke and Descartes. Locke is the quintessential modernizer, proclaiming that human beings are in some fashion free, equal, and rational. Rousseau is a modernizer, too. He accepts Locke's three premises, and builds on them himself, but he sees how each of them could take a wrong turn, and, in his warnings about the possible disastrous consequences of the Enlightenment's ideals, makes himself into the first great countermodern intellectual, the first to insist on the need for a new polity, a new culture, and new modes of child-rearing to neutralize the acids of modernization. The dialogue between Locke and Rousseau thus reflects the emergence of that cluster of social forces and ideas we vaguely call "modernity." I am using the term to mean the triple revolutions of modern times: the great transformations in science, industry and the capitalist economy, and politics.

Some recent work in social history stresses shifts in the character of the family from an economic unit of production to a unit of consumption, leisure, and child-rearing. The parent–child bond changes from something mainly economic to something mainly emotional. And closely bound up with all these changes was the rise of institutions consciously designed to

8

offset the collapse of traditional institutions. Schools were part of the institutional response to modernity. Schools represented rationalizing progress in the minds of figures like Horace Mann; they were also meant as communal counterweights to the imbalances of unchecked economic and technological change, the chief of which were thought to be the destruction or at least the weakening of the fabric of traditional life.

Our debate does not have a very long history. Since Philippe Aries's (1962) work, *Centuries of Childhood*, we have been getting used to the idea that our ideas about childhood—and our ideas about adolescence, youth, and, for that matter, old age—are very much time-bound and culture-bound. Whereas children in the West used to be thought of more or less as adults in miniature, masses of people around the world have come to view childhood as a distinct time with special needs. As a body of thought about children, their minds, and how they learn develops, the dialogue about children is influenced by the growing number of institutions for them. The institutions, for all their defects, mark a pronounced shift in the status of children in the West over the last 200 years. Our culture today places more value on children, makes more room for their uniqueness and diversity, and takes a greater interest in their learning than it did in the past. I am not saying we already are a child-centered culture, whatever that might mean. The absence of financial and emotional support for many children; the existence of hungry children; the presence of battered, bored, miserable, drugged, and manipulated children in our midst; the generally low quality of our collective institutional arrangements for children—all raise grave doubts about the place of children in our society. We do not have a great deal to congratulate ourselves for. But we are more of a child-centered society than we were in the past we sometimes sentimentalize so shamelessly. Large numbers of thoughtful parents and professionals appreciate children, and children themselves have moved from being marginal and exploited figures to being culture heroes of a sort, a position not without its own drawbacks.

ROUSSEAU VERSUS LOCKE

Rousseau is the great *moraliste* of modernization. He sees modernization in moral, political, and cultural terms. In all three realms, he is a psychologist, with both the weaknesses and the strengths of an essentially psychological approach. The psychology of modernity is the main thing, then. It consists of two parts: a moral pathology and a statement of human possibility. The moral pathology, the more famous of the two, is described in Rousseau's well-known account of the dividedness, alienation, and inner deadness of modernity. Rousseau portrays moderns as cut off from nature and a healthy social life alike. His pathology demonstrates the catastrophic consequences of the failure of community. A healthy person needs social support and a sense of self. Moderns lack both. In the artificial and unequal world of civilized life, our social nature conceals and deforms the underlying natural self. Rousseau frames his criticisms in terms of a quest for a norm of public decency that would mesh private and public selves, eliminating the need for masks and lies. Rousseau's ideal is a unitary, undivided existence, supported either by a protective family or by the polity. The chief threats to a self that is whole and of a piece are the fickleness of the imagination itself, change, inequality, social complexity, and the social division of labor. This is why "progress" is the issue. Rousseau appreciates the advantages of the division of labor, yet he sees the possibility of a society that is at the same time interdependent and at war within itself. He compares complex social life to a banquet in which workers all over the world toil so the rich can glut themselves. His essential metaphor for the underlying barbarism of all existing society is savage, unreflecting carnivorousness.

This morbid social psychology is grounded in a psychology of development, a norm of human possibility and "natural" growth countering Locke. Rousseau's qualified dissent from the psychology of John Locke and Descartes introduces an important theme: It is the effort to rescue Western man from the nihilistic consequences of one version of modernity, the dualities imposed by 17th-century science, which broke the world into rival realms of spirit and matter and suggested that the basic underlying reality was matter. Rousseau borrows Locke's psychology, but he tries to reintegrate mind and body, heart and mind, to achieve a unified, unalienated consciousness. Rousseau's complaint about his divided inner self is a crucial moment, the point at which the forces of modernization were producing a countermodern consciousness: "We ourselves are but the least part of ourselves." *Emile* is one of the greatest and most comprehensive attempts to balance contrary realms, to achieve what I shall call a high Romantic mediation of thought and feeling, a new countermodern and Romantic psychology that was to underlie the pursuit of what were later to be termed the New Education, the New Child, the New Man, and, eventually, the New Woman.

Education is a particularly fascinating window on modernization and the response to it, because the transmission of culture to the young across the generations becomes a highly conscious affair once a traditional culture starts modernizing, often the first item of articulate public policy. In the history of educational policy we can see the paradoxical attempt of each modernizing culture to become conscious of and to design arrangements that in an earlier day were not matters of conscious thought and policy at all. It is sometimes like the effort to make the instinctive something conscious and developed. Formal education is a symptom of the shock of modernization. The builders and rationalizers of our present educational system assumed they were confronting an immense crisis, that the traditional modes of passing on culture from families to children were breaking down, and that henceforth rearing and educating children would become more of a public responsibility. In all its forms, Rousseau's New Education and his utopian vision of the new educative and therapeutic private family explore the contours of the basic paradox of the effort to contrive by thought and artifice "natural" modes of child-rearing, teaching, and learning.

Childhood itself is, as Aries says, a relatively recent invention, in the West, at least, and by and large the dominant traditional account of children reflected Christian doctrines of original sin. Yet there is a clear minor strain of thought that drew on the New Testament and Jewish tradition to emphasize children's innocence, too. To enter the kingdom of heaven, Christ said, we must become as children, and a number of figures in Christian tradition pointed to the special importance of childhood. Very broadly speaking, the two alternative Christian responses to childhood reflected a larger tension within Christianity between the followers of St. Augustine and those who side with Augustine's great opponent, Pelagius. The Augustinians stress the utter sinfulness and wickedness of human nature; the Pelagians insist on its potential for goodness and autonomy. Throughout Western history the two points of view have prompted very different courses of conduct, alternative views of what we might nowadays call social policy. To order people's sinfulness and guide them in their weakness, Augustine wanted a total city of God on earth. He is like Dostoyevsky's Grand Inquisitor, who insists that, above all, people in their weakness need miracle, mystery, and authority. The Pelagians, believing in man's goodness, reason, and capacity for autonomous choice, have wanted not one city of God but a city of plural choices. By the time of the Enlightenment, figures like Rousseau are rebels against Christianity, but they also draw on Christian tradition in their rebellion. Aries ignores the way that these different strains of Christian tradition flowed into what he rightly sees as a new 17th- and 18th-century interest in childhood. And thus he misses out on the doubleness of the modern response to childhood.

Locke can be thought of as speaking for a predominantly repressive mode of child-rearing—an inner-directed mode, to resurrect David Riesman's useful phrase. Rousseau, on the other hand, represents a softer mode. But both want to do away with traditional modes of child-rearing. Both assume a new, highly self-conscious modern family dedicated to

consumption, leisure, and, above all, rearing children. Both are explic-
itly addressing fathers as well as mothers. And, of course, both were talking to a very thin crust in the upper strata of their times.

John Locke's thinking about childhood also drew on these contrary
strains of thought about childhood; because he was preeminently a philosopher of the mind and politics, his treatise on the education of children
reads like an extrapolation from philosophy and politics, even though he
drew on his own experiences as a tutor. Everything about Locke's ideas
on child-rearing suggests the disruption of the older, patriarchal orders.
In traditional orders, child-rearing is not usually a very conscious matter.
Locke rebels against this traditional world, with its received ideas, its
sacred notion of authority, including the authority of kings and fathers, its
inability to separate politics from religion and the sanctions of hopes for
heaven and fears of hell, and its incapacity to acknowledge new sources of
authority. Locke's rebellion is severely moderate, to be sure. In many ways
it is the anarchy and looseness of the older, feudal modes of child-rearing
that appall him the most, just as it is the irrationality and arbitrary character of patriarchal authority that he hates. Locke's animus against the
slovenliness of the regime of wet nurses and backstairs servants reflects a
new moralizing ideal of the family: It is to be a private institution, not a
crowd, and its function is to be deeply, anxiously concerned with the right
upbringing of children, which can no longer be taken for granted. Children
must be separated from the undisciplined elements of the adult world, and
their characters must be shaped. Locke's child-rearing is above all an exercise in the creation of a social character. It is antitraditional and fundamentally repressive.

Locke's ideas about authority and the proper sort of child-rearing reflected his new view of human nature. The mind was a blank at birth, a
tabula rasa. We are not interested in Locke's views for their influence, which
is always difficult to measure, but for what he shows about certain generic
issues in the long debate on childhood and modernity. Locke was willing
to compromise with religion. Yet he looked at children with wholly secular eyes. Sin was not an issue. Even so, the view of childhood he promoted
saw children as distinctly flawed and inferior beings. The Lockean child is
an incomplete adult, needing the constant attention of rational parents and
teachers to mature properly. The basic stance of adults is outspokenly repressive. Locke's theories were part of developments in the 17th, 18th, and
19th centuries that were to lead to the near-total Victorian division of sex
roles and in particular the feminization of child-rearing, teaching, and,
especially in America, culture itself. Yet in Locke's terms, it is plain that he
is also seeking to expand the role of the father now that childhood has
become, so to speak, a policy matter. Locke is promoting a new role for

fathers, a middle-class version of patriarchy in which authority is ultimately rational. And he is anticipating the 19th-century middle-class family style Freud was to interpret in terms of the myth of Oedipus. From today's perspective it is less the directly sexual character of the Oedipal problem that looks interesting and more the general question of power and authority: Locke is describing a mode of child-rearing that puts great stock in an internalized father. In the end, Locke's main concern seems to be to implant the right sort of conscience in children, to develop the right sort of social character.

Rousseau counters Locke down the line with an alternative set of propositions concerning childhood and the human mind, thus setting the terms of debates that are still current, such as the running controversy over the respective merits of environmentalism as against maturationalism (or, as it is sometimes called, nativism)—development from without versus development from within. Lockean psychology tends toward a rigid environmentalism. Cartesian thought tends toward a rigid faith in innate structures of cognition. Rousseau emerges as one of the great maturationalist opponents of Locke; he is faithful to Descartes in stressing the autonomous, rational power of the mind to order the world through its categories. However, Rousseau was also a close reader of Locke; he draws on Locke's empiricism in his rebellion against the dryness, abstraction, and cognitive tedium of Cartesian rationality. He is in pursuit of sentiment and the concrete, too, and for this he reads 17th- and 18th-century British psychology, as do all the Romantics intent on validating experience, stealing ideas from Locke in order to overthrow the scientism of Locke's universe. In fact, Rousseau's psychology of early childhood combines a thoroughgoing Lockean sensationalism and empiricism, especially in his account of the early years, with a developmentalist's account of the cognitive and abstracting powers of the Cartesian mind. Besides being a maturationalist, Rousseau is also an interactionist, one of the true sources of the naturalistic psychology of Jean Piaget and John Dewey.

The basic attitude toward the naked human impulse is a key issue. Locke wants to free the child from ancient mummeries, constraints, and artifice, but he is deeply suspicious of instinct, and mainly intent on molding free, rational, and equal beings into a social character that will conform to society. Rousseau believes, like so many of his Romantic followers, that the live instincts are more often right than the deadening dictates of social convention.

All along, however, there is a profound maturationalism behind Rousseau's portrait. And, off and on, the model of development is interactionist, the product of a byplay between Emile and his environment. This is, perhaps, unique to Rousseau: the profound, developmental emphasis on the forward drive of growth itself, the dynamism of a life force unfolding inside the child. This is what Rousseau thinks of as "nature," and it is why he and those who follow him believe that there is something elemental and even sacred about impulse. Impulse is the source of growth, the fountain of self-renewal—a corrupt and jaded civilization's last contact with nature itself. Rousseau's Romantic religion is life; the native impulse is its sacrament.

Consciousness is a good for Rousseau; it is not, however, the supreme good that it is for other high Romantics. He wants to damp down the desires the imagination prompts, to block out the lure of the past and the future in taking people away from experience in the present. His two educational goals—growth and inner peace—are the two contradictory impulses of the New Education. In spiritual terms, the contrast is between a nature that is abundant, and a nature that makes its home in stoical scarcity.

Although these ideals coexist in Rousseau's mind, fear that moderns will lose their way and themselves often triumphs; the Stoic defeats the high Romantic. In the end, what Rousseau wants for moderns most of all is surcease from change. This is why growth and consciousness of the sort admired by the high Romantics from Wordsworth and Keats to Dewey are not the bedrock of his position. It is why he is fundamentally a countermodern. In the end the rebel from Christianity sides with Augustine rather than Pelagius. He seeks peace for ordinary people because he despairs of human nature. This is why, at bottom, Rousseau can be profoundly totalitarian. Like the Grand Inquisitor and his 20th-century heirs, he is tempted to enslave the human race out of pity for its weakness.

The Enlightenment debate between Rousseau and the likes of Locke, Voltaire, and Condorcet echoes throughout the vast literature on social progress, reform, families, children, child-rearing, and schools. It is a debate between the two great rival myths of modernization: the Long Revolution and the Lost Community. The Long Revolution is the Western myth of science, progress, and uplift—the Long March to the music of secular Reason. The Lost Community is the great counter-statement—the lament for the communal webs of kin and faith and sentiment that have been destroyed by modernization.

Schools are part of the debate; so are child-centered modern families. They are symptoms of the world we have lost through modernization, or else evidence for the gains we have all won. For those mourning the old order, the nuclear family is a pathetic remnant of a richer social world or a sinister novelty; to proponents of the Long Revolution, the child-centered families of recent decades are an index of rising affluence, leisure, mass consumption, and changing standards of child care. Supporters of the Long Revolution point to the decline in infant mortality and the ravages of childbirth and to higher standards of health, housing, cleanliness, leisure. From the other point of view, children assembled in the state-run, age-graded, highly rationalized institutions we call schools are a perfect emblem for the loss of humanity in the bourgeois order—apt symbols of a rationalized society incapable of accepting diversity, death, old age, faith, or mystery.

Thus since Rousseau, it is impossible to speak of policy about children and families without trying to cast some sort of balance sheet on the ills and benefits of modernity. He had an instinctive sense that the meaning of the family was changing in the 18th century and that men and women and children were going to stand in a different relationship to each other in the future. He was scarcely a woman's liberationist—Emile's bride, Sophy, is a ghastly parody, anticipating what has been called the 19th-century's cult of true womanhood, and his ideas about the new ideal family are distinctly patriarchal. Nonetheless it is not hard to see the implications for other members of the family in Rousseau's destruction of authority and his sense that the quest for equality and autonomy would henceforth be shared by everyone, in many different realms.

The richest storehouse of these themes on education and modernity is, of course, that child-centered strand of thought we call the New Education. From Pestalozzi and Froebel to John Dewey, this is a line of thought that tries in a high Romantic fashion to blend the legacy of the Age of Reason with Romanticism. It is a set of arguments about modernity's implications for families and child-rearing, not just schools. The quest for a new education is an institutional expression of the search for the high Romantic synthesis: for learning settings that would offer an interplay of head and heart, science and sentiment, authority and freedom, civilization and nature, the concrete and the abstract—that would strike a dynamic balance between the claims of the self and community, and of the past, present, and future. Rousseau's familial utopia becomes part of the countermodern attack on industrial capitalist society in the name of a vision of a unified culture and a unitary consciousness, and also in the name of a vision of progress.

Rousseau's discovery of childhood is an episode in the West's changing appreciation of children, in the use of childhood as a countermodern symbol of wholeness and an unalienated outlook—a healthy imagination.

This interest in childhood is part of the Romantic interest in uniqueness. To generalize, as Blake puts it, is to be an idiot. Man is a meaning-maker, and he makes the unique conditions for his own renewal—especially, as Blake and Wordsworth followed Rousseau in insisting, out of the experiences of childhood. The Romantic cults of sensibility, the noble savage, and children's innocence—which Rousseau began—promoted egotism, nostalgia, sentimentality, and the other forms of evasion of reality we rightly attack when we think of the weakheaded side of all the various Romanticisms. And there is no doubt that such evasions occur in the thinking of the strongest Romantics, as when Rousseau sighs heavily over the supposed innocence of children, or when Dickens descends into the bathosphere. Yet, like Dickens, Rousseau can also be a vigorous high Romantic countermodern, insisting that the test of a culture is the individual's spontaneous life—the child's sense of wonder being an emblem of the human imagination's capacity for fully experienced vitality. In both its wonderful strengths and its appalling weaknesses, the Romantic intellectual tradition Rousseau contributes to is a religion of life. Harold Bloom calls it a doomed, yet self-renewing tradition, doomed, because in the end its prophets are destined to encounter the final constraint—death itself—yet self-renewing because the struggle against what the early Romantics called death-in-life recurs each day in the life of every generation. Romanticism remains the underlying cultural mode for Anglo-Americans and for many Europeans, too. We can hope to go beyond it—we have to—but we shall have to go through it, which means coming to a better appreciation of its strengths and delusions.

Rousseau's arguments about nature and childhood become part of an important assault on the world-view of Locke, Bentham, and Mr. Gradgrind (the utilitarian child-hating capitalist in Charles Dickens's novel, *Hard Times*). The attack is based on a fundamentally countermodern and developmental picture of human nature that emphasizes spontaneity and creative autonomy. For all its origins in the Romantic doctrines of individualism, individual growth, and personal development, the argument insists that the capitalist doctrine of materialistic, rational self-interest is in the end a philosophy of death. Casting social criticism in the form of a battle between life and death is the essence of this Romantic position, and from it have emerged some of the most powerful and moving critical accounts of modernity, as well as a very great deal of cant. The image of childhood in this countermodern tradition reflects the values of spontaneity, disinterestedness, love, wonder, and the capacity of every person to make meaning and fashion symbols of experience. As Peter Coveney and Tony Tanner have reminded us, the literature of childhood from the great Romantics on is an attack on industrial capitalism and a vindication of human nature, a criticism of industrial life from the standpoint of a religion of life. It may be called a religious literature—all Romanticism is, after all, a kind of spilt religion—but generally it is a religion of this world.

And what a mixed bag Romanticism is regarding childhood: on the weakheaded side, it expresses hostility to logical analysis, a contempt for form, a suspicion of intellect, and a reluctance to draw up a complex balance sheet on modern society and life itself. Its weaknesses are those of an intensely subjective and private sort—what we mean when we use the word "Romantic" as a term of disapproval. The strengths of this mode and its tradition are its integrity, its sense of wonder, its refusal to be complacent, and its profound understanding of human development. As in the *Emile*, the image of childhood can not only stand for sentimentality and escapism, but also for a spirit of undefeated life—the wholehearted, truthtelling integrity of Huck Finn's stance toward slavery, his courageous solidarity with Jim, the escaped slave.

Emile's education is at times a window opening onto life. At other times, it is clearly an escape from life, an idyll, a pastorale in the bad and sentimental sense, a retreat from life into a pervasive pity—Rousseau's endless, condescending pity for mankind and his own bottomless self-pity. Even the strongest figures in Rousseau's line sometimes retreat into subjectivity, nostalgia, and pity as they pursue the memory of their own childhood. This is a note that Dickens sounds too often, for all his true greatness. The path from *Emile* to J. M. Barrie's Peter Pan is the distance from a robust, engaged Romanticism to the end of a spent movement.

Some of the greatest figures in the line are mainly expressing a low Romantic rebellion against the monopoly of reason, but in the hands of the Blakes, the rebellion is rich in implication of the power of the mind to fuse and synthesize experience and thus to grow and to find harmony and that deep power of joy Wordsworth spoke of—to locate what he calls the secret path to the hiding places of power. For the richest figures in the line, as for Rousseau, the point of making use of childhood is not a repudiation of adult existence, but a search for essential continuities in the lifelong drama of renewal. Through the image of the child's sense of wonder, the great Romantic writers deal with the possibilities for human life and the imagination.

This tremendous doubleness reflects a division within high Romanticism. Rousseau describes Emile's childhood as a dynamic drama of development; he also paints it as a harmonious, insipid idyll.

The first expresses a retreat from life that is still at the core of many countermodern stances. The second captures the spirit of true engagement with life that underlies the deepest criticisms of modernity.

Over the years, too many of the high Romantic syntheses of contrary realms have had a bogus air, as Richard Chase (1957) used to argue, insisting that the Romantic American literary genius was at its terrifying, broken-hearted best in exploring the tensions and dialectics of contrary realms. I want to extend Chase's point to Romantic social thought, psychology, and education generally. Rousseau is at his psychological best when, instead of rendering an idyll out of Watteau, he shows growth as the result of a dialectic of conflict: between Emile and nature, and between Emile and his tutor. Love lies at the core of the child's life, but the key to development is conflict. Rousseau's pastorale, and those that have succeeded it, like Friedrich Froebel's nineteenth-century daydream of children's harmonious development, reveal some of the deepest weaknesses in this line of thought. No real childhood can ever be an idyll.

Today the heirs of Rousseau's foolishness are the sentimentalists and pop Freudians who have taken Freud's dark picture of development—his secular version of the sinful, tormented souls of religious tradition—and converted it into the simple idea that children can be made happy by an absence of restraint. Freedom is necessary for development; so, however, is conflict and grief and sadness. Adults can help, but no one can spare a child a successive series of inner crises which are inherent in anyone's relation to the world. To love at all is to risk loss, to know hatred and anger, and to learn sorrow.

No institutions could accomplish all that Rousseau and his heirs wanted families and education to do. Sentimentality is not just a surface aspect of the tradition, but points to some of its craziest misconceptions. Yet the good side of the utopianism is also plain; in asking whether there were alternatives to the modes of modernization that prevailed in the West, the thinkers in Rousseau's line were raising critical issues. Defending utopian thought, Martin Buber (1949) once pointed out that socialist tradition has yet to arrive at an adequate portrait of human nature and human possibility. I agree. In looking for a balance of modern and countermodern, the utopians in Rousseau's line struggle toward a more complex portrait of people, their possibilities, and their needs. High Romantics like John Dewey insist that there can be a mediation between head and heart, between the rival claims of the Enlightenment and Romanticism, science, and sentiment. Above all the utopians have helped us to reject the total narratives of progress or loss. Rousseau's democratic heirs demand that we make critical choices and act rather than let History dictate human fate. They are sometimes unrealistic about institutions like families and schools, but they raise fundamental issues: alternative possibilities, the meaning and purpose of life and death, the forms the religious impulse might take in a secular world.

Family Matters

O NE PARTICULAR SUBJECT illuminates both the breaks and the continuities in recent history especially well: the rediscovery of the family as an item of popular attention, scholarly writing, and public policy discussion. This phenomenon has a good deal of political interest, and opens up a window revealing a strange time and an unsettled national mood. It is a time in which many find it hard to resolve the tension between deeply conservative impulses and a host of radical ideas that have not in fact disappeared from the intellectual scene, even though the politics have changed so much. The examination of the fundamental nature of our institutions that was such a noisy aspect of the time of confrontations we think of as "the 60s" continues—although in a more sober and restrained form—with the family often the focus of the inquiry.

Reminiscences, novels, and academic studies of those troubled times are already appearing—the authors walking onstage with an air of embarrassed prematurity: "Aren't you rather young to be writing your memoirs?" We wonder. On the face of it, the contrast between the present and the recent past does seem striking. A time of public turmoil marked by demonstrations, marches, and a peculiarly intense involvement with events has been succeeded by a very private age in which people turn inward to themselves, their families, and various consolations of escape: nostalgia, science fiction, food, and jogging. In what follows, I don't want to wholly discredit the legend of the wild, lost 60s, but I do definitely mean to knock a few dents in instant history's belief that everything has changed.

The sense of foreboding attending the topic of the family may reflect a kind of secular religious crisis. Familism and child-rearing are close to being religious values for many Americans, perhaps especially for those who have watched all the other idols crumble. Family life and its love could do all things. For many reasons, this faith is now wavering. There is an uneasiness about the family that reflects a widespread suspicion that the Beatles were wrong—love may not be all you need.

Academics, journalists, and ordinary people in schools and living rooms argue whether the family is collapsing or whether it is alive and well. Evidence of disintegration is matched by data suggesting that families are merely shifting form and function as they adapt to change. Most of us debate these matters from our general instinct of where history is tending, from our own lives and those of our friends, and from what we see going on under our noses. One of the difficult things about the family as a topic is that everyone in the discussion feels obliged to defend a particular set of choices. We see families on the skids, in terrible trouble, and we also know families that are thriving. Even the statistics yield ambiguous interpretations.

What is bewildering for many people, I suspect, is not that the phenomena of marriage, families, and child-rearing are in some sense exiting from the stage of history, but that many things that were once taken for granted are now becoming matters of conscious choice. Marriage is voluntary; so, for a growing number of people, is the decision to have children. We often forget that the voluntarism works both ways: Many people are choosing to stay married, to raise children, and to allocate the division of family labor in traditional ways.

Two things remain clear. First, the family in some form continues to be the paramount institution for child-rearing. Despite the rising divorce rate, 98% of American children are in some form of family setting. This is undoubtedly a greater percentage than in the past, whose family stability we romanticize so shamelessly. Nostalgia is one of the great enemies of clear thinking about the family. The disruption of families in the 19th century through death, separation, and the other convulsions of an industrializing economy was much more catastrophic than we imagine. The image of a stable past by which we measure our present disarray and uprooting may also be quite false. In 1880, 57% of the population lived in rural isolation or in the anonymity of big cities. Today, two thirds of Americans live in small towns and suburbs where, for all the real disadvantages, neighborliness and community may be easier to establish. The second fact is that a more equitable division of sex roles at home and at work is crucial to any effort to expand possibilities for both men and women. We continuously confront the tangled nature of the social web. Changes in the stereotyped roles of women imply changes in the standard relationships of both men and women to the three crucial realms of work, child-rearing, and leisure. The family remains the main school in which the young learn about sex roles, for better and for worse. If a wider range of roles is to be available to both sexes, changes must begin within the family. The future of the family is thus bound up with the hopes for women's future liberation and for men's emancipation from the prison of traditional masculinity.

Nostalgic pictures about family life in the past are nothing new. Our national religion of progress, boosterism, has for a long time carried an undertone of deep worry over what the forces of unchecked economic and technological change are doing to older ways. This concern is often expressed as nostalgia, the quintessential conservative emotion in American life. There is a strong link between boosterism's worship of the future and nostalgia's regrets over the lost past. Boosterism is sentimental about the future; nostalgia is the same feeling directed backwards in time. Both avoid the task of living in the present.

The family as the centerpiece for nostalgic, historical tableaux has always been tied to a certain set of narrow, moralizing norms about family life. It is WASP in ethnicity and traditional in format, sex roles and the division of labor. The American family came in one model: Mom, Pop, Sis, Bud—all grinning out at you from the snapshot. This model seems to be breaking down, although it is puzzling to imagine what will replace it.

We look beneath the media images for more solid truths about the family, but we continue to shadowbox with symbols. It is a fact that the proportion of children in our population is shrinking. The proper stance to take toward this fact is also part of the current family debate. Much of the conversation on families revolves around the fact that the great World War II and postwar baby boom is over. The cohort that made up the population boom is now grown up. They are one reason for the enormous current interest in such topics as child-rearing and families. The articulate and highly educated children of the baby boom form a huge, literate market for books on various issues in parenting and child-rearing, and, as time goes on, adult development, divorce, midlife crises, old age, and, of course, death. In sheer numbers, this particular cohort and its concerns will probably continue to exert a disproportionate influence on our society. It is a well-educated group, raised to affluent expectations, seasoned by the upheavals of the civil-rights and antiwar movements, suspicious of institutions and authority. It will make more trouble before it is through. Speaking as one standing near the beginning of the age cohort—I was born in 1940— I take a particularly wry pleasure in looking forward to seeing my friends marching in the inevitable radical old people's movement of the year 2000.[1] In the meantime, however, there is the ocean of adulthood to be navigated, and this poses special problems for the grown children of the 60s. This is one of the reasons why discussions of the family and its commitments resonate now with such intensity.

Americans have long, perhaps too long, thought of themselves as a young nation, ignoring the old and settled nature of our institutions and their historic dilemmas. We want to stay young; that hasn't changed. Yet the cause of the young—the party of hope and the future—has for the time being lost what the Chinese call the mandate of heaven. It is no longer as easy as it was to imply a fundamental critique of this society by showing the inadequacy of its arrangements for children and youth. Now the grown-ups, some of them products of vanished youth rebellions, must step forth and speak for themselves. There is less cant about the young now, and more vindictiveness. Popular films show children as devils, possessed by demons and powers. The Supreme Court, our national arbiter of symbols, has in the case of *Ingraham v. Wright* upheld a rather shocking instance of corporal punishment in a junior high school.

The 60s outlook was Romantic and of the left. It tried to connect the personal and the historical, to trace necessary yet treacherous links between public and private life, even though in the end it succeeded in analyzing neither. What remains is an outlook, a stance toward politics and history, not a cogent analysis or, least of all, any clear prescription for political action. In midlife, I notice my friends are much more interested in their own family history. We were always reluctant to think historically about our lives and the lives of our parents; we read about the past, but somehow we never thought of our own lives as part of the same grand tapestry that included the 19th-century Irish farmers, shtetl peasants, Renaissance cardinals, 17th-century Puritans, African warriors, and London mechanics. We were struggling toward a future, trying to live in the present. This is a matter of age partly—the young have the twin duties of escaping history and family life. That often meant cutting ourselves off from the past and our families, a break that was seldom as final as it seemed at the time.

The way the family illustrates the continuities and breaks with the 60s is easy to see in these policy debates. The family is emerging as a key symbol in an ongoing assault on institutions and professions, a continuation of Romantic mutinies against a modern professionalized service society. In a host of fields deinstitutionalization of one sort or another has become the mode, and with it usually rides an implicit argument that the alternative to the institutions we now face is some form of family existence. Much of the new interest in families reflects a fundamental disenchantment with the optimism of the domestic programs of the Kennedy–Johnson reform eras. The disenchantment comes from both the right and the left; critics on both sides see government, bureaucracy, and the professions as the enemy, and the family as a victim of the intrusive power of the centralized state. Disillusionment with the "service" strategies of the Kennedy–Johnson years is one of the most popular current readings of the legend of the 60s; but the disillusionment itself draws on the themes of the 60s. In sociology, the work of Coleman (1966) and Christopher Jencks (1972) on education has become the new orthodoxy. These revisionist educational sociologists hold that schools do less than we think to promote either academic achievement or social mobility, and that family background is the most important measurable factor in predicting the future of the young. (It should be noted that the tendency to assume that what cannot be measured precisely can safely be ignored mars a good deal of this work.) Current interest in the family expresses this loss of confidence in education, which in turn reflects the loss of faith in politics and government.

In the 60s, many of us became conscious that a century and a half of institutional reform had left a deeply problematic legacy in the array of service institutions that were this culture's response to the dilemmas of capitalist modernization. Revisionist scholars began to study the past and present workings of schools, hospitals, mental asylums, prisons, and juvenile courts. The inquests into the pathologies of these institutions go on. As their stock sinks, the stock of the family rises. Here again there are interesting precedents. In the mid-60s, the controversial Moynihan Report (1965) stressed the pathology of the Black family and the supposed legacy of slavery, arguing for government policies that would support families. The Moynihan Report offered us a warning for the 70s and 80s in the way it tangled its plea for full employment with its own therapeutic and moralizing arguments. In confusing the issues of family health and full employment, it echoed a very old pattern in public policy: Stressing the peculiar pathology of the families of the poor is a consistent thread in an ancient, stylized, and highly moralizing public conversation. But the report also stressed direct help for families.

Out of the upheavals of the 60s and the responses to them emerge two clear themes. Both express the notion that families need support. The first theme stresses the need for income and jobs. This is not necessarily a repudiation of the service strategies of the Kennedy–Johnson years, although now it is often couched in the language of the prevailing populist and revisionist distrust of professions, bureaucracies, and government action of any sort. Social critics like Christopher Lasch are not alone in making the attack on the professions a major focus. The income argument can of course suggest simply that the social services by themselves cannot overcome the effects of extreme inequality; they require equality to function properly. This would be my argument. The extremes of inequality and power that now exist create systemic deprivations and distortions in the delivery of social services of all kinds. The main generic dilemmas of the social services from education to medical care arise from the general contexts of inequality and the play of market forces in which they operate. A second, lesser theme running through all these reports is the vague yet insistent 60s' demand for something called "participation." The clients and consumers of services of one kind or another are increasingly critical of the consequences of a century or more of professionalization, and they are demanding a share and a measure of control from the professionals. The historical era of imperial meritocracy and unchallenged neutral professional expertise is running out.

Thus the 60s' Romantic and countermodern assault on the professions is still very much part of the current scene. It can feed into a rancor against all state and professional intervention in the lives of private citizens, producing a strange ideological alliance of the anarchist left and the conservative right against statism. Or it can translate into the argument that the services we have built are a social good, but that they cannot operate in a healthy fashion in such a radically unequal society. To be sure, this argument implies that more government action of some kind is needed to redistribute income so that support services are available to those who have been unable to purchase them.

I agree completely with the need for income and jobs, yet it is one thing to underscore income and redistributive issues, to point to the decisive necessity for family support and full employment, another to forego thinking about the services children and families need and to lapse into the current defeatism that says anything government does is terrible. This in effect is what many policy statements do. In this I detect the spirit of a bruised and rather frightened liberalism that is now very common among those who have not abandoned liberalism altogether. The current focus on families reflects the prevailing populist suspicion of merit, privilege, and inequality, the continuation of the 60s' revisionist attacks on the professions and the typical "service" strategies of the Kennedy–Johnson years, and the new sense of conservatism and the appeal to traditional values and countermodern symbols. The chastened liberalism met in many circles has absorbed the lessons of instant history. It is therefore suspicious of programs, experts, bureaucracies, and professionals, and inclined to look for policies that bypass them, just as Lyndon Johnson's War on Poverty once tried to bypass the agencies of state and city government to reach the poor. The strength of this new outlook is its realization that inequality is the central issue, and that the major long-term item on the national agenda for families has to be income redistribution. This strength is accompanied, however, by certain intertwined weaknesses.

A shortcoming of the new liberalism is that it rests on an essentially atomistic and economic view of life. It says families need money. Income needs redistribution. And that's all. In essence, the new liberalism still relies on a market model of society, and says that the task is to restore competitive power to the poorer atoms by boosting their income. That's good, but the framework remains atomistic. The new liberalism expresses compassion for people; yet at its roots it remains the philosophy of Charles Dickens's (1854) Gradgrind, who believed that only self-interest holds society together. The new Gradgrindism reflects the prevalence of economists in our policy debates, a curious phenomenon, since conventional economics has virtually admitted that it cannot solve inflation or unemployment problems. This basically economic outlook shows its roots in classical liberalism through its constant efforts to restore vanishing market mechanisms and to bypass any sort of solution that might require people to work together. We are used to Gradgrindism of the right. Now we are hearing it on the left. Today's Gradgrindism is based on a particular view of the 60s, which holds that money was simply thrown at social problems in the form of expensive and useless programs mainly of benefit to the professionals—trying to feed the sparrows, as the phrase goes, by feeding the horses.

The problematic, sometimes sinister, and often tragic role that professionals play in dispensing services in a multiethnic and profoundly unequal society is one thing; the assumption that we can water down and dispense with the services we now have is something else. Our suspicion of bureaucracies and professionals has a great deal of validity: It is a valuable and enduring truth that self-perpetuity is the dominant impulse for most organizations. The professions are, at least in part, in conspiracy against the laity. So far, the revisionists have had some useful warnings to sound. The idea of professional service is not so valid as the old working-class vision of fraternity and republican virtue, or even the older Christian ideal of love and charity. Unfortunately, not one of these four admirable ideals has sufficiently strong roots in our public life. In a time of financial crisis, people are tearing down pathological professional and bureaucratic structures without much attempt to put anything in their place.

A more revolutionary, fraternal, republican, or Christian social vision might be better able than the current Gradgrindism to supply two things generally missing from current policy perspectives. One is that many people do in fact need help. The second point is that public policy ought to be about providing contexts in which people could help each other. As matters stand, the need for help subjects people to ideological hazing, class and racial disdain, and the power of bureaucrats and professionals; but the need is still very real. Here Kenneth Keniston (1978) has much the better of Christopher Lasch (1977); families with children are indeed often isolated, beleaguered, and in need of assistance. The challenge is to frame contexts that offer families more choices about the kinds of help they receive. Help should augment family life rather than diminish it.

We need to fight on two different political levels at the same time. On the national level, we need egalitarian coalitions to assert democratic control over the power of corporate privilege. The major arena for egalitarian change has to be the national government, since it alone has the potential for controlling the vast private governments represented by the corporations. At the same time, however, many local institutions are atrophying from lack of citizen participation. We need a revival of voluntarism and pluralism too. The 60s' puzzled quest for participation goes on, especially in the continuing assaults on the professions.

What is required is coalition-building and institution-building. A more fraternal society would rely on common sympathy and common effort. Gradgrind and all his allies, right and left, traffic in solitude and self-sufficiency. Those who share the new outlook are alert to the weaknesses and the errors of older service strategies. Their populist faith in the family is attractive and their suspicion of the state is not unwarranted, yet, in effect, they advocate a social order that guarantees that some will end as losers. The market model of society is already a nostalgic anachronism in an age of international corporations. An antistatist position, pure and simple, is a tacit endorsement of rule by the giant corporations. Gradgrind's view overlooks the many ways in which we are all implicated in each other's fates, for it is precisely its intention to see that every man and woman remains an island.

Few people on the right, naturally enough, and, oddly, fewer and fewer on the left, are willing to admit that our system has collective consequences, and that changing it, therefore, entails collective actions and responsibilities. Social policy these days operates on a fundamental loss of faith in social sympathy. Economics may be good mental discipline, but it is not good for the heart. An economist's viewpoint emerges readily enough in capitalist society. It tends to be the natural idiom of businessmen, lawyers, and economists. What is strange these days is to find it in the idiom of the left, where too many are ready to dismiss whatever we arrange collectively or communally, without acknowledging that this condemns us to a world of unrelieved competition.

Analytically, the current debates on policy often lack any sense of collective consequences, such as how the sum of individual decisions generates systematic consequences. Philosophically and spiritually, today's debates forget the heart, neglecting the fact that social sympathies are as real as the GNP. Tactically, Gradgrind's liberal and radical heirs are blind to the fact that any gains we will make on any of these fronts will be a result of common action: political coalitions and alliances. We have, in recent history, only two instances of such alliances: the working-class union movement and the civil rights coalitions. The precise, profoundly influential current distinction between income and service strategies makes good analytic sense and fodder for learned articles. In actual politics, gains on both service and redistributive fronts tend to emerge out of the same cauldron.

We also have to learn to live on at least two levels. One is the level of the basic vision of a just and equal democratic society that we may never reach. We need our utopia, for without it we don't even know what questions to ask. The other is the level of intermediate tactical goals, worth gaining in and of themselves, and also worth fighting for because the struggle to get them promotes collective action. We are not facing a high-level "policy" decision over whether to stress "income" rather than "service" strategies. It is ludicrous to talk as though we were imaginary brokers of social capital, choosing to invest in income rather than services. The real political question is what kind of intermediate goals we can develop to build alliances among the poor, the minorities, the working class, the middle and affluent classes, and the professionals. Here the tidy distinction between income and service strategies breaks down even further, because the main goal is collective action on a host of fronts. Gradgrind is not only morally obtuse in thinking that you can reduce policy to atomistic individuals or atomistic families. He misses out on the means by which both service and income gains tend to come about—various forms of collective action.

What is dismaying about the current shift to the family as a symbol in the writings of figures like Lasch and Keniston is its underlying privatism. Both are, to be sure, calling for public action: Keniston for redistribution of income and Lasch, much more despairingly, for a revival of democracy at the local level. Yet neither has any great faith in collective action and the public realm, and this is worrisome. For without collective action, without linking ideas to ongoing social movements and forces, thought itself is bound to be ineffectual or even harmful. The Moynihan Report on the Black family should remain as an awesome warning on the relationship of ideas to politics. By cutting itself off from the very social movement it was trying to help, it exposed itself as a particularly vivid example of what William James in another context used to call "vicious intellectualism." It tried to argue a case for supporting poor families, but got so wound up in trying to demonstrate the supposed pathology of Black families that it lost its message completely. Does anyone recall that the main points of the Moynihan Report were full employment and family support?

Something similar to the Moynihan Report might come from current concern over the family. Unless this concern gets tied to collective action on a host of fronts, it could mean a new era of essentially private and even psychological solutions to our public problems, an era of empty therapizing and empty spiritualizing. An age of familism has a difficult time not turning into an age of psychology.

What I am suggesting is something that neither liberals nor radicals enjoy hearing. There is a tandem relationship between liberal reform and the pursuit of more radical goals. Liberal coalitions make it possible to propose radical visions, even though one of the chief aims of liberal reform is to defuse radical violence. The liberal domestic reforms of the Johnson era were a mixed bag, but we are significantly better off with them. Despite the current parable of the 60s, it is not always easy to maintain the distinctions among programs that are redistributive, those that aim at better services, or those that encourage collective action. The Johnson era domestic reforms came about in part through executive initiative, but more through mass movements forged from various kinds of coalitions. Those resisting further change in our society now point to these programs as evidence that we are essentially a healthy society and do not require further radical action. This response is typical of American reform history.

The very real changes in society over the last 15 years have come from outside of what is loftily called the policy system. They were the result of various kinds of social movements; one tragedy in recent years is the general fragmentation of these movements. In the process, our perception of how change occurs has become murky. We debate service and income "options" as though mass movements didn't exist; as though the progressive labor unions weren't the major support for both social services and income redistribution; as though there is no political potential arising out of the welter of middle-class movements. In our debates, we proceed as though the heart of the matter is ideas, not politics.

The tragedy of the present moment is the extraordinary disarray of the traditional progressive coalitions. In principle the present administration favors full employment and support for families, but its tax and welfare policies are mired, and it's hard to see where they will go. It is easy to say we need common coalitions, but at the moment the Gradgrinds hold the floor. The biggest danger in this age of the new familism is the very clear tendency to retreat to private and apolitical answers to collective political problems. Families may become an important symbol in the battle for a new and more communal society, but the times are hard and the politics of these matters are badly confused. The appeal for more equality is right, but in a time of immobility and retrenchment such fundamental appeals can ring hollow in a disheartening way. Even small victories are preferable to no victories at all; they feed a sense of possibility that is more important than any specific program. We need small victories.

The family is such an elusive symbol. It is perfect for an uncertain age presided over by a president who seems at the same time a decent man and a Cheshire cat. Ambiguity seems stitched into the family as a topic. The greatest stories, from "Hansel and Gretel" to *War and Peace*, tend to be family stories, and we read them hungrily, looking for ourselves. Public pronouncements on the family matter never seem to do justice to the dense poetry of the subject. I don't mean only the poetry in children's laughter and the sense of solidarity in good and bad family times, or even the delicate, unpredictable beauties that flicker into our common family existence like the birds we keep encountering above the broken glass in city parks.

Besides the essential joy of families I also mean the trouble: the sad poetry of selves trying to reach out and connect through the self-imposed and external obstacles; the tragic weight of past errors; the smothered poetry of men and women imprisoned in roles; the nightmarish poems of childhood's terrors. These are poems of rage and hate and fear and loss, poems of the past and the cycle of the generations, the poetry we weave around our own children in grief and happiness as we grow old and leave the world for them and their children. Lacking this richness and complexity, public and political discourse about the family always sounds abstract, hypocritical, and shallow.

The committee reports, legislation, and policy documents fall so short it is hard to know where to begin. We need the poetry, the profound joy and sadness of families, for a very solid reason. With a grasp of the poetry comes a way to shake off our perennial blindness to the meaning of other people's lives. When we meet across the chasms of class, race, sex, age, and all the other ancient and contemporary gulfs barring human beings from one another, the one experience most of us share is the family. There is very little difference between one person and another, William James once said, though what difference there is is very important. You learn this by studying families. For those like me, who want a more democratic and equal society, a sense of the elusive, complex poetry of family matters is a reminder of how resistant families can be to public policy, meddling, good works, and other efforts of reformers to straighten out the human race. Try to break up a family fight, and you end up getting socked yourself. Unhappy or happy, the specific poetry of any particular family will leak through all the grids laid down by the experts. In looking at families, we are struck again and again by the mysterious capacity of people to give and withhold themselves on their own terms.

All this is a plea for compassion first, and then modesty. Giving more support to families is not going to end the grief of children and parents. More generous family policy would do only what any public action can do. It can help parents and children meet the inevitable tragedies of life with more dignity and less needless pain. This is not the millennium, but then family life is not a millennial sort of thing.

There is another side to this matter of poetry, and it bears on what kind of family scholarship we might look for over the next few years. I've touched on a number of reasons why the topic of the family has peculiar political resonance, but the resonance is not only political. Few other subjects carry such a burden of mythology. The family scholarship these days is iconoclastic and revisionist in spirit, yet it is also intensely personal. One reason why the grown-up children of the 60s find the family fascinating as a scholarly topic is that it poses the question of subjectivity and objectivity so clearly. You can't discuss families the way you might talk about fruit flies. Indeed, one of the most striking things about current work on families is the way that it tends to express profoundly personal meanings. Perhaps all scholarship is a form of autobiography, but in few other realms is it as imperative that scholars examine both their own family experiences and their relationships to the families they are studying. The most interesting scholarship on the family tends to be romantic in one sense or another. It dissents from the conventions of objectivity, yet is bothered, as all Romantic scholarship ought to be, by the question of validity. Here, as elsewhere, it is evident that the troubled soul of the 60s goes marching on.

Our conversation begins to resemble that in the last scene in Eugene O'Neill's (1956) great family drama, *Long Day's Journey Into Night*. Sitting together in a dwindling pool of light, the darkness growing, the family talks on. Fathers, mothers, brothers, sisters are trying to explain: not understanding, but comprehending; loving one another, but hating and hurting each other; tangling and untangling like badly cast fishing lines, a group of inviolate, wounded selves. O'Neill's characters, like the rest of us, are speaking about the family in order to explain their attitudes toward life itself.

NOTE

1. With great regret we note that it is now 2002 and the "radical old people's movement" has not yet emerged. But we can certainly still hope!

An American Education

I WANT TO TALK about some of the elements that go into a complete education. I assume that the aim of education is a more conscious and complete self. I want to suggest that a sound education is the product of a mediation between certain of the great contraries of existence. For example, remembering and seeing. There's a circle involved in becoming a really conscious person, a circle of seeing and memory. To see things, you need to remember, and in order to remember, you need to see. This sounds theoretically impossible. But people round the circle all the time: They see and remember and see again. Seeing and remembering may be the roots of anything we call a self, and some balance between these two is critical. Some people, and even some cultures, are too haunted by the past to see clearly now. On the other hand, we know people—and cultures—so used to squinting at the glaring present that they have no memory.

In *The Book of Laughter and Forgetting*, the Czech writer Kundera (1980) talks about modern times as the "age of the airbrush." You blow away the part of the picture you don't want, a convenient 20th-century form of amnesia. Kundera describes a famous photograph of the founders of the Czech People's Republic. One aide lends the prime minister his fur hat, and then the picture gets snapped. Some years later the aide is purged and, of course, airbrushed out of the famous picture. New copies of the photo are sent around to schools and public offices, but the prime minister is still wearing the missing aide's hat. This is not only a phenomenon of totalitarian societies: In my 11th-grade American history course I speak of America as the United States of Amnesia. Americans of each generation seem surprised to discover poverty and inequality, even though these were settled features of the republic as early as the 1830s. Again, some people and some cultures are so haunted by the future that they can't face the present.

Clearly in any sound existence the present should hang in balance with the future and the past: They should balance like the parts of a mobile, righting and correcting each other in the dance we all do. Right now in President Reagan's America, most poor kids have lost the sense that there will be a valid future. The grotesque unemployment rates for the young are

31

our biggest educational problem, because they cheat young lives of the necessary sense of a future. A remembered past, a seen present, and an imagined future need to hang together in some balance that each of us must strike. You could say that arranging them in the right proportions is one of the basic tasks of an education.

Another big step is learning to free up your imagination and yoke it to reality. Thinking of education as a process of disciplining the imagination is a classic American tradition. This is the way that our classics—Emerson and Whitman—saw the task of living and learning. Walt Whitman was our first developmental psychologist: Perhaps it's time for him to step out of the closet. He had a formula—he stole it from Emerson—that goes like this: The Me plus the Not Me equals the Real Me. Development is not just the influence of external forces on you—that would make you a machine, as B. F. Skinner and the behaviorists would like you to be. Nor is development a flowering from within, independent of reality. That's sappy, sentimental Romanticism. Whitman and a long line of tough-minded American Romantics believed that a true sense of self—the Real Me—arose out of an interaction of the self with nature and with other people. The Real Me, a conscious self, a liberated and disciplined imagination, is a product of this developmental dialectic. Education, in this classic American way of viewing life, emerges out of the interplay, the dialectic, of the imagination and reality.

This line of thought says that education involves discovering a particular kind of romance and a particular kind of science and seeing that the two are interwoven, part of the same imaginative rhythm of living. The quest, then, is for true romance and for a valid science. True romance is the myth-making power—the self-renewing poetry that rises when the imagination marries the world. It's what makes the imagination come alive, and it is akin to science. Valid science arises in a disciplined encounter of the Me and the Not Me, and involves the courage to front the facts, as Thoreau says, and publish them to the world. I'm talking about true romance, then, as opposed to sentimental and narcissistic romanticism, and about valid science, as opposed to a scientism that tries to reduce all of existence to the laws of inanimate matter. I think, at bottom, an education in true romance and valid science is making yourself at home in the world. If "at home in the world" has a cozy and comfortable sound, like the picture of the sleeping bears on the cartons of "Sleepytime" herb tea, I don't mean it that way—though keeping cozy in a chilly world is getting to be a major accomplishment. Scrabbling any kind of a home out of the rocks, in the Stone Age or now, can be a desperate business. For one of the most appalling truths about this world we try to find a home in is its fundamental uncertainty. When you really understand that, then you may begin to see what an achievement it is to make a home in the world. Nothing stays the same. Nothing we make lasts. Sleep, love, life itself—all pass. But what we create—art, human art—can last, some art longer than another. And, like the crew that has to keep rebuilding the ship out on the open ocean of uncertainty, we keep making and remaking our homes in the world. The process of making, of homebuilding, endures.

I think the best account of growing and learning in the classic American vein I'm tracing is the wonderful first half of Mark Twain's (1883) book, *Life on the Mississippi*, a book about his education as a master pilot. Twain is a very young man who has to grow up to be at home on the river. He connects the search for truth with the quest for virility, insisting that the imagination grows best by confronting reality: It's what happens when the active mind encounters the actualities of the river. Seeing and memory are important parts of this encounter. Memory comes into play at each step. Seeing and remembering, you learn every sandbar and shoal and snag in the river. You learn them, and then you have to forget them, and learn new things, for the mighty river never stops changing its course. You never stop knowing the river; you're always in the process of learning about it. Although the fundamental truth about the river is uncertain, Twain learns that knowing is better than not knowing, and that a kind of provisional, ever-changing knowledge can save your life.

This may be the hardest lesson Twain has to learn—the lesson about uncertainty. When Twain first discovers that his knowledge is turning obsolete the minute he learns it, he's tempted to despair. Like many of us, like students everywhere, his shocked response to the fundamental uncertainty of things is despair. Maybe knowing isn't any good. If nothing is sure, then nothing matters. If there isn't one right answer or the right way to paint or even to read a text, what's the point of making any distinction between ignorance and knowledge? Twain shows that even if all knowledge is provisional and there is no absolute, the pilot who keeps learning the changing river is safer than an ignoramus. Safer, and more alive and conscious. Knowledge is provisional, he says, but it can guide you along in the shifting, flowing reality. Knowledge is fluid and not solid. It's something you make and remake and remake again, and in the process you remake yourself, to be born again.

Instead of memorizing the maps, you need the more basic knowledge of how to draw and redraw the map itself. You need to learn how to make the maps, because you always need new maps. Making new maps, however, is not just a matter of gathering information. The river boat pilot is engaged in a life and death business: He saves lives. Twain insists that knowing has much to do with self-preservation and self-renewal. The river boat pilot makes the sleepy little towns along the river come to life—Twain describes him as a kind of modern-day Orpheus whose steam whistle wakes communities out of their sleep, to live again. In Twain's account knowledge has something to do with self-renewal and the battle we all fight against inner and outer death. He suggests that renewal is a product of the marriage of contrary realms of existence: the Me and the Not Me, the self and nature, the self and society. He refuses to see science and art (or poetry) as rivals or antagonists, precisely because he believes that the imagination thrives on a constant engagement with reality. The dialectic of the river and of the self—the interplay of the objective and the subjective—is what makes a truer and more conscious self, a Real Me.

Clearly this emphasis in our tradition on the blend of science and romance means that knowing is not only a matter of the head: Knowing draws on memory, courage, creativity, and the unconscious. Among other qualities, this kind of knowing draws on the courage to act on your knowledge and to take responsibility. Creativity thrives by the courageous and virile engagement of reality in the midst of today's profound uncertainty. It involves a blend of what an older psychology called the heart and the head.

Twain's teacher is Mr. Bixby. He tells the boy: "I'll learn you the river if it kills you." There's no doubt in Bixby's mind that he can teach the boy or, more properly, learn him the river. Lucky students at our own school find a teacher or another student to be their Mr. Bixby. Even mean pilots, like ornery teachers, have something to teach you.

Writing about his youth from the vantage point of middle age, Twain saw that steamboat America represented a time when there was a balance in the culture. A balance of the great contraries, but also a right proportion between villages, human beings, and steam technology. The wonderful first half of the book ends with the boiler explosion that kills Twain's brother and turns his own hair white at the age of 23. Plainly Twain was thinking in social and collective terms about a time when the path to development still seemed free and open. He showed how important community is for making yourself at home in the world. Most of the equipment we use in building our homes in the world is collectively created, like our knowledge. Twain says that the pilots formed an association—today we might call it a union—getting together to pool their knowledge of the river. They set up a system of boxes with messages about changing river conditions, so one boat could tell the others about the shifting river. Knowledge keeps changing, it's never fixed or final, and it's something that people make and remake collectively, a communal creation.

Later on, Twain gets so pessimistic about America and its possibilities that it's good to remember his having stood proud in his pilot's uniform: a free man among other free men in the fellowship of masterless equals. He was celebrating the marriage of mind and reality, and also celebrating the importance of craftsmanship, what Thorstein Veblen (1914) called the "instinct of workmanship." Piloting was Twain's metaphor for the spirit of creativity that ran against the grain of what he called "the Gilded Age." Piloting stands for true value in a fake world. In the big steamboat race at the end of the book, the men stripped away all the decoration and even got rid of the paying cargo in order to do something clean and first-rate for a change, something esthetic. The ideal blend of workmanship, creativity, and freedom—in life and in education—comes out in Twain's adjectives: "gold-leaf, kid-glove, diamond breast-pin piloting." It comes out in one of Twain's favorite words, "gaudy." Among other things, the pilot represents the spirit of gaudiness in a society often starved by its Philistine realism and tin-pot pragmatism. Praising the pilot's sense of craft and beauty, Twain is also speaking of his own development as a writer, finding the words to write about becoming a pilot: In doing so, he shows that he's become master of his second art, writing.

Twain's self-portrait places the pilot in a time and place when things were balanced, when Orpheus, the spirit of the arts, stood with Prometheus, the spirit of technology: The steamboat, in its scale and in the human art that goes into its piloting, represents the right balance.

We prize Twain's account of his education for the profound individuality it breathes, the way it points to the excitement of the free individual learning to be at home on the river at a time when White males on the American frontier were among the freest human beings who ever lived. He wrote of one kind of American possibility we never want to lose. And yet, as Twain shows in the last half of the book, the time is past, and the place is gone. How to sustain true individuality in a different time is one of our challenges today. As Twain's pilots' association shows, the question of true individuality is at bottom a question about politics. Ultimately, as even Twain realized, enhancing and nourishing true individuality and creativity may involve scrapping the obsolete and destructive cult of rugged individualism espoused by President Reagan and his political allies. Like so many Americans since his time, Twain eventually retreated to nostalgia and sentimentality, growing more and more bitter about his own time. He grew fearful of the future, too, and wrote *A Connecticut Yankee in King Arthur's Court* (1889) to show how the modern technological imagination could sever its ties with nature and human sympathy and produce a nightmarish war to save the hearts and minds of a "backward" people by destroying them with modern weapons.

Our age is going to be a more collective and communal epoch than Twain's 19th-century America. Some form of collectivism is inevitable on this shrinking and hungry planet in the nuclear age. Will it be a democratic collectivism with room for the individuality our tradition so rightly prizes, or another variety of totalitarian collectivism? Surely our time demands a form of community that can honor the wonderful vitality of the individual celebrated by Twain and Whitman. Twain was on to something very big when he showed how his own more conscious and creative self emerged out of the relationship with the older pilot, Mr. Bixby, and when he pointed to the profoundly communal grounding of the master pilots' kingly individuality. True individuality—not the selfish rugged individualism of the Marlboro ads—arises out of common human bonds and ties. Our cherished sense of self, at its best, is a product of life together in a community. If I'm right, then learning to be at home on the river now in 1982 can be learning to make ourselves at home in communities like the Commonwealth School.

Five Big Ideas

2002

"PROGRESSIVE" CLASSROOM FADS come and go, but a stance toward childhood that pays careful attention to kids, their individuality, and their concerns and needs and minds is, I would argue, a horse of another, more permanent, color. The world's democratic revolutions first touched children's lives as matters of family practice and parenting, as much as classrooms and pedagogy. Pierre, in Tolstoy's *War and Peace*, spouts all the fashionable radical ideas he picks up from Rousseau but is then shocked when his wife, Natasha, takes the step of actually nursing the baby. Over the last two centuries, many families in many different world cultures have moved toward a more egalitarian family practice that marks an important shift toward listening to children. Kids and their thoughts and voices count for more in the minds of more grown-ups. I'm not denying that the lot of children in many places is miserable—even growing worse: child labor, child soldiers, starving children, neglected and abused children—the reports are many and grim. And yet as Amartya Sen (2001) and others have noted, there is also a worldwide story of how, along with women (their fates are always intertwined), children in many cultures are stepping into the light of new recognition as persons in their own right. It would be a good thing if more schools across the planet felt free to follow the lead of the world's families.

Five very large ideas animate democratic teaching and family practice as it has spanned the last 200 years. First, children (like adults) are social beings: Kids can and do learn a great deal on their own, but much learning flows from trusting relationships with adults and other kids in an educating community. This is an aspect of child development often ignored in U.S. educational policy circles today—although it is of course an assumption underlying daily practice for most families and many classroom teachers.

A second big idea is that children are prodigious "natural" learners; childhood is a time above all of intellectual construction, exploring meaning, and amassing information. Before school, all children of all social groups, for example, collect (daily) an impressive vocabulary—at a far faster rate than in school. Wise parents and teachers understand that children, when they begin school, bring much knowledge, complex understandings, and ways of learning how to learn. This is why a teaching regime with opportunities for active learning and participation is preferable to passive rote and the classroom style Montaigne derided centuries ago as "thundering in children's ears." Of course there is a lot kids don't know—entire worlds, civilizations, alphabets, facts, phonics, numbers—and that is where schooling and a rich curriculum should come in. But all sound teaching builds on the powerful constructive capacities children bring to school and makes use of their individual knowledge and strengths and passions as bridges to more disciplined school studies.

A third big idea is that children are unique. This individuality is not only a stubborn reality but an important set of clues pointing to how best to raise and teach them—like wise parents who understand that a sister is not the same person as her brother, a good school learning environment is prepared, on occasion, to develop children's particular interests and passions, as well as more universal curriculum goals. Listening to individual children is at the core of good teaching, as well as good parenting.

A fourth idea touches on the crucial role of adults and their judgment and authority in kids' development. At home, of course, but also in schools: Teachers and parents are the ones who constantly adjust the balances—between the individual and the social, the child and the curriculum, work and play, needs and responsibilities. These are site-specific matters requiring constant, specific, changing judgments by both teachers and parents. There is always a new, running balance to strike—you can go too far in either direction. (Dewey perpetually and vainly warned us to keep Child and Curriculum in some balance.)

A fifth big idea emerges from all these others: an old critique of the conventional formal 19th-century schools modeled on the old factory system. Schools have never sufficiently capitalized on "natural" and "informal" modes of learning used in families and communities.

These five ideas are part of a dissenting democratic countertradition to the school establishment we have inherited today. If they were more influential, I believe we would be making more progress in educational reform. In particular, they can help us in grappling with the big educational challenges of our time: family diversity, and especially immigrant diversity; the need for first-rate child-care settings; and the ambition to give every child an education in academic and intellectual complexity.

These first two items stare us all in the face; it is embarrassing that they are not more central to educational policy today. We are living in a time when both city and suburban schools face unprecedented immigration and family diversity. Yet, puzzlingly, one of the big policy themes of the era is the effort to standardize and tighten bureaucratic control over teachers and classrooms. The diversity of families today would be served far better if more educators would adopt the stance of Leonard Covello, the principal of Benjamin Franklin High School in the 1930s and himself an Italian immigrant (Perrone, 1998). Covello saw the need for schools that operated as democratic communities, welcoming families and capitalizing on diversity; he devoted much thought to ways of reaching families, personalizing learning for individual kids, and helping schools become networks of contact between grown-ups and families and communities. For Covello, teaching was a form of community organizing.

The other huge family/school issue today is child care, and the amount of time kids are spending outside the family in formal institutions such as schools, day-care settings, after-school programs, and the like. This development, which touches families across the spectrum of social classes, seems to me yet another important reason why a more personalized and communal vision of all education as a social, as well as an academic, apprenticeship of the young meets the needs of the times. Instead of pushing for schools that are more and more impersonal, test-driven, and bureaucratic, we should be making schools places where children can live well-rounded lives that support academic and intellectual achievement. All families would benefit from schools where conversation and play were part of a balanced and human routine. Instead, some of today's policymakers and school managers are actually pressuring preschools to become more rigid and prescribed. Childhood, like our forests and wetlands, is at risk.

The last challenge is society's growing sense that we need to educate all children for intellectual and academic complexity. Americans disagree today, as they have for many generations, about the elements of a decent education. But most would agree that the demands of work, citizenship, and even (perhaps) such aspects of life as parenting have grown more abstract and intricate. Formal schooling and educational credentials play a greater role in people's lives. A fair expectation, for example, is that most students in school now will at some time enroll in some form of higher education. Being good at school matters more than it used to. Being bad at school is particularly disastrous if you are working-class or dark-skinned, or poor. We all have a stake in helping schools become places where most kids (not just a few) know and understand more than in a simpler past.

Instead of looking for ways for students to master intellectual and academic complexity by offering many connections to learning, however, more of our schools today are under pressure to further standardize and in effect simplify learning, and push for the old factory-style, one-size-fits-all curriculum. This is especially and disturbingly true for schools dealing with working-class children, poor kids, and kids of color. The radical inequality of American society in the last 20 years is harshly reflected in current school practices: We are dramatically standardizing and dumbing down education for the poor and working class, on the one hand, while for the children of the affluent, learning is becoming more individualized, and more intellectually demanding. In the Brave New World we are building, some children get simple, K-Mart lessons; others get to purchase intellectual sophistication and complexity at Nieman-Marcus.

On this score, I would argue, the big ideas about family and educational practice I have just outlined have a lot to offer. An important feature of complex learning is that, unlike a regime of simple right and wrong answers, it actually requires periods of living in ambiguity, confusion, and uncertainty. At least some portion of the school curriculum in all subjects should deliberately develop and stretch the crucial human capacity to work in the dark—the hallmark of all truly serious thinking. The dark is best mastered in the good company of other students, with much conversation and scaffolding, and a thoughtful well-educated adult guide, but mastered it needs to be, or you may never become an educated mind, confident, free, upright, and whole. You cannot interpret a good poem, or come to a deeper understanding of the causes of the Civil War, or sift through the causes and politics of global warming without some ability to sort through competing meanings, arguments, and explanations—and some sense of why any conclusion will have to remain tentative, subject to further evidence. And at least some portion of the school curriculum in all subjects should reach for the kind of passionate understanding and intellectual commitment students get when they are able to dig deep and long into topics and projects of their own choosing.

Historically, it is significant that large numbers of adults in both families and schools today can take children and their thoughts and imaginations seriously—not to exaggerate the genius of the young, or rhapsodize about their stumbling efforts, but to make cultural space on a large scale for their thoughts and voices in families and classrooms and other settings as apprentice thinkers, scientists, artists, creators, problem-solvers, and citizens. A big question today is whether our new appreciation of children's intellectual and imaginative capacities will ever get reflected in the daily life of our schools. I have to say that there are grounds for worry.

I hate to imagine that the schools and districts now cutting recess and slashing budgets for real books and art and music and adopting reforms that attempt to control and script teachers' performances are the wave of some grim Orwellian future for kids in public schools.

The discovery of children's minds, their inventiveness and their creativity, is one of the great human intellectual accomplishments of the last two hundred years. All over the world, parents and teachers have built their practice on this discovery—to make learning more pleasurable and solid, and childhood a time of apprenticeship to art, reason, and a richer and better life. To neglect this wonderful historic discovery—that our children are thinking and imagining, and that this intellectual work can be one of the most significant forces in their own healthy development—is both a sin against the spirit and a terrible waste of young minds. I believe that the pleasure—the fun—of using your mind creatively and well is one of the implicit natural rights of childhood around the world. Beauty is a necessity for kids, as much as food and water and love. Children's play is not only recreation but also the early version, the dress-up rehearsal, for all the rest of human culture, including what we used to call "high" culture. It would be a terrible irony—especially in this democracy of ours—if in the name of "standards," our schools turn away from being places where children explore, joke, pursue passions, speak the poetry of their lives, and have wonderful ideas—just as this ambition for them and their lives was shown to be utterly realizable.

PART II

School and Society

FEATHERSTONE'S IDEAS about the classroom have deep roots in his ideas about politics and society. He came of age as a journalist in the 1960s, but his political tradition is an older one, one that might be called socialist, but is in love with—and takes seriously—the promises of American democracy. He is, he writes—and the pieces in this section show—"deeply sympathetic to the argument that the cure for the ills of American democracy is more democracy." This democracy is economic as well as civic; these writings frequently suggest that the one may be impossible without the other. Featherstone's democracy is a poet's vision as well as that of a political thinker, as much John Keats as John Dewey, a place where "every human might become great."

Although he writes mostly about schools, Featherstone recognizes that that vision will not be realized through school reform alone; indeed, school reform without economic and political democracy is unlikely even to reform schools, as Featherstone suggested in his 1969 essay "The Problem Is More Than Schools." Some of the essays in this section reflect on 1960s and 1970s political struggles over community control. As a writer for the *New Republic*, Featherstone reported on the nation's most famous such battle, in the Ocean Hill–Brownsville sections of Brooklyn, New York (we reprint a small sample of this extensive reportage: "Ocean Hill Is Alive, and, Well . . ."). Several years later, he explored similar themes in articles about the results of court-ordered school desegregation in Boston, where some White neighborhoods fiercely resisted busing, both out of racism and out of a desire for their children to attend neighborhood schools. In these complex, ambivalent sketches, he grapples with the effects of race, class, and inequality on schools. He also reflects on the urgent need to improve the relationships between schools and the communities they serve, writing, "Schools cannot continue as colonial garrisons in suspicious and hostile neighborhoods."

These political concerns turn out to be inseparable from the classroom. He persistently points out that the most pressing American
educational dilemma is not the lack of informality in classrooms but
instead whether we can build a more equal, multiracial society. More
than 30 years later, as we face political debates over testing, charter
schools, vouchers, and the privatization of public schools, Featherstone's
observations still ring true, and his more recent writings have continued
to explore the ideal of better schools for "everybody's children."

For Featherstone, education should prepare children for citizenship
in a democracy; without sacrificing standards, it should be an "apprenticeship to freedom," as he recently wrote. Although painfully aware of
schools' failures in this realm, he remains keenly interested in why a
few succeed in teaching the children of the poor. The answer sounds
so much simpler than it is, he knows. Writing in 1995 ("Democratic
Vistas") on Deborah Meier's Central Park East High School, he observes
that teachers and children there have "what many of us . . . still lack, a
structure of respect."

Ocean Hill Is Alive, and, Well . . .

MARCH 29, 1969

O N DIFFERENT OCCASIONS this winter and spring I've been making visits to schools in the Ocean Hill–Brownsville demonstration district in Brooklyn, New York. It's neither possible nor desirable to weigh the merits of a venture like this after one turbulent year; what follows are simply some impressions of the schools, and some thoughts about where they might go from here.

One of the problems in creating good schools is that there is very little solid information, of the sort easy to generalize from, about how children learn—not just poor children, the "deprived," and the "disadvantaged," but all children. No one knows very much about how children actually learn to read, for example. There is some very good evidence that a good background in phonics is useful for many children. Nevertheless, sensible teachers in classes where phonics is stressed soon discover that a lot of children need other things; quite a few are completely idiosyncratic in what helps their reading along. An ideal "program" would offer many different ways to pick up reading, and this is in fact what the people at PS 144 are trying to set up, although the kids, like those in most Ocean Hill schools, are still on the BRL-Sullivan programmed workbooks (whose main and only virtue is that kids can work through them on their own, freeing the teacher to work with individual students).

Some of the things we know about good schools are so obvious they're platitudes: They are generally run, for example, by good principals. Successful principals are by no means alike: They differ widely on such matters as discipline. No one formula could be devised for all the necessary talents, but it should be apparent that the city's ranked list and its special examinations are not likely to be much help in finding good people. Appointment of principals has been a key issue in decentralization battles so far, and rightly so. The Ocean Hill governing board, after a number of court battles, has been permitted to name "demonstration principals" whose credentials meet state certification standards or an equivalent. It seems to me that its appointments have been first-rate, as even many opponents will concede.

Schools and teachers succeeding with ghetto kids do different things and in different ways—they do not present a "model" or a "program" that can be duplicated and done by somebody else in a routine. This suggests that "models" are not necessarily what we ought to be looking for. Recently much was made of research showing—not very surprisingly—that teachers' attitudes toward children are important. (So is the attitude of the administration toward teachers.)

What are the teachers like at Ocean Hill? Many are untrained, of course—college graduates and graduate students who came this fall because of social conscience or the draft, or a desire to try their hand at teaching. It's hard to convey a general impression of what classes are like, because the schools are so big—1, 000 students and more—and because even in routine schools a variety of teaching goes on.

There are few classes where chaos reigns. In some schools there aren't any. They exist though. In one, with kids fighting, the teacher practically cries as he asks me to leave. Next door, an equally inexperienced young man presides over a formal, altogether serene and quiet class. Several doors up, children form a strange, ragged sort of moving reading group with a cheerful young Black lady who tours the room, holding court: It looks impromptu, but the reading seems to be coming along, and the kids are having a good time. An aide works seriously and for a long time with one little girl who has troubles. In another school are two young men, graduate students, just the sort of people you'd like to see in teaching, intelligent, joking with the kids before class starts. They tower over the tiny fourth graders. With the bell, the whole scene changes. One teacher stations himself in front and angrily hollers questions to the increasingly restless class about some very simple words on a boring phonics chart, while the other patrols the edges of the room beating out brushfires of talk and squabbling. When class ends, everybody relaxes and fraternizes in the trenches, old buddies again. It's crazy: Two hulking men and 16 fourth graders and this is how they teach. Yet I'm sure they could make fairly good teachers.

Another school has some fine kindergarten classes with plenty of books and phonic games—a number of kids are reading—they remind you by contrast how bare most of the classrooms seem. Most need more teaching materials, although I saw a lovely room full of kids' drawings, and one young Black teacher had a handsome display of Africana in his classroom.

It is hard to pin good teaching down: Most good teachers like kids, care about their learning, make demands, set standards, and tend to think in terms of individuals. They are more ready than others to take advantage of opportunities—something somebody says, a new interest, an occasion when most youngsters are busy—to teach something. There aren't very many good teachers in Ocean Hill yet, but a number seem to be learning fast, even when they are having trouble with discipline. In their inexperience, they rely too heavily on the phonics reading workbooks and the programmed materials. These are dreary and far from adequate at teaching reading. The kids, however, like them, and this is not as perverse as it sounds: They go through them at their own rate, working on their own, and most succeed in filling in the exercises, which they enjoy. The catch is you can get to be an expert at the workbooks without getting to read a real book. Many of the teachers have discovered this, and have started filling up the classroom with readers and real books, and there are some efforts at encouraging writing in the form of dictated stories and so on. It seemed to me that these sorts of materials can serve a function for beginning teachers: They free them from the burden of formal teaching, to some extent, and they make it easier to work with individuals and small groups. They could be a first step toward a much freer kind of classroom.

The Problem Is More Than Schools

DESPITE THE CHAOS in New York City, a number of cities are gingerly moving toward some form of decentralization and local control. Worried administrators are trying to read the murky lessons of New York's disaster: It is obvious that any planning for decentralization has to include representatives of all the important political elements in a city. There should be one single plan, instead of half a dozen. Guarantees of teachers' rights have to be spelled out. And if decentralization is preceded by any experimental dry runs, such as the demonstration districts in New York, it will be necessary to delegate powers and lines of authority with a great deal of precision. Such experiments may be necessary on political grounds, but they inevitably work as lightning rods, attracting trouble, offering easy marks for sabotage to those opposing change, and exposing the fundamental issues at stake. The experience of New York with its demonstration districts resounds like a funeral bell with one practical lesson: Any experimental districts ought to include some White middle-class areas, and probably should include poor and lower-middle-class Whites as well. White parents have to be persuaded that they, too, can benefit from lay participation in school reform. The failure to do this in New York—to name, for example, the integrated Joan of Arc district on the Upper West Side as one of the model districts—was a major error.

These and other tactical considerations must be weighed, but when all is said, there is no set of techniques for dodging the underlying dilemmas posed by the movement for community control. Lurking like carp below the surface of the school disputes are a number of shadowy issues very nearly without precedent in our history. There are intellectual issues arising out of the new communitarianism of portions of the middle class, and new challenges to the professionalism of the urban bureaucracies. There are the political issues raised by the minority revolutions. And intertwined with these are the educational issues. One of the difficulties in the school crises is that all the questions—each complex and baffling enough in its own right—fuse together, so that protagonists find themselves forced to take sides on a whole range of complex concerns all at once. It seems to me that, under the circumstances, only ideologues and

48

bigots can look at what is happening with undivided minds. Two concerns, both as yet badly defined, form part of the intellectual background of discussions of decentralization. The first—the widespread sympathy with demands for increased local control—is still only a mood. The second—the attack on professional monopoly of the professions—is as yet reflected in a few weak stirrings of rebellion. Both may become more important as time goes on; ultimately the constituency for community control and reform of the professions may include more than just the oppressed urban minorities.

Race and the collapse of services for the poor fire the movement for community control now, but it also draws on wider currents of feelings. Resentment at the way the cities work has been festering for 20 years. As Nathan Glazer (1969) says, the program for community control antedates the Black revolution—it was drawn up by middle-class theorists like Paul and Percival Goodman and Jane Jacobs.[1] Nor was it an exclusive concern of a few White intellectuals with a taste for anarchism. In moving out to the suburbs many people were choosing, among other things, to sacrifice certain amenities of city life for a setting in which they had some leverage on government and access to the authorities—or at the very least, choices about such matters as the educational environment in which their children were to grow up. Clearly there were many other reasons for the middle-class exodus, not least of which was the desire to escape the presence of the new Black immigrants. And of all places, the suburbs illustrate the extent to which American life is organized in mass national units: Their chain stores and their similarities of landscape are reminders that there will always be a limit to how much local control any of us will have in a continental, and even international, economy. But granting all this, I still think Glazer is right: One aspect of the growth of suburbia has been middle-class dissatisfaction with urban services, distrust of the vast city bureaucracies, and aversion to being administered.

This resentment of a distinctly modern condition of powerlessness is shared by portions of the population in all the advanced technological societies. It unites conservatives and radicals—like an SDS woman I spoke to who had worked with some John Birchers against an urban renewal project in South Boston. It is accentuated by the recurring incapacity of majoritarian democracies to come to terms with their ethnic and cultural diversities—an incapacity that has produced waves of separatist (and often reactionary) movements in countries like Britain, Belgium, and Canada. In America, attention has focused on the rise of Black nationalism, but a similar mood of resentful communitarianism lies at the roots of the spreading White middle-class revolts against urban renewal plans, superhighways, and ABM missile sites; it is responsible for a measure of the campus unrest, as well. In distinct ways, Eugene McCarthy, George Wallace, and Robert Kennedy were able to tap into these feelings in the last presidential campaign, invoking what Richard Goodwin (1969) has called the sources of our public unhappiness. So far it remains simply a mood: It has not been able to crystallize itself into any institutional shape. The main intellectual failure of those who share it has been a reluctance to grapple with the problem that demands for participation and local control have to be squared with the fact that this is a nation of 200,000,000 people, many of whom are organized into hierarchies, bureaucracies, and unions. What is called for is the kind of intellectual enterprise that Paul and Percival Goodman began in *Communitas* (1947), an attempt to spell out real alternatives to our present urban life. What we are getting, instead, is simply a reiteration of the dim aspirations of a troubled middle class for accountability, participation, and a politics of private expressiveness. Nonetheless these dissatisfactions with the urban order, and the call for more participation and local control, are very much in the air: Even though their intellectual sources are different from those of the minority revolutions, they have contributed to the declining legitimacy of the urban institutions now under fire.

This mood informs an assault now under way against the bureaucracies and professions. In an explosive new context, the advocates of community control of the schools have revived a traditionally stormy issue in American education: whether laymen or professionals will run the schools. This may signal the slow beginning of an important shift in thinking—not just for Blacks but for the White middle class, too. In the past, radicals and reformers have tended to assume that virtue must dwell with the professionals, whose standards are usually more progressive and universal than those of their clients; local control in the South, everybody knew, spoke in the accents of parochialism and bigotry. This is a classic argument; it remains true today. Its force has been somewhat blunted in recent years, however, as it also becomes plain that large numbers of professionals—in medicine and other fields as well as education—are digging in to protect vested interests from reasonable public scrutiny and accountability. In many cases the professionals are hiding behind obsolete and self-serving credentials and licensing systems. The furor over schools has obscured how general these problems are becoming. In the midst of the Albany legislative sessions on school decentralization, for example, there were a number of skirmishes over hospitals—particularly Harlem Hospital—that raised similar issues. Both hospitals and schools are failing the poor, and lack of money is only part of the problem. In both, the professionals have a natural stake in keeping themselves in charge and the public out—although there are indications that a number of disgusted doctors may end up crossing over to the ranks of a community control movement.

Reform of structures that have simply grown up over the years is clearly long overdue, although this may not be the most opportune moment for a sensible debate. Many children of the affluent are talking as though they want to repudiate all professional standards. A few teachers, doctors, lawyers, and others are seriously working to define a new professionalism—one that would serve clients instead of the profession. Up to now, their influence hasn't been great.

Intolerable schools and collapsing health services give the revolt of the urban minorities more of a focus than middle-class longings for participation; but while it is more specific, it shares many of the same battle cries and poses, with one great exception, similar challenges to the professionals. The exception, of course, is race. A new Black community consciousness is stirring; and we are witnessing an ambitious attempt to organize the Black ghettos into a political force around issues like community control of schools.

To take the measure of all these stirrings is far from easy. As with the middle-class left, a good deal of Black revolutionary rhetoric barely masks a profound despair; and politics too often becomes a matter of inflammatory gestures rather than programs. And for all the organizing that is going on, Blacks in the cities are still dismayingly weak as a political force. The needles turn in the old, old grooves: People don't vote, leadership in the "community" is divided and greedy, few organizations are capable of surmounting the grinding factionalism. As a political fact, it is wise to remember, Black Power is still a slogan: Real power in the ghetto remains the same as ever, an occasional veto power over the White armies of occupation.

Nevertheless there are signs of a change, particularly in the aftermath of the various community action programs of the War on Poverty. In many ways these programs were a bust, provoking long, senseless quarrels among the poor over bones devoid of any meat. In the absence of massive employment and income programs, bitter fights over participation seem rarely to have been worth the candle. But veterans of the poverty programs have been trained to organize; and they emerged from the whole futile process with a conviction that there are plenty of things wrong with the institutions serving ghettos besides lack of funds. The community action programs didn't produce a revolution, as their hysterical enemies charged; they didn't alter the feelings of the poor about being powerless, as sentimental advocates hoped. They have, perhaps, established an important precedent in the ghetto: Successful programs to help the poor probably can no longer be run without the active participation of representatives of the poor. This includes schools.

In the course of a curiously ambivalent assessment of the community action programs, Daniel P. Moynihan (1969) pointed out that one of their principal results has been the creation of a new Black leadership at a time when minorities are struggling for more power in city politics. Discrimination and the decline of opportunities for unskilled work in the inner-city cores have made Blacks more dependent on public institutions than earlier immigrants. At the same time, civil service reform and the professionalization and upgrading of municipal services have denied many entry into the sorts of jobs that were once available through patronage to the old-time ethnic political machines. In a sense, as Moynihan says, the poverty programs have been a substitute for Tammany, a political apprenticeship. Much of the drive for community control of schools in New York has come from people trained to hold meetings, write proposals, operate mimeograph machines, and make trouble for bureaucrats by the various community action programs of the War on Poverty. There is no cause to romanticize this process of political development or to exaggerate its progress. Harlem has its full share of the oldest politics of all—jiggery-pokery and corruption. It is too early to say with any confidence that the new leadership emerging will in fact be an improvement on the old. What is clear is that the school crises have joined this new ghetto leadership to another new group, Black professionals, ambitious and eager to reform the schools.

There are different priorities in this alliance: For some, schools come second—they are merely a focus for organizing a community. For others— for most of the professionals, and, one suspects, for most thoughtful and active parents—reforming the schools is the main task.

If the new forces in the ghetto succeed, they will in the end have to make a settlement with a society that is increasingly meritocratic and committed to more "objective" criteria in advancing people to better jobs. Perhaps they will be able to link up with general reform aimed at loosening up rigid professional structures, making qualifications for jobs rest on performance rather than credentials. Right now this seems a long way off. The experience of earlier groups with the bureaucracies suggests the need for some perspective: Once you break in fully, the walls can help protect you, too, a consideration that will not escape the attention of Black professionals as they start defining their roles in community-controlled institutions. The push to organize the ghettos poses questions that time may answer, but which now look close to insoluble. The rhetoric of the organizers masks a basically conservative aim: Many argue that the way to join up with a society that has excluded Blacks up to now is to organize as a group. But conservative or not, this tactic exposes the uncomfortable truth that life in America, for all our universalistic pretensions, is organized on the basis of competing racial and ethnic groups. Ethnic identities persist in voting patterns and ways of living: They are vital realities, not a survival from the past. Earlier groups, it must be said, have not usually managed to break into established institutions, which is what Blacks are attempting: The more common pattern was to create their own, on the margins of society—political machines, the crime syndicates, and the Catholic Church being prime examples.

There are no other levers of power within reach: Blacks have no money, and in most cities they don't have anything like a majority. They have two perennial weapons of the underdog: the appeal to the universal values— equality, justice—America says it lives by and the threat of disruption. The first has produced some gains but is not likely to carry them very much farther, and the second is wearing dangerously thin. So they have to organize, knowing as they do that any effort to organize along racial lines will cut them off from White allies. Many admit the risks involved, that community control will always be something of a sham without massive national jobs, income, and housing programs. An administrator in one of the New York demonstration districts thought about this and conceded: "The reason why we're picking on the schools is that everything else has failed."

Sooner or later discussions of these matters come round to the need for national political coalitions, for which there would seem to be no realistic immediate prospects. The decentralization crisis is in part a reflection of this political failure. Behind the struggle for community control of the ghettos lies the somber truth about America in 1969: Groups pursue self-interest to the edge of self-destruction.

Community control of the schools spells deep trouble; many of the criticisms leveled at it strike me as quite sound in theory. There are always going to be sharp limits as to how much one can accomplish simply by staging elections in unorganized communities. Community control will not mean more money for public education—indeed, one danger is that it could signal further withdrawal of White support from ghetto institutions. It raises risks of confrontations between hysterical Whites and Black extremists; as in New York it can provoke a conservative and racist backlash. And it always has to be remembered that it does not necessarily mean any change either in teaching or in learning.

Finally, however, such reservations are beside the point. The school system is shaking to pieces. There is a crisis of authority, and there has to be a political settlement. The opponents of the movement for community control have said—correctly—that it is a threat to order because it discredits many existing institutions. It does this for the good reasons that they aren't representing the interests of ghetto residents. In that sense it is revolutionary, although we should remember that most trade unions, including the UFT, used to operate on the far side of the law, and that peace usually comes about when organized groups know that they have enough strength to come to terms but not enough to destroy each other.

The opponents of community control have been unwilling to admit how much authority has ebbed away from institutions in the ghettos. They have been unable to pose any political or educational alternatives. Legitimacy can only be restored by a redistribution of power. The unanswered question in New York City, and elsewhere, is the extent to which any redistribution of power has to be along ethnic and racial lines.

Peace of sorts can come to the schools and other ghetto institutions. How much better they will then be is another matter. Less bureaucracy will be an improvement, as will more parent participation and local accountability, but there is no evidence that any of these reforms will necessarily improve children's learning. The movement for community control is a political phenomenon. It has been the focus of debates on education because there seems no way of moving schools in any direction unless the political dilemmas are first resolved. Educationally speaking, it is not a program but simply a response to what are believed to be the failures of integration and compensatory education. Actually, integration, like Christianity, has rarely been attempted in any intelligent way. (A notable exception is Berkeley, California.) Its failure in places like New York was political: Not enough people wanted it. The same thing is true of compensatory education: No dramatic, expensive attempt has been made anywhere to make schools for Black and poor children *better* than schools for the middle class. This, too, has been a political matter: Few people are willing to spend that kind of money. (For one thing, it might be better spent on jobs and income programs.) For some time to come, it will be chimerical to hold out promises of either integration or adequate compensatory programs in most districts of a city like New York.

Throughout the discussions of education, little has been said about parents' involvement, aside from a number of misleading claims on this subject from the ranks of those supporting community control. Yet some of the most promising schools in our cities have been on a scale sufficiently small to make participation work. The experience of small privately financed "community" schools and storefronts has confirmed what some of the better preschool and Head Start programs have discovered: that apart from political considerations, there is a powerful case for parent involvement in younger children's schools—because what parents do and say is more important in the lives of small children than anything a teacher does.

Some thoughtful people in the ghettos say that these private ventures, at present financed by string and chewing gum, point toward a day when public education as we know it will be dead in our cities, a victim of its inability to resolve its besetting dilemmas. Despairing activists in the community-control movement are saying that they have given up on the public schools, although nobody has any idea of how sources of public money could be tapped to feed private ghetto schools. Over the next few years there may be some experimenting with public tuition grants to groups of parents interested in setting up their own schools. Like decentralization and community control, this will be sold as a sovereign remedy, guaranteed to cure every ill that man or horse is heir to. Again, some skepticism will be in order: The poor have not traditionally fared well at the mercies of the free market. One look at the fraudulent schools supposedly teaching computer programming to ghetto residents should convince anybody of the limits of free enterprise. Still, the crisis may push us that way, and if it does we may have to change some of our historic ideas about education. As David Cohen[2] puts it, the state might come to be seen as the regulator of the schools rather than the agency that actually operates them. There have been glimmerings of this notion throughout the decentralization controversy in New York: All the different community-control proposals tacitly assumed new responsibilities for state education authorities—regulating such matters as civil liberties and the teaching of bigotry, maintaining standards, and overseeing the distribution of state and federal aid according to equitable formulas.

There is plenty of educational experimenting left to be done, and out of all the present turmoil there may emerge schools that are diverse and better than those we have. One of the few clear lessons in this whole muddled business, however, is that the schools mirror the society. Its political failures have generated a crisis that schools alone can never solve. At long last, we are learning that the schools won't be able to pick up the marbles for the rest of the social order.

NOTES

1. Jane Jacobs is a writer and thinker on cities, communities, and economic morality. Her 1961 book *The Life and Death of Great American Cities*, arguing that most city planning destroyed neighborhoods and fostered sterility, had a tremendous influence not only on the field of urban planning but on the emerging New Left.

2. David K. Cohen, a longtime friend and colleague of Featherstone, studies education policy.

Busing the Powerless

JANUARY 1976

IT'S CLEAR IN BOSTON in 1976 that the era in which race was thought of as a Southern dilemma is long dead and gone. The issues are American, not Southern. Schools in the most defiantly resistant Black Belt counties in Mississippi and Alabama have desegregated, while Boston is in turmoil. Times of defeated ideals make people especially sensitive to hypocrisy, and the symbolism in Boston's present resistance has not escaped many observers. Massachusetts has a liberal and progressive reputation, which in many ways it deserves. Senator Brooke is the first Black person to sit in the U.S. Senate since 1881, and recent Massachusetts leaders have by and large presented a decent set of faces to the world. Much Massachusetts liberalism has taken on an abstract, ceremonial, and symbolic cast in recent years, however. There are signs that the progressive promises of recent years are about to be broken. Budget problems have mounted. There are pickets at the State House protesting cuts in all the social services. The governor and the legislature are dumping people off the welfare rolls and cutting off money for medical care; long lines of unemployed stand outside the state offices. The temptation to opt for a reactionary populism is enormous.

Boston, too, has a reputation as a civilized place. Visitors think of it as a repository—perhaps a museum would be a better word—for a good many ideals about American life, education, and culture. Some of the Bicentennial visitors may picture it as the home of the abolitionists, which is accurate so long as you remember that Garrison preached an end to slavery here at the clear risk of his neck. The fact that mobs spat on Senator Edward Kennedy because of his stand on busing is difficult to square with the ideal of Boston and its past, or, for that matter, with the legendary love affair between the Kennedys and the Boston Irish. Yet it was in Boston the other day that someone firebombed the old Kennedy home, birthplace of JFK, scrawling "Bus Teddy" on the sidewalk outside. The desegregation issue has done a lot to drive a wedge between liberal elites and the constituency for egalitarian change. Busing may yet inaugurate a new national era of fake reactionary populism of the sort symbolized by the paradox of Governor Wallace's popular appeal and his program for the state of Alabama, which enriches the corporations.

The desegregation issue has become badly tangled. The attack on the legally mandated Jim Crow dual systems of the South is now almost complete. Southern desegregation has worked well in some places and badly in others. Some systems in the South are turning into models of race relations that pose a shameful contrast to a good deal of what is happening in the North. Others got rid of dual schools by firing all Black teachers. Extending the law to the North proved to be difficult. For a long time, the lawyers were bogged down in the distinctions between *de jure* and *de facto* segregation. Old-fashioned Southern segregation was a matter of law and official policy, whereas Northern-style segregation was the product of extralegal forces—the housing market and so on, and therefore beyond legal remedies involving the schools. Or so thinking ran. By 1970, however, civil rights lawyers began persuading the lower federal courts to give much more detailed scrutiny to the facts of urban segregation outside the South. The notion that a clear line separated *de jure* and *de facto* segregation has not in fact stood the test of evidence. Lawyers representing Black plaintiffs in many cities outside the South have been able to show that a good deal of segregation is the result of action taken by school boards and school officials. Testimony in case after case shows similar patterns. Officials built schools in all-Black neighborhoods, shifted school district lines to maintain segregation as Blacks moved into new neighborhoods, or worked the old scheme Linda Brown encountered in Topeka years ago, long-distance busing ("forced busing") of Black children to far-away Black schools instead of to nearby White schools.

It is this sort of evidence of official action, and not a hunger for radical social change, that compels sober and generally conservative federal judges to conclude that a good deal of Northern-style segregation throughout the country is a violation of Black schoolchildren's constitutional rights. This is what lies behind the wave of court decisions in Pasadena, Denver, Baltimore, Detroit, Louisville, Boston, and many other cities. The question becomes what remedies the courts can offer, for rights without remedies do not exist.

Here desegregation has run into some very big snags. While it is often not hard to prove that school officials are contributing to Northern-style segregation, it is also clear that there are other, unofficial forces at work: zoning, patterns of housing discrimination, realtors, mortgage, insurance and loan policies of the banks, and so on. Even when the responsible agencies are in some sense official, they operate at different levels of government, involving multiple jurisdictions. Schools are often implicated, yet the sources of much Northern segregation also lie outside schools. The circle of remedies is drawn far too narrowly if it only includes schools, yet there are no precedents for widening it.

The other snag arises in cities with a majority Black population. There, what Black plaintiffs seek in the courts is an end to discriminatory pupil placement policies. The Constitution entitles them to this. In terms of the other, wider, goals of desegregation—moves toward integration, better racial balance, or access to enriched resources for education—there are clear limits to what schools can accomplish with a majority Black student population. For those still eager to pursue these wider goals, the remedy would seem to lie in metropolitan schemes linking city and suburban schools. In 1974, however, the Supreme Court shaped by President Nixon's appointments seemed to say that the lower federal courts may not reach out to the suburbs in the search for remedies, even if plaintiffs can show that suburban schools are implicated in segregation. It is not clear what the ruling really means or how final it is; a number of suburban–city desegregation cases are still pending.

The Supreme Court decision did not stop the legal drive for desegregation within the cities. To Blacks mainly concerned with ending discriminatory placement policies, the goal is not necessarily any kind of racial balance. For them, discussions of suburbs and metropolitan schemes are beside the point. But for others, both Black and White, who still think that racial balances are desirable and educationally productive, the Supreme Court ruling has for the moment added a special air of futility to the desegregation battle in cities like Detroit and Washington, where most school children are Black. The ruling offered Whites and Blacks in the cities an unusually clear illustration of the fundamental and growing injustice of our whole network of urban boundaries. The legal units of our urban geography have always operated as fences for privilege; but the isolation of the poor and dark-skinned has never been as great. In effect the Supreme Court suggested that the suburbs may be left alone. Shifts in both Black and White thinking on desegregation also cloud the issue. As a tactical matter desegregation is still widely supported by most Blacks. Many oppose busing, however (especially to hostile neighborhoods), and many do not hold with the racial balances implied by the courts, even though these seem the simplest remedies to enforce. Many insist that the issue is not racial balance at all but putting an end to discrimination and giving Black students equal access to the best education a school system has to offer. From this point of view, mainly Black schools and all-Black classes are fine. (There always was something inherently racist about the notion that Black students need to sit near Whites in order to learn.) Some are outright separatists. Still, even separatists you talk to are mindful of the tactical point that Black children have a better chance at access to a full range of educational offerings in classrooms where White children are present as hostages, so to speak, of the system's good intentions.

The whole question of racial balance is obscure, and the confusion does not only exist in the mind of the public, which imagines that the courts in each case are insisting on a fixed racial balance. Contrary to what most people think, federal judges have by and large been studiedly ambiguous in the way they have talked about the demography of desegregation. Often the decisions imply some form of balance, but the specifics are left vague. There is a wide spectrum of opinion, too, among Black observers. Some focus mainly on an end to discriminatory pupil placement policies, which can still produce mainly Black schools. Others insist on racial balances of some sort, either because they are intrinsically desirable, or because they may help guarantee Black students' access to better education. In cities with a majority of Black students, this second position extends into an argument for metropolitan schooling. These two quite different, not to say contradictory, emphases are seldom openly discussed in national debates on desegregation. In part this is because many Blacks and civil rights lawyers are profoundly ambivalent on the question. And in part it is because people's positions are based on the local situation, which may be unique. Metropolitan solutions may be good in some places but not others. This is not the only area where the necessity to frame policy in national terms generates new problems of its own.

The Black dialogue over nationalism and universalism is old and tortured. It shifts over time, and there have been further developments since the separatist and community-control impulses of the late 1960s. The demand for community control in New York City arose primarily from the failure of school desegregation, and the seeming futility of desegregation as a policy in huge urban ghettos. The ideal also picked up on the quite real breakdown of lay democratic control over unresponsive, chaotic, and indifferent school bureaucracies. Desegregation still remains an enormous puzzle in large ghettos of cities where Blacks are not a majority, and the question of democratic control over the schools is far from being solved. Yet the tragic and ultimately futile contest for community control in New York City convinced many that the fight in that form on that turf was not worthwhile. Community control today is now much less of a despairing ideological battle cry, because it has shifted to places like Newark, Detroit, Atlanta, and Gary, with their Black majorities. It is now a pragmatic affair, conforming to some of the older patterns of American ethnic politics. The advent of Black mayors, school boards, and—perhaps—political machines means a great deal. Like the electoral gains in the South, it gives a historically outcast group a chance for more political power than it had before. At the very least, some old racist ghosts have been laid to rest: majority

Black school boards can make competent decisions and Black mayors can govern, just as all-Black schools can teach.

The rise of Blacks to political power in all these places has prompted, predictably, a rash of proposals for metropolitan government. Blacks are suspicious of these schemes, and will rightly resist giving up the influence and political power they are winning, although they may be open to proposals for making special services, such as schools, metropolitan. (Many current metropolitan schemes recall earlier Yankee attempts to shift power to the state level, as immigrants captured the cities.)

These pragmatic forms of community control are, however, no more of a panacea than the earlier ideological demands. The old joke that community control meant Black ownership of Harlem in exchange for White ownership of General Motors was never very funny; it no longer seems funny at all in Detroit. Cities like Detroit, Newark, and Gary are not exactly brimming over with resources; they are ailing badly, and suggest new and gloomy variations on the old misleading theme of separate and equal. Separate in America never has been equal and never will be.

It is clear that the pursuit of political power in cities with Black majorities and near-majorities is in many respects at odds with the pursuit of school desegregation. If we were less of a national society this would matter less. Unfortunately policy gets framed nationally; there is a national politics of education as well as a profoundly local politics. It is very hard to understand that and to understand that the situation in Detroit is very different from that in Boston, even though what happens in majority-Black Detroit now helps shape the political climate in Boston, where Blacks are a distinct minority.

There remains a pressing need for minorities to join with Whites as part of egalitarian and majoritarian coalitions that do not exist. Many Blacks and Whites still think of school desegregation as a step toward a truly integrated society, but the civil rights movement is in political tatters, a victim of its success, and also of its failure to translate its demands into a broad program of economic justice. For a long moment in history, as these things go, an immensely creative national moment fused traditional and novel modes of lower- and working-class protest with traditional and novel middle-class styles of action and reform and created unprecedented changes. The French writer Charles Péguy (1910/1958) said that everything begins in mysticism and ends in politics. The American version of Péguy's aphorism needs rewording: Everything begins in mysticism and ends in the federal courtroom. Legal professionals have finally built a solid structure of precedents for attacking Northern desegregation, but Black support for it is weakening, and White pressure against it has risen. The mysticism has evaporated—"Were you looking to be held together by the lawyers?" Walt Whitman (1860) asked—and this has left integration-minded Blacks and Whites speaking in subdued, practical, and tactical tones. Schools are important but no substitute for jobs or political power, where power is accessible. Desegregation is right but it isn't likely to lead to a multiracial society terribly soon. The evangelism that made so many martyrs and produced so much change couldn't last forever. In Boston, where the parents and children are showing so much courage, where the grievances are extraordinarily clear-cut, where racial balance is still possible to achieve, and where the alternative of political power for Blacks is not an option—even in Boston, supporters of desegregation wonder whether it is worth the political consequences. The plans the courts have seized upon seem the most enforceable schemes for upholding the law and remedying trampled rights, yet in some places they are self-defeating, and probably do accelerate the flight of the middle class out of the city. The busing issue is building up extraordinary political countercurrents.

No federal desegregation order has been reversed by any court, yet the opponents of busing believe they can win, that "Never" is not just a slogan. They believe this because local leaders have assured them, and so, in veiled ways, have our nation's leaders. Richard Nixon signaled clear retreat on desegregation and so has President Ford. The government speaks with a babble of tongues on the issue, and federal civil rights enforcement has slowed to a creak. (Last year's violence in Boston convinced federal officials of the need for a strong federal presence this year.)

"Busing" and "neighborhood schools" are slogans. Over 40% of the nation's children ride to school in altogether uncontroversial buses. If you add in other kinds of public transportation, the figure is over 65%. Busing is scarcely new in Boston. In the days before court orders, the Boston school system bused more children than it is now doing. (Admittedly it had a larger school population then.) "Neighborhood schools" drawing on cohesive neighborhoods have for some time been the exception rather than the rule, even in Boston, where the sense of turf is unusually strong. Yet there are many real grievances lurking beneath the slogans. Given a choice, parents do prefer nearby schools. Neighborhoods do count with people. In 19th-century Boston, Stephan Thernstrom (1964) shows, the working class and the poor were the most geographically mobile people. Elites were local and stayed put; it was the working class that had to hit the road. This may be one reason why we have an erroneous impression that the past was more stable than the present. If so, it is not the only instance where our collective memory has been refracted through the lenses of privilege. Since the depression, however, the working class has moved less; the most mobile Americans tend to be the middle class and the very poor. The fight in Boston today involves a clash between the values of some of the most mobile groups and the values of some of the most geographically stable groups. Besides being racial, it is also a cultural and class battle between cosmopolitan professionals and locals, between people who identify with neighborhood and local values. This feeds the neighborhoods' resentment of the professionals, the courts, the lawyers, and the media.

Desegregation would not be such a divisive issue if those supporting it could point to a host of gains for the working class in other realms. Governor Reubin Askew of Florida and Senator Walter Mondale of Minnesota come to mind as examples of the sort of leaders that might pull off the coalition we need, but they are rare. One of the tragedies of the political era we've lived through is that the most dramatically oppressed groups got much more attention and sympathy than those whose oppression was less well publicized. The recession has hit the Boston working class very hard; and now desegregation is reminding them how little society has attended to their concerns in recent years. This makes White workers terribly vulnerable to fake populists. Local fakes wave the bloody shirt of past ethnic grievances and promise that busing can be stopped. National fakes nurse more current grudges and dangle the slogans of busing and popular property rights in front of the electorate without doing a single positive thing for any working man or woman. The failure of politics to cast people's grievances and aspirations in universal and democratic terms haunts the period of reaction we are living through.

Our traditions of school reform tend to be elitist. Often in the past democracy at the local school level has meant thwarting elitist versions of school reform. In the progressive era, for example, reactionaries in New York City tried to rework schooling into an outright caste system. This was stopped, although tracking and other policies favoring the children of the middle class came in. Common people have been able to veto elite plans for education, on occasion. This, in part, accounts for the continuing legitimacy of schools. They have not, however, been able to do much in a positive way for the education of their children. Some reformers had excellent ideas about sound practice and good teaching, but in practice the reform style has rarely aimed at winning over teachers, let alone parents. This has been one of the minor tragedies of American education. Desegregation fits the old reform mold. It is meant to help Blacks, a group historically cut off from opportunities in Boston's schools. It is initiated by Black plaintiffs. And yet the whole way it is being done rehearses the old elitist patterns of reform. Sometimes in our cities today it looks as if we are getting an updated Northern version of the old Southern alliance of planters and Blacks against poor Whites, which never really benefited anyone except the elites.

Once again, the egalitarian promises of public schooling are being over-whelmed by the realities of inequality.

The fact that the residents of Charlestown and South Boston are re-sisting elite social planners, that they are defending community and neigh-borhood and even, in their prayer marches and American flags, the symbols of patriotic and religious nationalism, gives them a more respectable hear-ing now than they might have had 5 or 10 years ago. The contrast between the country's universal ideals and the actual diversity of its peoples, races, and cultures has made for a history that swings between periods of uni-versalism and periods of tribalism. The universal ideals for the republic often serve as a mask for nativist and racist definitions of America: This is why, periodically, they fall into disrepute. Periods of tribalism are often healthy responses to the failure of the American consensus to acknowledge the genuine pluralism of the culture. The line between legitimate ethnic pride, nationalism and self-respect, and tribalism is not easy to draw, how-ever. And it is never altogether clear whether the angry tribes really are simply protesting their abuse by successive groups of hypocritical elites. The distinction is important. You can share a sense of rage over the nar-row definitions of America that have prevailed in the past and still feel that the elements of the common culture that have emerged are very much worth preserving and defending. I'm thinking of the political tradition that has fitfully offered levers to outsiders; of the language of rights; of the law, which seems so fragile in Boston today; of urban pluralism; and of the ter-rible failure of the progressive movements of recent years to translate their aspirations for minorities into the universal language of rights.

Judge Garrity's decision does not set a formula for racial balance. Like many other federal judges he has selected remedies that leave the ques-tion of balance ambiguous. But there is no ambiguity over the fact that Boston's has been a virtually dual school system with two sets of policies, one for White children and another for Black children.

Whether desegregation is the main cause of the White exodus or not, schools probably are a factor. Resegregation is not a happy prospect. People have a constitutional right to remedy when they are sent to a segregated school on the basis of the color of their Black skin. Nobody has a constitu-tional right to live in a city with a White majority.

Social scientists have played a curious role through the history of de-segregation. Social science has influenced policy; it has also mirrored the changing politics of the issue. Studies of the effects of desegregation have been ambiguous, because people have seldom been precise about what it was intended to accomplish. Complexity of aim is not necessarily a bad thing; education itself usually reflects a variety of goals. But it makes research difficult. No one said what exactly the goal of desegregation was: higher achievement scores for Blacks, racial harmony, shifts in racial attitudes, more political leverage for Blacks, or simply a remedy for discrimination. The Brown decision quoted from the celebrated research of Black social psychologist Kenneth Clark to the effect that segregation hurt the minds and hearts of Black children. This was plausible in a broad sense; yet further research came to focus on lower achievement scores on tests. The idea developed that desegregation would in and of itself raise Black children's test scores. Yet the evidence that desegregated schools would eliminate differences in achievement was very spotty. Some observers, seeing that desegregation does not automatically produce equality, have been led to argue that we must redefine our conception of educational equality to mean equality of outcomes. It is not clear how this could be done in education except by massive compensatory programs. Compensatory education has not always failed, as its critics say; it has in fact sometimes worked. But real gains in achievement require a great deal of money that is not apt to be forthcoming in a time when many cities are on the verge of bankruptcy.

Recent academic debates on equality have emphasized that improving schools is no substitute for more fundamental social change. That is an important point to keep in mind, particularly in following the elusive symbols in the desegregation issue. This is the sort of understanding that is useful if it provides perspective on the schools, and pernicious if it discredits educational reform without offering any real alternatives. It was perhaps never sound to rest the case for school desegregation on the shifting sands of social science research. The American public has yet to be educated to the fact that social science is both faddish and profoundly political. All along desegregation has been a legal matter—a question of the redress of rights—and a political matter—a way of giving some of our society's strangers more of a chance at access to educational resources. For many, too, it has been and continues to be a moral issue.

It was also to be predicted that talk of desegregation would range over all the hurts and inadequacies of our national life without really focusing on the subject of education. Today children in Boston are learning important lessons about the law, race, and other aspects of our society, but this was not exactly planned in their curriculum. And yet the instances of reasonably successful desegregation are now so many that, in fact, a good deal of practical educational knowledge is at hand. Knowledgeable people say that the number of non-Whites in a desegregating school should probably not go over 40%, if resegregation is to be avoided. (The numbers must not be token, however. David Riesman[1] and others have long warned about the psychic costs paid by token minorities, including women, in newly desegregated institutions.) Desegregation of course seems a rather sad joke if the schools children are bused to are in fact inferior to the ones they originally attended. And schools children are bused to should be near enough to their homes for their parents to stay involved in school affairs. Places like Denver—and increasingly Boston—are also showing how important it is to make use of city-wide advisory groups of Blacks and Whites; such groups are even more important at the school level. (There seems no way in the 1970s to escape the need for participation, as unclear as our ideas on the subject remain.) Special classes must not become dumping bins for minority children. Schools in some places have gone beyond desegregation—an end to discriminatory placement policies—and are actually working on integration, getting Black and White students to know each other. Real integration has to take place at the classroom, not the school, level. It means paying careful attention to such decisive symbols as cheerleaders and football teams. It means finding alternatives to the kind of across-the-board tracking that is becoming more and more common in our schools. There is nothing inherently wrong with ability grouping in individual subjects, like math and English. The problems for integration (and I would argue, education in general) are posed by tracking systems that relegate masses of students to second-rate curricula, on the premise that they will meet second-rate fates in life. Integration is more promising when it begins in the early years of school. It requires interracial staffing and planning.

Numbers of our schools have desegregated; in some, integration is going on. Numbers of schools are segregated and others are resegregating. One of the real difficulties with the whole desegregation issue is that it gets debated as a national policy matter, yet many of the crucial facts differ from school to school, and even from classroom to classroom. Geography and demography make current desegregation remedies pointless in some places and apt in others. This complexity has attended all our discussions of school reform and social policy in recent years, and yet we have continued to speak the language of a strange one-eyed rationalism, an either-or language of national policy that bypasses the inconvenient muddle of American life. And it is not only the variousness of the landscape that we have oversimplified. We debated desegregation versus compensatory education, for example, as though the two were mutually exclusive, when in fact, many schools need both. In recent years we debated school reform versus other forms of social change, as though we were master planners in the war room and the Great Computer were offering us a clear choice between alternatives. In reality there is no central war room or master planners. There is no Great Computer. Our choices are far from clear. By any realistic political reckoning, it seems altogether probable in fact that school reform and social change will operate in tandem, if they operate at all. Our thinking remains woefully apolitical.

Small pieces of reform and change are occurring in some of the schools in Boston today. There are many in the city who do not like what is happening, but who are working hard to keep the peace and do their jobs. Many in the mainly Irish teaching staff of the schools and the mainly Irish police force sympathize with the antibusing protesters, but they are making the law work. Teachers and parents have shown more guts than anybody, always excepting the schoolchildren. All are being asked to live up to ideals few in the city honor. When one thinks of what a troubled place this is, a despairing quote from St. Paul comes to mind: "Here we have no continuing city." St. Paul (Heb., 13:14) was being a little melodramatic, as usual. Boston does continue. The schools are working, and seem in many ways healthier than other institutions in the city.

The issues in desegregation are shadowy and symbolic; they are important, because we live by symbols, but a steady diet of such symbols hardens the heart. Some good and altogether ordinary things are taking place in Boston's desegregated schools, but the situation is shameful. The law is clearly the creature of the rich and the powerful, who are exempt from its consequences. Schemes of social engineering that confine desegregation to the deteriorating core cities and let the suburbs off free insult the intelligence of a democracy. Supporters of desegregation have not said that enough. Those defending their neighborhoods and their children and protesting busing have also not admitted that the issue is race and the constitutional rights of Black children. Next to injustice, hypocrisy stings people hardest. People in South Boston are right to be outraged by the suburban liberals who call them bigots and racists, and wrong to think that Black children's legal rights can be ignored merely because larger remedies involving the suburbs do not exist. They are mistaken, too, in thinking that their very real grievances, values, and sensibilities outweigh other people's constitutional rights.

These things can't be said enough. Nor can it be said too often that the depth of danger in the present situation is in large part the work of the old Boston School Committee and the other local and national politicians who are making such a good thing out of encouraging resistance to the law. The threat of violence has come to be so commonplace that we forget what a menace it is to democracy. Too many people in this country have got to hoping that somehow someone else's violence will advance their cause. This result has been a corrupting sense that violence is normal. In the long run of history it has been, of course. That is a troubling thought. Bicentennial visitors wanting a taste of history should pause and test the air of Boston. Monuments, embalmed artifacts, restored buildings, pictures of porcelain statesmen wearing powdered wigs do not give the real feeling of history. History feels like this: a city of frightened people making choices with divided minds, picking not right against wrong, but what they hope will be the lesser set of evils, and wondering what the consequences will be.

NOTE

1. Featherstone refers here to the sociologist David Riesman, who is best known for *The Lonely Crowd*, his 1950 study of a changing American middle class.

John Dewey Reconsidered

———

1972

———

JOHN DEWEY LIVED A LONG TIME, from 1859 to 1952; some of his best work was written at an age when most men have retired. The single most persistent thread in his far-ranging career was a determination to establish the unity of all experience, to reunite separate realms and distinct modes of thought in a culture splintered by its philosophical dualisms. The search for a continuity between literature and life, thought and action, mind and body, self and society, carried him through three phases.

In the first, which lasted up to the early 1890s, Dewey was a philosophical idealist. He followed the British Hegelians in defining knowledge as a kind of participation, seeking to connect the mind to the objects it knows. Hegel was important to him because Hegel promised a resolution of dualisms and contradictions, a vision of life that was whole and of a piece. Even after he abandoned Hegelianism, Dewey was permanently indebted to Hegel for a social conception of the human mind, for the idea that freedom was rational self-realization, and for the view that logic and morals were evolutionary phenomena, changing over time.

From the 1890s to the early 1920s there was a second phase in Dewey's thought. This was when he put together his basic philosophical outlook—he called it instrumentalism—and elaborated a pragmatic approach to logic, ethics, psychology, education, and social thought. Now Dewey followed Charles Darwin in attempting to integrate human knowledge and human action into a framework of nature and natural processes: The mind was an instrument of evolutionary adaptation, and the terms of Hegel's dialectic became those of a biological creature interacting with its environment in a never-ending spiral of mastery and adjustment. Indirectly, Darwin gave Dewey the idea that philosophy itself was a sort of evolutionary criticism, an ongoing critique of old ideas in the light of new circumstances. Like Thorstein Veblen[1] and Karl Marx, Dewey had a particularly vivid sense of the oppressive weight of dead ideas on the minds of the living.

Dewey fused certain traditional values of Protestantism, its reverence for experience and its belief in the application of intelligence to morals, with ideals of science and democracy. Like other disciples of Hegel on the left, he emphasized the realm of action as a vital concern of philosophy—developing his own concept of what the Marxists call praxis. The function of thought was to guide action; to believe a proposition was in some sense to act on it; the test of meaning and truth was experiential. Dewey warned genteel America of the folly of idle abstractions, cut off from real experience—what William James (1909/1977) termed "vicious intellectualism"—and, equally, he reminded Teddy Roosevelt's admirers of the danger of all action not informed by intelligence. He contended that ethics was a branch of knowledge, and he developed a logic that tried to end what he saw as the "scandal" involved in the culture's divorce of science from morals. Along with William James he laid the foundations for a new psychology, and he worked out the outlines of a new philosophy of education.

This Dewey was an extraordinary, Protean figure, who immeasurably enriched American thought, putting his decisive stamp on a vast range of issues in a dozen fields. Certain flaws kept surfacing in his social thought, however, and they are worth pondering because they suggest general weaknesses in the outlook of many members of Dewey's generation, the progressives who came of intellectual age in the years between 1880 and 1920.

William James and Dewey were the two opposite poles of American social thought—James with his supremely Romantic emphasis on individual experience, and Dewey with his characteristic emphasis on the social context of all experience. Both were inclined to talk a good deal about "adjustment," a term that derived from pragmatism's central metaphor, the Darwinian adjustment or adaptation of the creature to its environment. Applied to social life, the biological metaphor was misleading in one respect and ambiguous in another. It was misleading because it pictured a cooperative struggle against nature, building bridges or fighting epidemics. Most social situations lack the unity of purpose given by a common natural enemy: The social "problem" is the exploitation of some people by other people. Like many progressives, Dewey kept defining social problems in technical and technological terms, which evaded crucial considerations of power, class, and race.

The ambiguity in the term "adjustment" lay in the fact that Dewey meant two nearly opposite things by it. He meant a passive adaptation to the social environment, and he also meant mastery and control of it. In his educational writings Dewey sometimes talked about the need for workers to become conscious of the meaning of their work. This had a fine radical ring to it, but, put in terms of consciousness alone, it had a distinct oily flavor of "human relations" capitalism—ending the labor troubles in the cotton mills by treating the hands to edifying lectures on the history of the textile industry. Late in his life, when Dewey spoke of social adjustment, it turned out that he meant a revival of local democracy and workers' control of industry. That, however, was not always what he actually said. This ambiguous meaning of the term "adjustment" was a particularly serious drawback in the American context, because it reinforced the tendency of Dewey and other progressives to conceive of social reform as a matter of assimilating immigrants into a society that despised them.

Many of the progressive intellectuals saw a new collectivism arising out of the central historical experience of their time, the industrialization of American life. Some were corporate collectivists, dreaming of rule by enlightened captains of industry. Others, like Thorstein Veblen, dreamed of technocracy, rule by expert Bolshevik elites, scientists, and engineers. Unlike the technocrats, who made no bones about their elitism, Dewey remained a democrat; he was nonetheless profoundly influenced by Veblen, sharing Veblen's uncritical awe of the utopian potential of American industry. Dewey believed that modern technology promoted a rational, matter-of-fact industrial mentality among the masses, and like Veblen he bootlegged all sorts of hopeful moral, humane, and scientific virtues into his descriptions of the industrial order. Inevitably, he thought, a cooperative industrial commonwealth was going to replace capitalism.

Now it may be that, in the long run so derided by Lord Keynes (1924),[2] Dewey and Veblen were prophets; it may be that the imperatives of an advanced industrial order will move us all toward a society directed by intelligence. What was certainly true was that the progressives, like more recent theorists of industrial development, drastically underestimated the strength of the corporate order and the grip of profit on American life. They hoped that planning would take the place of drift or the forces of the market, that the standards shaping social policy would be human needs and the welfare of the whole community; they were certain that history was rapidly converting these hopes to realities.

With the progressives, Dewey thought that government and science would operate independently of politics. He shared their profound revulsion against politics, their weakness for technical solutions to political questions, their vain hope that institutions could do the job that only politics could do. The hope was reflected in Dewey's educational thought, for example, where, though he was a superb guide to the educational and social nature of the school community, he was a typical progressive reformer in promising that schools could solve basic issues of justice and equality.

With important exceptions in his ethics and educational writings—particularly Chapter 7 of *Democracy and Education* (1916)—the progressive Dewey took values for granted. Assuming that society was progressing toward good ends, he preoccupied himself with instrumental means and techniques. He criticized American life, but it was true, as Lewis Mumford (1926) charged, that he acquiesced in too much of it. In his own mind Dewey thought of himself as a populist radical, but from the outside he too often looked like a social engineer, preaching adjustment.

Two incidents illustrate the lack of critical political judgment in progressive reform. The first is the strange case of the Gary, Indiana, public schools. Both Dewey and Randolph Bourne (1916), the *New Republic*'s cultural and educational critic, praised what came to be known as "The Gary Plan," a series of ideas put into effect by the Gary superintendent of schools. Dewey and Bourne liked these reforms because they made the schools lively and because they exemplified scientific principles of economy and efficiency—sacred words to progressive ears. They were not prepared for what "scientific management" actually meant to most educators: In practice "The Gary Plan" boiled down to getting double and even triple use of the school plant by having twice as many children in one building and a rotating schedule of activities and rooms. The educators, in short, viewed the plan wholly as an administrative technique in the service of business and bureaucratic values totally at odds with any standards for a decent education. When the scheme was introduced to the New York City schools, Dewey had an opportunity to see a classic example of that exercise in bureaucratic manipulation, reform entrepreneurship, and ethnic and class warfare that Americans call education innovation. The reform mayor of New York and a motley coalition of reformers pushed the plan against the wishes of Jewish ghetto parents—who thought it was a plot to give their children a working-class education—and against the wishes of teachers and principals, who had never been consulted in the first place. There were riots all over the city—10,000 parents and children demonstrated in Brownsville—and the outraged voters threw the reformers out in the 1917 election. Dewey was slowly learning that school reform without the backing of teachers and parents was bound to be autocratic and reactionary. The reformers claimed to represent the public, but of course represented their own kind of interest group. This did not automatically discredit their ideas: It did make it imperative to analyze their class and ethnic biases.

Dewey was equally uncritical about war as a weapon of reform. He feared Prussian absolutism; when World War I seemed inevitable, he argued that the war effort could unite America, teach people how to cooperate, and bring about a new culture to replace the individualistic and capitalist culture. So for a time he was a booster for war, making the case for intelligently applied violence, and attacking pacifists like his friend Jane Addams[3] for their sentimentality. What made Dewey's defense of the war so appalling was his opportunism, his identification with the warmakers, and his abdication of any responsibility to think clearly. Most of the *New Republic* staff shared Dewey's crackpot realism and his desire to be hardboiled and effective; in fact they carried sentimental *Realpolitik* even farther than Dewey, tying their absurd dreams of national and international regeneration to such unlikely champions as Woodrow Wilson and the batty Colonel House.[4] Dewey's enthusiasm for the war was brief, and it was tempered by a habitual skepticism about great leaders and his growing alarm over the wartime suppression of civil liberties. In the end he had committed the same sin as most of the rest of the *New Republic* editors: He had surrendered his critical judgment and his sense of common decency to a presumed direction that history was taking. Randolph Bourne's famous attack on Dewey over the issue of the war is usually interpreted as Bourne's farewell to pragmatism. I think Bourne (1917) was making a point that Dewey later came to agree with: that instrumental values are only part of a complete philosophy; without vision, an articulated set of values, and a grasp of politics, pragmatism could be twisted to serve any ends. Bourne was confessing that all the prewar reformers, including himself, had been insufficiently critical of American life. The men and women who had been raised in what Henry James (1886) called the "fool's paradise" of the prewar years had imagined that their private Utopias were being realized by what turned out to be questionable and sinister means. Dewey finally saw that there was no conceivable relationship between his ideals and the ends for which the war was fought, and his basic vision underwent a change. This was the third phase of Dewey's career, beginning in the early 1920s and continuing for the rest of his life, a period in which he was more publicly active than he ever had been before, producing an enormous amount of polemical journalism, as well as his two masterpieces, *Experience and Nature* (1925) and *Art as Experience* (1933). He changed his emphasis from the instrumental realms of science and technology to the human values to be served by science and technology, and radically deepened his critique of American life.

From being a progressive social engineer, Dewey became a utopian social critic, skeptical of progress, more and more aware of what was good about the good old days, and what was ominous about the industrial order. Morton White (1972) has pointed out that American philosophy before Dewey traditionally conceived of its task as the mediation of contrary realms of human experience; Romantic American philosophers like Emerson have characteristically vindicated morals, feelings, and esthetics against mechanistic and rationalistic science. In his progressive phase Dewey was a modernist rebel against these classic Romantic American traditions in the name of a new vision of science. Late in his life it became clear that Dewey's rebellion against Emerson and American philosophical tradition was strikingly Romantic and Emersonian in its aim: to make philosophy a criticism of experience from the standpoint of human aspirations. The late Dewey was trying to salvage the aspirations of American

Romanticism without its craziness, to restore its deepest insights on a modest and empirical basis that did not exclude science.

The late Dewey continued to emphasize the scientific method as the only path to knowledge. He never abandoned his admiration for science as a model of all intelligent inquiry. He kept hoping that the spirit of science would pervade daily life. Yet now he drew an increasingly sharp contrast between the abstracted findings of science and the intrinsic, richly human "consummatory" values of art, conversation, and shared experience. Once his inarticulate major premise had been the idea of scientific and industrial progress; now his central insight into industrial society was that it made people into machines. He still thought the industrial order could lead to a good life. He still believed in cooperation and planning; now he also insisted on workers' control of industry and a revival of local publics and face-to-face communities.

Art as Experience was the best statement of the late Dewey's chastened Romantic vision, with its profoundly esthetic core: Good art was a paradigm of fulfilled experience, life at its most complete. Art was an exploration of imaginative possibilities, and hence ultimately, if indirectly, critical and moral. *Art as Experience* revealed Dewey's standards for a healthy society; it joined him to the great tradition of cultural prophecy attacking capitalism and industrial society in the name of an ideal of an integrated culture. From Samuel Coleridge and Matthew Arnold to the Leavises[5] and T. S. Eliot, this has been in the main a traditionalist and elitist body of thought, although there has been a running socialist minority report from John Ruskin[6] and William Morris,[7] R. H. Tawney,[8] Dewey, and, in our time, Raymond Williams.[9]

In writing *Art as Experience*, Dewey was in fact reopening an important debate that started when George Santayana,[10] Henry James, and Henry Adams had attacked American life from an esthetic point of view, seeing art as a haven and a refuge from slums, immigrants, robber barons, boosters, bosses, philistines, and the consequences of unchecked technological growth. In the 1890s, Dewey disliked the esthetes for their scorn for science, their escapism, their elitism, and their denial of the possibility or desirability of creating a democratic culture. By the 1930s he still disliked these things but was prepared to acknowledge the penetration of the esthetes' critique of the prevailing forces in American life. This deepened his critical grasp of what was wrong.

There are interesting tensions in *Art as Experience*. One source of tension arose from Dewey's view of a common culture in which the arts would be a force, esthetic but moral too, educating the community and preserving and extending its better values in the face of greed, vulgarity, and ignorance. Dewey was committed to a humanist art, yet he was aware of the fact that much of the best, as well as the worst, modern art and literature has been produced by artists whose values were far from being humanist or liberal. Dewey never reconciled his ideal of a healthy culture with the deep alienation of 20th-century art.

There was another tension in the book. As a work of esthetics, *Art as Experience* was curiously reticent about standards of judgment; yet in a sense its entire theme was the need for critical intellectual standards. It reflects the cultural dilemma of every American democrat who wants to establish a basis for making artistic, intellectual, and moral judgments. On the whole, American democratic and populist traditions have tended to deny the possibility of ordering American life by any common values. The reason for this is obvious. Those who appeal to standards of any sort have usually been elitists; our history is full of ugly attempts on the part of elites to straighten out the masses. Thus Dewey's intellectual ancestor, Horace Mann,[11] argued that citizens in a democracy required the moral discipline of social institutions like schools, because democracy demanded more of human nature than other forms of government.

This was not a bad point, in theory. Given the actual class and ethnic realities of the American scene, however, a plea for social and moral discipline was a political weapon in the hands of ascendant groups against immigrants and the lower classes. Recent historians have done a good job of dissecting American reform, and we now take a more interesting and dour point of view about the motives of reformers in general. Having unmasked many benign figures in the traditional reform pantheon for the elitists and racists that they often were, those of us committed to democracy should be prepared to concede that American popular traditions have also left much to be desired. Some of the reformers stood for ideals that, however abused, were sadly missing from American life: the ideal of a public good that was more than the numerical sum of private goods; the belief that American life could be ordered in terms of values. Dewey was attempting the very difficult task of infusing American populist traditions with a concern for common moral, intellectual, and cultural standards. In the end he came to appreciate what most progressive reformers missed, the enduring vitality in American pluralism: its revolt against any single group's definition of what was American. He leaned more and more toward traditions of local democracy and pluralism. Yet he also saw that a revival of these traditions would be reactionary without a commitment to universal values and shared standards. Standards would not be handed down by tradition or religious authority. There was no legitimate source of authority in the modern world except the rational, democratic process of thought and evaluation—the common social pursuit Dewey kept calling, vaguely and misleadingly, "the method of intelligence."

There are problems in reading Dewey today. One major problem is his writing style, which has the monotonous consistency of peanut butter. William James cursed it as God-damnable (Hofstadter, 1963), and Justice Holmes[12] once captured both the excitement and the difficulty of *Experience and Nature* by describing it as "what God would have spoken had he been inarticulate, but keenly desirous to tell you how it was." Like many in his generation, Dewey was in revolt against lofty sentiments and fine writing; his style was in part a rebellion against Style. He was helped in this studied disregard of the graceful by a tin ear that simply could not hear the difference between "irrelevant" and "irrelevancy." Like Emerson he was at his best lecturing, but there was a lack of control and discipline even in the best lectures. The emotion filtered through the dry cracks at the wrong moments. In its energy, its mixed modes, its appetite for information, its dullness, and above all in its groping, muffled desire to say something about all of experience, a book like *Democracy and Education* resembles the formless, unfulfilled novels of Theodore Dreiser.[13]

Among other things, a style tells you whether someone is thinking clearly. Dewey did not always want to think clearly. He wanted to erase many of the distinctions by which philosophy, common sense and good style have sought to order discourse about the world, to reintegrate mind and body, self and society, truth and morals. He had a radically Protestant dread of idolatry, a sense of horror at the scandalous worship of words and images instead of the shifting precarious, beautiful reality of actual experience. At his best, Dewey was attempting to write a natural history of experience, to portray our logical judgments and moral decisions as they actually occur in encounters and transactions with other people. This enterprise took him to the borders of art, which is why *Art as Experience* is so important for understanding him, a guide to his ambitions and a key to the sense of incompletion and frustration that pervades so many of his works.

The desire to do a natural history of living experience, thinking and valuing on the wing, lay behind Dewey's Socratic insistence that knowledge and virtue are one. It was probably responsible for his frequent confusions of fact and value, which also stemmed from something he shared with the late, metaphysical William James: a conviction that any healthy sense of virtue had to reflect our actual biological and social natures, which were subject to empirical investigation. This and the insight that in actual fact truth and morals are intertwined are aspects of pragmatism's legacy that are worth preserving.

In the realm of educational thought and practice, Dewey's legacy is still very much with us and remains a lasting influence on our own struggles for better education. Although his progressive hopes soured and history made him a very misleading guide to larger macro issues concerning schools, he continues to be an extraordinary source of insight into the micro realm of classrooms, learning, and pedagogy. Thoughtful educators keep returning to Dewey's efforts to reestablish a high Romantic synthesis of science and feeling on a modestly empirical footing. The marriage of science and Romanticism that the best progressive minds sought remains a goal today, although we are certainly no nearer to it than Dewey or his contemporaries. He tried at first to make a clean break with America's Romantic past, but later he attempted to come to terms with it. Each generation in our profoundly Romantic culture fights this same battle in different terms. Romanticism was as central to Dewey's educational thought as the issue of populism was to his social thought. Both are central issues for us today.

All the manifold varieties of Romanticism are protests on behalf of the concrete and the organic against the abstract and mechanistic. There is, however, a distinction between low and high Romanticism. In education and other realms, low Romanticism has traditionally exalted the heart over the head, celebrating the irrational and intuitive, and fearing science and rationality. It is a viewpoint and mood that is perhaps especially widespread today. High Romanticism, on the other hand, is the recurring search for a saving middle ground between the icy reductions of analysis and the undisciplined craziness of the solitary Romantic ego. High Romanticism welcomes science and reason within their proper domains. Its real enemy is not reason, but scientism—all the partial, limited modes of thinking that deny the power and autonomy of the imagination and falsely claim to render a complete account of human existence. High Romanticism is thus a quest for a mediating vision in which reason reinforces emotion in the exercise of the imagination. This was pragmatism's ultimate goal; it was a Romantic goal, even though no one was ever less of a Romantic by temperament than John Dewey. In the end, for all his commitment to the scientific method, Dewey was trying to be Emerson's heir in mediating between the abstractions of science and the values of concrete experience. *Art as Experience* was an effort to transcend the Romantic past and to preserve its best insights. Its difficult, unfinished program meant acknowledging the validity of the standards and instrumentalities of science as well as legitimating the intrinsic "consummatory" values of art and shared human experience. Dewey's grand educational synthesis was never completed; his educational views suffered by being a product of his middle years. *Art as Experience* contains the richest educational implications of any of his works; yet education is not listed in its index.

Dewey was trying to place mankind within the framework of a scientific universe and illuminate the ends science should serve to naturalize humanity and to humanize science. For Dewey, the activity of art offers some important hints at what a synthesis of science and feeling might look like. Art and science were both deeply intellectual realms to Dewey, calling for discipline, standards, and judgment. Each, however, was involved with different sorts of meanings. Science dealt with that class of meanings posing abstract claims to truth, or what Dewey ended up calling "warranted assertability." Art dealt with concrete meanings. Science mapped the world. Art told what it was like to walk through its greenness.

There is another point about science and education that the philosopher David Hawkins (1974) makes in a recent book, *The Informed Vision*. Hawkins, long interested in the education of young children and sharing some of Dewey's views, argues that the practice of science—the actual process of discovery, the blend of synthesis, guess, and analysis—is more akin to art than the actual results of science. It is true that scientific results have to be expressed in terms of abstract symbols and universal standards of verification; nevertheless, pursuing science as a concrete endeavor involves an interplay of hand, eye, materials, and intuition that has parallels with creative work in art. In thinking of science as something apart from the intuitive and the concrete, and in thinking of art as something divorced from thought, education has neglected the true richness of both science and art.

Dewey thought that the old idea of science as analysis and art as synthesis was a misleading simplification, having no more validity than the Cartesian fiction of the mind as a lonely ghost inside the body's machine. Nor did he believe that science and art had to be in conflict, although he was painfully aware of the remoteness of the two realms in the splintered American culture. Art and science for Dewey were different points in the rhythm of the same dance of human imagination over experience. In both we come to understand the world by acting upon it.

As Hawkins also points out, Dewey was profoundly right to see something in common between one style of scientific work and the active probings and explorings of children in good classrooms. Anyone who has watched the practice of art and science in such settings recognizes the quality of absorbed participation that reigns. Good learning in science and art and other subjects has common elements of freshness, absorption, and participation. The play between children's minds and materials illustrates the fleeting high Romantic goal of reasoned reinforcement of the imagination.

Like Dewey, Hawkins urges teachers today to look beneath the surface of achieved and codified scientific knowledge to the underlying life of scientific inquiry so few people ever take part in. Dewey looked with anthropological horror at the spectacle of a culture whose material base was profoundly shaped by science, but whose people did not understand science. This problem has grown worse in the years since Dewey wrote. Science has become an enormous, often malign force in our society. Although it raises the GNP, it also fights our wars, helps ruin our environment, and threatens us with annihilation. This is the side of science we see most clearly. Most of us are less able to perceive that science is also a way of thought and action that ought to enrich our lives. The fact that specialized science expresses a mode of living and thinking available only to an elite minority dismays Hawkins as much today as it dismayed Dewey years ago. The concern is political in part; if knowledge is power, as it surely is, then elite control of science is a threat to all of us. Politics aside, however, there is something disgraceful about a culture whose people are ignorant of their material and intellectual underpinnings; in which the sullen victims of the perversions of science and technology curse the day the genie ever left the bottle and stand superstitiously and passively awaiting the next catastrophe. Dewey took insufficient account of the fact that his ideal of science as an individual artisan's craft did not square with the bureaucratic workings of that highly political institution we might call Big Science. The progressive intellectuals did not anticipate the nightmarish potential of Big Science. Yet Dewey's contemporary followers are surely right in noting that science is all too rarely pursued for its own sake, as a way of informing and liberating our vision. Like education itself, science is made to serve too many questionable outside masters.

Dewey never reworked his later emphasis on concrete values back into his formulations of science. As Hawkins puts it, he seems to have been ignorant of the actual practice of science, and was thus apt to emphasize scientific method to the neglect of the actual content that all vital method must feed on. He understood, but sometimes forgot to mention, the intrinsic pleasure of science. Although today we find Dewey's efforts to understand science and art essential first steps in framing our own ideas about education, there are moments when Dewey seems singularly exasperating. Most of all, perhaps, we balk at the tone, the blandness, the rhetorical ease with which he achieves his harmonies and mediations of divergent realms. We grow impatient with the innocent limits of his social imagination, and his failure to see the way that schools are implicated in issues of power, social class, and race. Yet we keep coming back to his vision: We too work toward a style of education that would reflect a high Romantic synthesis of the values of reason and human community. We, too, are looking for a mediation of reason, feeling, and imagination, an education that, beginning in play and evolving into apprenticeship, encourages children to learn both a reverence for concrete experience and an active mastery of the proper place of symbols and abstractions in a scientific world.

The utopian complexity of Dewey's commitments means that each generation of his readers picks out a different set of emphases. Recent progressive thought and practice has not shared Dewey's interest in schools as social, democratic, and moral communities. This seems to me a pity. The reasons for our neglect of the social dimensions of learning are many; some of us are still spooked by the way classic progressive thought kept getting twisted into a rationale for conformity and groupiness. Much of the best recent work in Dewey's footsteps has concentrated on two problems: the high Romantic synthesis, and the challenge to make knowledge accessible to children's active explorations along myriads of individual pathways. Both are aspirations, scarcely achievements.

Anyone speaking on behalf of even a portion of Dewey's grand program must speak humbly and doggedly, with what somebody once called the authority of failure. Plainly we must live with more pain in our hopes for the schools than the progressives felt, or showed. In part the pain reflects America's continuing lack of two necessary perspectives on schools. We are, like the progressives, still largely unwilling to admit that school is only one part of children's lives, and not the major part at that. We continue to make vast claims on behalf of the schools. And the very size of these claims leads us to the second error in perspective, our habitual neglect of the smaller, daily possibilities of our educational institutions. In the end, what allowed Dewey to shake loose from his grandiose progressive utopianism was his hardheaded focus on the importance of the present moments in teachers' and childrens' lives, the day-to-day quality of life in the classroom.

Dewey would have been a friendly but severe critic of the second round of the New Education. He was deeply disappointed by the turn the first progressive era took, and he would have been critical of much recent work too. He was ever impatient with the New Education's chronic susceptibility to low, irrational romanticism, with its anti-intellectualism, its lack of confidence in legitimate adult authority, and its quite mistaken notion that its ideas invalidate all traditional practice and standards. Yet good recent ongoing work shows the strengths of progressivism at its best. Child-centered progressives like Dewey believed that education's most radical step was helping children learn to think. Without discounting the importance of skills, they pointed to the significance of the kind of active learning that goes on in play, and showed in actual practice the effectiveness of pedagogies that move children from play to more disciplined work. They thought that children's present lives ought to be as important to their teachers as their futures are; that schools—in a valid, if much-abused formulation—are life, as well as preparation for life.

The child-centered progressives had hopes for the social functions of schools as well. They wanted schools to become democratic, cooperative communities of adults and children. They worked against the historically conformist grain of American education, with its obsession with superordinate goals, its neglect of daily practice, and its search for a one best system to impose on teachers and children. They emphasized children's diversity and stressed the educational importance of the fact that childhood is a time of intellectual construction.

Implicit in much of what figures like Dewey wrote was a dissent from an essentially economic view of the role of education. Dewey opposed the mainstream progressive educators, the administrative progressives, as historian David Tyack (1974) calls them. They were busily intent on reordering schools along corporate and managerial lines; schools were to be sieves for sorting out students according to their future jobs. Since Dewey's time, child-centered thought and pedagogy has been a distinctly minority viewpoint in American education, generally more influential at the lower levels of schooling than in higher grades.

The New Education appears in fits and starts in educational theory and practice partly because we are a faddish culture and rarely build on the past in a cumulative way. It keeps reappearing, however, because it raises perennial questions. Each generation reexamines Dewey's complex educational legacy on new terms. Dewey's progressive faith in science itself does not move us very much today. We are skeptical of his assumption that the anguish of living will diminish as knowledge grows. For one thing, the social sciences do not seem impressively cumulative in their wisdom; Dewey plainly underestimated the practical and moral problems involved in applying experimental science to people. He made a characteristic progressive mistake in neglecting the political character of all institutions, including science. I would agree with Dewey on the validity of the ideal of science. What else do we have to go by but science: broadly understood—the appeal to evidence, to logic, to inquiry validated by open public processes of criticism and debate. But the ideal is only fitfully represented by the institution called science. This is more obvious to us than to Dewey's generation. Every day we witness scientific rationalism harnessed to evil and even crazy political ends. In the middle of a panic-stricken flight from rationalism and the consequences of a perverted science and technology, it is useful to remind ourselves, with Dewey, that science ought to be a humane liberal pursuit, a path to liberation.

In social thought we are apt to prefer the late Dewey to the progressive social engineer. Dewey was wrong to ignore the politics of institutions—like the Bolsheviks, the progressives kept forgetting that what they were mainly doing was building bureaucracies—but he was right about the need to create institutions. Being more conscious of the dangers of bureaucracy, we will want to fashion our institutions after the voluntaristic, pluralistic spirit of the late Dewey. Going beyond the world the progressives left us will involve creating institutions on a human scale, and professions that truly serve clients.

It will involve working for political coalitions to redistribute wealth and power, for without politics, attempts at reform will repeat the history of progressivism. Lacking politics, progressivism was in the end merely the ideology of liberal professionals and reformers. For a time Dewey looked like the ideal spokesman for the new bureaucratic order of professionals, managers, and experts. Just as John Stuart Mill[14] outgrew the desolate calculations of Jeremy Bentham's[15] utilitarianism, Dewey transcended the bleak managerial scientism of the progressive outlook. Like Mill, Dewey will be remembered for the way he carried liberal thought to the edge of something quite different from what it started out to be.

Dewey's philosophy, which was really quite simple, reflected an enduring outlook—the outlook of Daedalus, the legendary Greek craftsman who built the famous maze, designed wonderful gold jewelry, and mastered the secret of flight. Daedalus is *homo faber*, he believes that we know what we can make and he scorns superstition, hero worship, and irrationality of any sort, glorying in the triumphs of artisans, builders, engineers, and artists. The temperament has practical strength and a number of theoretical weaknesses. It is not sympathetic to contemplation; it is suspicious of politics; it often does violence to nature; and it is afraid of the past. Dewey never conquered his fear of the past, which is perhaps why so many ghosts of old philosophical issues hover over all his work, and why his psychology has so little to say about the inner life. He never examined his own history, and he never understood the American past—the American history taught in Dewey's experimental elementary school was a pageant of technological cooperation, not the chronicle of violence and oppression that were equally part of the story.

Dewey's basic point of view was never tragic. It was comic, based on the healing potential of ordinary social experience, but his outlook deepened and he came to appreciate realms he had once neglected. *Experience and Nature* is far in spirit from the technological imperialism of Dewey's earlier instrumentalism, suffused with a serene sense that humans stand within nature like Jonah in the belly of the whale. It turned out that Dewey's instrumental universe had room for many mansions, including the houses of contemplation, pain, and death. In politics, after he stopped believing in technical solutions, levers to pull to bring about Utopia, he emphasized grass-roots change, and the necessity of diverse political coalitions to move a diverse and various country. He worked to build alliances between workers, professionals, and the public in various ways, ranging from active support of democratic and highly political union movements to consumer and parents' groups and third parties, never quite settling on one means, never discovering a single source of social salvation, an increasingly lonely *philosophe* of a wispy revolution that never came about. He did not give up on the possibility of a democratic cooperative America. The wholeness of his late perspective, the cumulative nature of his concern, the steadiness of application, the lack of bitterness, made up for his terrible vagueness. He closed a late autobiographical sketch with these words: "Forty years spent wandering in the wilderness like that of the present is not a sad fate—unless one attempts to make himself believe that the wilderness is after all itself the promised land."

George Orwell (1940) once called Henry Miller "a Whitman among the corpses." He was pointing to the difficulty of working within the celebratory Romantic vein on the grim material of 20th-century life. Dewey was struggling to be an Emerson among the dynamos, the bureaucracies, and the colossal wars of our recent past.

NOTES

1. Victorian-era social theorist Thorstein Veblen was one of capitalism's most articulate critics.

2. Featherstone refers here to the British economist's famous joke: "In the long run, we're all dead."

3. Jane Addams is one of the best-known social reformers of the Progressive era. The reference here is to her involvement in the peace movement and commitment to internationalism. Active in the Women's Peace Party, which later became the Women's International League for Peace and Freedom, she opposed the U.S. involvement in World War I. As a result of this work, Addams won the Nobel Peace Prize in 1931.

4. Colonel Edward M. House was chief adviser to President Woodrow Wilson.

5. Literary critics Francis Raymond and Queenie Dorothy Leavis.

6. Great Victorian art critic and environmentalist John Ruskin.

7. A poet, translator, publisher, and decorative artist, William Morris was also, in the 1880s, probably Britain's most outspoken socialist.

8. British historian Richard Tawney, a Christian Socialist, wrote about education, economics, and politics.

9. Raymond Williams was a British Marxist literary critic and a great influence on the student radicals of the 1960s and 1970s.

10. George Santayana, the philosopher, poet, and novelist.

11. Massachusetts's first secretary of education, Horace Mann was a 19th-century advocate for public education and for the idea that it could be the basis of a more democratic society.

12. Justice Oliver Wendell Holmes served for 20 years on the Massachusetts Supreme Court and 30 years on the U.S. Supreme Court, retiring in 1932.

13. Theodore Dreiser, a Dewey contemporary, wrote naturalistic novels, the best known of which are *Sister Carrie* (1900) and *An American Tragedy* (1925).

14. When 19th-century philosopher John Stuart Mill, a child prodigy, read Bentham in adolescence he felt that "all previous moralists were superseded." But later he recognized that Bentham's utilitarianism had both moral and intellectual limitations.

15. Early 19th-century philosopher Jeremy Bentham is best known for his theory of utilitarianism or "the greatest good for the greatest number."

Democratic Vistas

JUNE 19, 1995

THE NINTH AND TENTH GRADERS at Central Park East Secondary School in East Harlem are putting on scenes from *Macbeth*. Deborah Meier, the principal and founder of the school, writes, "They knew that the laughter from the audience was the laughter of colleagues working with, not against them." Later, a much-loved friend of the school dies. Meier says, "We stopped to take stock of her life. . . . We can do such things not because we are more caring than other teachers . . . [but] because we have a structure and a style that enables us to show our care effectively."

This extraordinary high school is part of a cluster of three small public elementary schools and one high school serving largely poor families. Over the years the cluster has created a community of mutual respect. But saying only this risks sentimentality. That's why it's important to pay attention to these two examples in relation to the title of Meier's (1995) book, *The Power of Their Ideas*. The book is about the uses of the intellect, the deliberate cultivation of habits of mind and heart and literacy. One constant thread is the notion that intellectual values are not divorced from qualities like sympathy and care. Another implicit assumption is that the life of the mind—the habits of thinking and doing that go into intellectual work—requires a variety of social settings in which teachers and kids take turns acting as talkers, thinkers, artists, scientists, activists. The mind's work is social business. We need company to do it, even when the company is imaginary. Poor kids breaking into the vaults of "high" academic culture probably need such company even more than the rest of us.

The school's production of *Macbeth* and the memorial service both reflect an effort to make certain values manifest in public settings: to enact them with the school itself as the audience. Visitors soon realize that the kids perform—for one another, for teachers, and, at graduation, for outsiders gathered in as special witnesses. Teachers in many other schools share the same values of respect and intellect, but the places they teach in often lack common structures that make such habits as commonplace as gossip and horseplay in the halls.

The Power of Their Ideas is in part a memoir of the creation of this structure of respect. It is in part an outline of some general principles that might allow for the creation of similar schools in other places. And it is a stirring manifesto for democratic, public education—hurled into the teeth of the times. Doing *Macbeth* well and taking stock of a friend's life both involve respect and imaginative empathy. If you add healthy intellectual skepticism to the mix and then work it into daily classroom habits, Meier argues, you begin to arrive at a curriculum designed for democratic participation.

A democratic education ought to educate all the people to rule. Up to now, most democracies have done a really ambitious job only with the children of the elite. Middling folks and especially the poor have received educational leftovers or worse. Meier skewers the nostalgia that is such a powerful, twisted force in U.S. politics and education. She rightly argues that the good old days in education never existed for more than half the population. Poor kids in particular got the shaft. Her school's work over the past 20 years is an imaginative vindication of the revolutionary idea that all kids are created equal, that the many can graduate high school with the intellectual competence that history usually reserved for the few. Moreover, the school's work shows that an education ambitious about the having of wonderful ideas (in Eleanor Duckworth's grand phrase) is not a luxury gained at the expense of the three Rs but a way of making the three Rs come freshly alive.

The lesson hits home all the more because U.S. society is now trained to expect less of poor and dark-skinned ("inner-city") children. Work crews in the nation's Congress are busy striking the remaining safety nets and ladders. No one expects a poor kid to produce reasoned views about whether *Hamlet* is a better play than *Macbeth*. And few in a time of civic despair are prepared to hear that the public schools are the proper vehicle to nourish the extraordinary untapped capacity of all our children. Central Park East shows—every generation requires fresh testimony—that the question is not whether democratic and truly public education is possible. The question, as Meier says, is whether we want it badly enough.

Meier's compelling argument for rethinking the American high school root and branch comes out of a school where half the kids are African-American, one third Latino, and about 10% White. More than half qualify for free lunches. Twenty percent qualify as handicapped. In a city where half the students don't finish high school, Central Park East Secondary School (CPESS) sends more than 80% to college, where they stay and get degrees.

Institutions always come out of a history. Teachers, parents, kids, and reformers operating today need to know that there is a past to build on. Most of the staff of the original Central Park East Elementary, the ancestor

of Central Park East Secondary School—White, Black, Latino—were products of progressive political and educational movements, particularly the
intertwining of open education and the civil rights movement of the 1960s.
Many also had roots in earlier progressive politics and traditions of democratic education. Some were students of Lillian Weber's City College Work-
shop Center. Some, like Meier, were veterans of early childhood education,
that classic seedbed of progressive thought and practice.

Meier and her associates fused an intellectually tough, durable, and
social vision out of the eclectic and creative 1960s scene. She and her allies
were uneasy with the individualistic focus of what was called open education. They criticized the anti-intellectual side of progressivism and the
sentimental 1960s rhetoric claiming that kids would bloom like flowers if
left to their own devices. She and her allies believed that adults have important and even necessary things to teach kids. She took a thoughtful early
interest in testing and assessment, looking for serious alternatives to the
usual quantitative methods of settling kids' fates. Intensely political, Meier
and her colleagues were staunch public school progressives. Through the
1970s and 1980s they kept a clear focus on the big problem in U.S. education, which was of course not "mediocrity," as we were often told, but rather
the lives of poor kids. After the civil rights movement waned, these disciplined people stayed on, as many have, finding their own cracks in the
system. The long-distance runners with graying hair attracted younger
colleagues to the idea that a teacher could be an artist, an intellectual, and
an advocate for poor kids.

Given the rich and successful history of progressive education with
younger children, it took perhaps only a small miracle to create terrific
public elementary schools in the city. Central Park East Elementary was a
notable addition to the roster of schools of choice in New York City's District 4. The truly astonishing thing was to invent a fresh and brand-new
progressive version of high school for poor city kids. Meier's vision of the
high school constitutes—even apart from her inspired practice—a powerful contribution to progressive thought. One startling idea still rocks her
audiences: the notion that a high school should combine the best features
of kindergarten and preschool tradition, on the one hand, and the spirit of
elite graduate education, on the other. Meier argues that kindergarten and
graduate school are the only places where students are routinely encouraged to have ideas and to follow their own interests, two essential features
of any deep education.

Another striking idea was Meier's sense of the importance of the community of adult teachers. The child-centered rhetoric of the 1960s echoed
a bad old progressive habit of implying that teachers can do incredibly
demanding sorts of teaching all alone—in effect asking the impossible.

Meier saw that support of kids' learning hinges on the possibility of an ongoing education for teachers. This comes out in her early thinking: "I chose to consider how to create the optimum conditions for making teaching as interesting as it had been to me, and at the same time how to offer the collegially respectful settings that I had missed (in public education)."

Within the standard New York City high school budget and the standard package of big city constraints, CPESS has indeed made it new. No teacher is responsible for more than 40 students, as opposed to the 150 that many high school teachers see daily. The schedule is ruthlessly simple: two periods, a 2-hour humanities block and a 2-hour math/science block. Teams of teachers decide exactly what goes into these interdisciplinary periods. The school has an elaborate advisory system, and a schedule that includes generous time for planning and consultation and meetings, including a civilized hour for lunch that supports the school's emphasis on thoughtful talk. The original entrance requirement was that families visit the school when a kid is admitted. That still applies, only now admission is by lottery.

CPESS has pioneered important alternatives to testing and grading, especially an elaborate practice of requiring that students present portfolios and exhibitions in different intellectual areas for graduation. As in so many other realms, the school's rigorous stance toward assessment is evidence of a tough-minded progressivism that stresses performance from students and teachers. It focuses less on the standard academic way of looking at high school learning and more on performance and the actual uses of literacy. Characteristically, the school's stance also dramatizes an important principle: the root of the word *evaluation* is *value*.

Along with a host of other reformers in the 1980s and 1990s, the school has pushed for a complete rethinking of the standard high school curriculum. Students at CPESS have to know a lot—portfolios and exhibitions for graduation are, after all, ways of displaying knowledge—but the school is more concerned with helping teachers frame experiences that will make certain habits of mind and action available to students. In my own work I've found CPESS's basic categories for habits of mind immensely fruitful for helping teachers and communities to rethink the aims of curriculum. CPESS teachers in all subjects want students to have the habit of inquiring about point of view: Who says what, from what angle? They want them to ask about evidence: How do you know? About cause and effect: What led to this, what connects this to that? Hypothesis: What if? What's another way to look at this? The fifth CPE habit of mind is the one most neglected in U.S. secondary education, the habit of asking, So what? Why would anyone care? Why is this worth knowing? [To see all this and more in action, rent Frederick Wiseman's wonderful 3- (yes, 3) hour film about CPESS, *High School II*.]

CPESS has become one of the most influential symbols of one strand of educational reform pushing for a rethinking of school structures and pedagogy in the interests of having kids use their minds well. It is an early member and prize exhibit of Theodore Sizer's Coalition of Essential Schools, which has had important successes in popularizing an intellectually demanding and progressive image of the U.S. high school. It represents a powerful argument for the advantages of small schools. Deborah Meier has recently moved from CPE to preside over a new effort to create a network of 50 or more small public high schools within the New York City system. The general platform is that of Meier's book and the reform movement it grew out of: the deliberate creation of small high schools; schools of choice; school autonomy over critical decisions involving hiring, teaching, and learning; lots of time built into schedules for building relationships and for reflecting on experiences together; a culture and structure of mutual respect and a set of habits of mind that foster inquiry and responsibility in all realms. In a desperate time, some powerful ideas may take root.

I have no five-point program for creating such schools—only two images from Wiseman's superb film. The first is a teacher trying to make sense of one bewildered kid's meandering about a paper topic. The kid mumbles in a teenage fog. The tired teacher persists. Hundreds of years seem to go by. Slowly, painfully, teacher and film audience start to get a glimmer. The paper, perhaps, is about how Christopher Columbus lived in the time we call the Renaissance, but how in his intense, fanatical narrowness, Columbus was not what we would call a Renaissance Man. Incredible as it is, an idea is taking shape in this kid's mind. This is the work of teaching in all its tedium and glory. This, ladies and gentlemen, is what it will take for all kids to develop powerful ideas.

My second image is the CPESS staff disagreeing about standards. Some feel their main job is to prepare kids to meet the standards of the real world, like the A.P. English exam. Others disagree: The main job is building up the kids' confidence in their own power to make sense of experience. Both sides surely have a piece of the wider truth sought by Dewey and Du Bois and by generations of forgotten schoolteachers. Even more, though, the quarreling teachers at Central Park East have what many of us in America in the 1990s still lack: a structure of respect.

Democracy and Education

JUNE 2002

I
N HIS GREAT PRIMER on democracy, the Gettysburg Address,
Abraham Lincoln created a modern myth of U.S. history as each
generation's struggle to balance equality and liberty. He spoke of
America as an experiment in creating government of, by, and for the people.
The educational corollary of this was an education of, by, and for the people.
The cultural corollary was an ideal of democratic culture that has not yet
existed, not even in ancient Athens, with its slaves, and its assumption that
women were inferiors. Walt Whitman and John Dewey and generations
of schoolteachers like my grandmother—an Irish Catholic teaching principal in Pennsylvania coal country—dreamed of such a culture for the children of all the people. As with government and politics, the essence of such
a democratic culture would be active participation. To grow up independent thinkers and strong free citizens, kids need to participate intellectually in the school subjects they are taught. That we are still a long way from
this goal may be sad, but not particularly surprising.

Like modern democracy, public education is a new invention, an experiment, too—only a few generations old. In our current despair over
public schools we forget how new the experiment is. Around the world,
hopeful little girls are stepping inside a classroom for the first time. It should
not astonish us that a planet that has so far concentrated on educating the
privileged still lacks a good model for an education system that prepares
everybody's children to participate fully in life.

Nowadays those who see the schools in terms of such rich old American values might insist, with me, on high school graduation and access
to some form of higher education as goals for everybody's children—an
updated, democratic version of the old elite idea of the liberal arts.

I believe that this older, more complex, and humane vision of teaching and learning is in fact well suited to the challenges of an information
age, a swiftly changing economy, and an interdependent world of many
cultures and peoples. Narrow, utilitarian versions of education—aimed at
acquiring information alone or training for specific jobs, for example—look
more efficient on the surface, lend themselves better to batch-processing,
and can be more readily measured by computer-graded tests, but will not

lead us to a system where most students are richly prepared as workers, citizens of the country and the world, and participants in culture itself.

As a democrat (with a small d) and a progressive interested in kids' minds, I would readily make an alliance with some of today's thoughtful conservatives—E. D. Hirsch, for example, and Diane Ravitch—to stand this older American vision of the purposes for public education against corporate and consumerist visions of schools as places where students just get basic skills or training for jobs. In a democracy, producing thoughtful, informed citizens is the real point of schooling, and the real basics are what the next generation will need to continue what Lincoln thought of as a great democratic experiment. It turns out, of course, that a broader, more liberal vision of schooling probably prepares students better for a world of changing jobs and lives in any case—but it's important to insist on schooling's proper role in preparing future citizens and participants in politics and culture, as well as in the economy.

Although we might—against corporate and philistine forces—be allied in our broad, liberal, democratic goals, Ravitch and Hirsch dissent from what they see as the debased means pursued by educational "progressives" in the last century. To read their works is to get a very dim view of those they label as progressives in education. Hirsch blames "progressives" for a Romantic cult of child-centeredness that undermined chances for a solid curriculum with basic cultural content (1987)—he has promoted an interesting version of such a curriculum in many schools. Hirsch makes a very good point about the link between information and ambitious thinking in all the school disciplines—you do have to know a lot of stuff in order to think intelligently about the Civil War—but he is wrong to imagine that many "progressives" from John Dewey to Theodore Sizer have not been deeply interested in this very issue. As for thinking about the Civil War, or any other subject, Hirsch lacks curiosity about kids' minds— it's not at all clear that he is interested in teaching children to think. Perhaps thinking is reserved for grad school. Kids don't bring a lot to his version of the educational transaction. For all his intelligence, and his robust commitment to democracy, Hirsch often manages to sound like today's stony school reformers, abolishing recess as they write long lists of words on the blackboard.

Ravitch's *Left Back* (2000) is a polemical history of U.S. education in which it turns out that the left and "progressives" generally have not been on the side of equality, as you might think (and as I still believe), but rather have promoted systematic educational inequality—tracking and a system of differentiated education. Rather than crediting unions, the civil rights and women's movements for egalitarian reform, Ravitch instead claims that it's been conservatives all along who've been battling for democracy and educational equality. Ravitch's idiosyncratic efforts do indeed uncover a number of attractive conservatives who fought for an academic education for all—my kind of conservatives. But her concentration on a very pure (nearly Hegelian) version of the history of ideas completely overlooks the many strong social forces, including racism and an unequal capitalist class system, that surely have shaped U.S. high schools even more than a handful of leftist professors at Teachers College, Columbia. I can't find my grandmother or the thousands of people like her anywhere in Ravitch's grand historical tableau. She is right that "progressives" can be anti-intellectuals, with a disdain for liberal learning and its values—early in the last century, many shared in the widespread U.S. effort to create second-class curricula for second-class students in our tracked high schools. (Though today, conservatives are often among the chief opponents of proposals for detracking.) She skewers the old philistinism of the left—the humorless "progressive" school where kids study the local road system instead of learning about Renaissance Florence or the Mayans.

Ravitch is especially vituperative in her treatment of the 1960s, when a cast of barbarians appears to have sacked Rome, leaving a smoking educational ruin. Then, at the end of a book-long critique of all and anything "progressive," Ravitch takes a surprising turn, one ignored by conservative reviewers. She ends with the highest praise for a small group of "intellectual progressives"—such as Theodore Sizer and Deborah Meier, who, she warmly concedes, do indeed have rigorous humane and intellectual goals for classrooms, and have put them into practice with actual teachers and live kids. And much of whose work, Ravitch does not say, owes debts to the rich curriculum, preschool, psychology, civil rights, and other movements of, if you will pardon the expression, the 1960s. Like Ravitch, and myself, these "intellectual progressives" have long argued for some democratic version of the liberal arts for everybody's children, schools where all kids get to use their minds well. Ravitch writes: "My own children grew up in New York City, where they attended a private progressive school that was academically rigorous and pedagogically venturesome." She speaks of teachers "who dreamed up projects that fired their students' minds and imaginations. If I could wave a magic wand, this is what I would want for all children."

So why not aim for such terrific classrooms for all our children? Ravitch's answer is terse and fatalistic: "Whether intellectual progressivism . . . could grow in a typical school setting was uncertain. At century's end, the typical public school was bureaucratically controlled, contained numerous inconsistent ad hoc programs, and lacked intellectual coherence. Intellectual progressivism in the late twentieth century tended to flourish best in private schools or in small public-sector alternative and charter schools."

Having spent over 30 years on just this matter, I have to agree with Ravitch—it's uncertain whether a progressive or any other intellectually ambitious version of the liberal arts for all will in fact become the norm for "the typical public school." On the other hand, why give up the long historic struggle so readily? Ravitch is an optimist in the short run—she seems to approve of the current style of school reform narrowly focused on top-down standards and vigorous high-stakes testing. She is a pessimist about the long run—it sounds as though she thinks public schools can never be as good as the private schools her kids attended. Would it be unfair to make her despair a symbol of the current state of the nation's mood in education? If bureaucracy and scale are as baleful as Ravitch says, then surely it is a mistake for today's influential conservatives to boost the very school reforms that push all schools toward more bureaucratic, scripted versions of teaching; perhaps we need a broad coalition of educators and the public to worry more about such endangered species as imaginative teaching and smaller schools. Many parents and students would agree with me that it ought to be possible to have high standards without the standardization we are presently getting.

I, on the other hand, am a short-term pessimist, worried about the unintended consequences of some varieties of current school reform, but more optimistic about democracy and education in the long haul. The apt quote, again, must come from John Dewey (1907): "What the best and wisest parent wants for his own child, that must the community want for all of its children." The task in a democracy is to persuade parents and voters of at least some compromise version of wisdom, a balanced education for the whole child.

PART III

Teachers and Classrooms

S PANNING 30 YEARS, Featherstone's writing on teachers and classrooms—which includes both journalism and critical essays—begins in the British primary classrooms of the mid-1960s. Published in pamphlet form, Featherstone's writings on British schools circulated widely—*The New Republic* sent out over 100,000 reprints. Featherstone also takes us through Herbert Kohl's literary classroom in Harlem and Frances Hawkins's observations of a nursery school classroom for deaf students. Some of his schoolrooms are less geographical than conceptual, as in his essay on *Helen and Teacher*, Joseph Lash's portrait of the intense, troubled, yet deeply engaged classroom of Anne Sullivan and Helen Keller's life together. More recently, he defines the "Living Classroom," a place where teachers and children work out the pressing and constant question of just what learning involves.

Along the way, Featherstone pushes his reader to see the intelligence of these teachers and students. The heart of his vision lies in these portraits and commentary; it is in this journalistic voice that we find the useful tension between the visionary—even the romantic—and the pragmatic practitioner. The portrait of British primary education with its inventory of supplies and detailing of the "Wendy House" might almost be taken as a kind of "how-to" manual—and some wonderful classrooms in this country were dreamt into being by teachers who read his series that way. We also find in these pieces the voice of the historian who elucidates the specific contexts and conditions of teaching and learning. For instance, on Anne Sullivan, he writes: "Her blend of child-centered pedagogy, a revived romanticism, and social reform expresses her generation and her time." Finally, contrasting the "enjoyment" in Jeanette Amidon's classroom to the environment in thousands of schools dominated by Mr. Gradgrind—Featherstone's fictional archantagonist, named for Charles Dickens's callous educator-industrialist who hates children and worships "facts, facts, facts,"—Featherstone enters into the messy theatrics of policy, and gently shoves the world of the classroom centerstage, spotlighting it with precision and clarity.

Finally, though he claims that "any attempt to describe what goes on in a good classroom fails," Featherstone's portraits of teachers and students in struggle help us to make sense of teaching. As he writes in his 1997 foreword to *The Living Classroom*, "Pin up this sentence on the wall: Enjoyment seems to be the key."

The Primary School Revolution in Britain: Schools for Children— What's Happening in British Classrooms

AUGUST 19, 1967

THE INTEGRATED DAY

M Y WIFE AND I have just spent a month in England visiting classes in primary schools, talking to children and teachers. Friends told us about good things happening in British classrooms, but we were scarcely prepared for what we found; in recent decades there has been a profound and sweeping revolution in English primary education, involving new ways of thinking about how young children learn, classroom organization, the curriculum, and the role of the teacher. We saw schools in some good local educational authorities—Bristol, Nottingham, Leicestershire, Oxfordshire—and a few serving immigrant areas in cities like London.

In what follows, I'm going to be as specific as I can about how classes work, how the room is laid out, what sort of things are in it, how the teacher and the children go through the day, and, in some detail, how a child learns to read—an example of the kind of learning that goes on. I know that American teachers, particularly good ones, are suspicious of most talk on education, because so little of what they hear relates to actual classroom practice. I hope I can be specific enough. The relevance of these British classrooms to American education is a difficult question, which I'll leave for later.

Primary schools in Britain divide into "infant" and "junior" schools. The infant schools in England take the children from the age of 5 to 7, and, in some authorities, 8. It is in the infant schools that people learn to read and write and to work with numbers. Junior schools take children from 7 or 8 to 11, when they go on to secondary school. Infant and junior schools sometimes occupy the same building, and some authorities—Oxfordshire, for example—have a policy of putting them together in one unit, like an American elementary school.

95

Westfield Infant School is a one-story structure like any of a thousand American buildings, on a working-class housing estate in Leicestershire. If you arrive early you find a number of children already inside, reading, writing, painting, playing music, tending to pets. Teachers sift in slowly and begin working with students. Apart from a religious assembly (required by law), it's hard to say just when school actually begins, because there is very little organized activity for a whole class. The puzzled visitor sees some small-group work in mathematics ("maths") or reading, but mostly children are on their own, moving about and talking quite freely. The teacher sometimes sits at her desk, and the children flock to her for consultations, but more often she moves about the room, advising on projects, listening to children read, asking questions, giving words, talking, sometimes prodding.

The hallways, which are about the size of those in American schools, are filled with busy children, displays of paintings and graphs, a grocery store where children use play money and learn to count, easels, tables for collections of shells and plants, workbenches on which to pound and hammer nails and boards, big wooden boxes full of building blocks.

Classrooms open out onto the playground, which is also much in use. A contingent of children is kneeling on the grass, clocking the speed of a tortoise, which they want to graph against the speeds of other pets, and of people. Nearby are 5-year-olds, finishing an intricate, tall tower of blocks, triumphantly counting as they add the last one, "23, 24." A solitary boy is mixing powders for paint; on a large piece of paper attached to an easel, with very big strokes, he makes an ominous, stylized building that seems largely to consist of black shutters framing deep red windows. "It's the hospital where my brother is," he explains and pulls the visitor over to the class-library corner where a picture book discusses hospitals. He can't read it yet (he's 5) but says he is trying. And he is; he can make out a number of words, some pretty hard, on different pages, and it is clear that he has been *studying* the book, because he wants badly to know about hospitals. At another end of the hall there is a quieter library nook for the whole school. Here two small boys are reading aloud; the better reader is, with indifferent grace, correcting the grateful slower boy as he stumbles over words.

The rooms are fairly noisy—more noisy than many American teachers or principals would allow—because children can talk freely. Sometimes the teacher has to ask for quiet. With as many as 40 in some classes, rooms are crowded and accidents happen. Paint spills, a tub overflows, there are recriminations. Usually the children mop up and work resumes.

The visitor is dazed by the amount and variety and fluency of free writing produced: stories, free-verse poems with intricate images, precise accounts of experiments in "maths," and, finally, looking over a tiny little girl's shoulder, he finds: "Today we had visitors from America . . ."

After a time, you overcome your confusion at the sheer variety of it all, and you begin making more definite observations. The physical layout of the classrooms is markedly different. American teachers are coming to appreciate the importance of a flexible room, but even in good elementary schools in the United States this usually means having movable, rather than fixed, desks. In these classes there are no individual desks and no assigned places. Around the room (which is about the size of one you would find in an average American school) there are different tables for different activities: art, water and sand play, number work. (The number tables have all kinds of number lines—strips of paper with numbers marked on them in sequence on which children learn to count and reason mathematically— beads, buttons, and odd things to count; weights and balances; dry and liquid measures; and a rich variety of apparatus for learning basic mathematical concepts, some of it homemade, some ready-made. The best of the commercial materials were familiar: Cuisenaire rods, the Dienes multibase material, Stern rods, and attribute or logical blocks. This sort of thing is stressed much more than formal arithmetic.)

WENDY AND PUPPETS

Every class has a library alcove, separated off by a room divider that also serves as a display shelf for books. Some library corners have a patch of carpet and an old easy chair. Every room has a "Wendy House," a play corner with dolls and furniture for playing house. Often there is a dress-up corner, too, with different kinds of cast-off adult clothes. The small children love the Wendy Houses and dress-up corners, but you see older ones using them as well. Some classes have puppet theaters for putting on improvised plays with homemade puppets—although many make do with the legs of one table turned upside down on top of another for a makeshift stage. Often, small children perform dance dramas involving a lot of motion and a minimum of words.

Gradually it becomes clear how the day proceeds in one of these rooms. In many infant and some junior schools the choice of the day's routine is left completely up to the teacher; the teacher, in turn, leaves options open to the children. Classes for young children are reaching a point in many schools where there is no real difference between one subject in the curriculum and another, or even between work and play. A school day run on these lines is called, variously, the "free day," the "integrated curriculum," or the "integrated day." The term scarcely matters.

In a school that operates with a free day, the teacher usually starts the morning by listing the different activities available. A lot of rich material is needed, according to the teachers, but the best stuff is often homemade; and in any case, it isn't necessary to have 30 or 40 sets of everything, because most activities are for a limited number of people. "Six children can play in the Wendy House," says a sign in one classroom. The ground rules are that they must clean up when they finish, and they mustn't bother others.

A child might spend the day on his first choice, or he might not. Many teachers confess they get nervous if everybody doesn't do some reading and writing every day; others are committed in principle to letting children choose freely. In practice, many teachers give work when they think it's needed. In this, as in any other way of doing things, teachers tailor their styles to their own temperaments and to those of the children. But the extent to which children really have a choice and really work purposefully is astonishing.

How they learn reading offers an example of the kind of individual learning and teaching going on in these classrooms, even in quite large ones. Reading is not particularly emphasized over other subjects, and my purpose in singling it out is purely illustrative, though the contrast between English classes and most American ones, where reading is a formidable matter, is vivid and depressing.

At first it is hard to say just how they do learn to read, since there are no separate subjects. A part of the answer slowly becomes clear, and it surprises American visitors used to thinking of the teacher as the generating force of education: Children learn from each other. They hang around the library corners long before they can read, handling the books, looking at pictures, trying to find words they do know, listening and watching as the teacher hears other children's reading. It is common to see nonreaders studying people as they read, and then imitating them, monkey doing what monkey sees. Nobody makes fun of their grave parodies, and for good reasons.

A very small number of schools in two or three authorities have adopted what they call "family" or "vertical" grouping, which further promotes the idea of children teaching children. In these schools, each class is a cross section of the whole school's population, all ages mixed together. This seems particularly successful in the early school years, when newcomers are easily absorbed, and older children help teach the young ones to clean up and take first steps in reading. The older children, too, benefit from a classroom environment where they can occasionally be babyish; they also learn a good deal from the role of teacher they adopt. Family grouping needs smaller classes, teachers say, because it requires close supervision to make sure small children don't get overshadowed and big ones are still challenged. Teachers using it swear by the flexibility it provides.

Teachers use a range of reading schemes, sight reading, phonics, and so forth, whatever seems to work with a child.

BOOKS IN PROFUSION

Increasingly in the better infant schools, there are no textbooks and no class readers. There are just books, in profusion. Instead of spending their scanty book money on 40 sets of everything, schools have purchased different sets of reading series, as well as a great many single books, at all levels of difficulty. Teachers arrange their classroom libraries so they can direct students of different abilities to appropriate books, but in most classes a child can tackle anything he wants. As a check, cautious teachers ask them to go on their own through a graded reading series—which one doesn't matter.

However a child picks up reading, it will involve learning to write at the same time, and some write before they can read; there is an attempt to break down the mental barrier between the spoken, the written, and the printed word. When a child starts school, he gets a large, unlined notebook; this is his book for free writing, and he can put what he wants in it. On his own, he may draw a picture in it with crayon or pencil, discuss the picture with the teacher, and dictate a caption to her, which she then writes down for him: "This is my Dad." He copies the caption, writing just underneath. In this way he learns to memorize the look and sound of his dictated words and phrases until he reaches a point where, with help, he can write sentences. Often his notebook serves as his own first reading book.

He also gets a smaller notebook, his private dictionary, in which he enters words as he learns them. "I got a new word," a 5-year-old brags to the visitor. Children are always running to the teacher for words as they find they have more and more to write. Good teachers don't give in without a struggle: The children have to guess the first letter and sound the word out before they get it. Thus they pick up phonetic skills informally, although some teachers do use sight cards and some formal phonics work. Gradually as a child amasses a reading and writing vocabulary, he reaches a fluent stage and you see 6-year-olds writing stories, free-verse poems, accounts of things done in class, for an audience that includes other children as well as the teacher.

As a rule, teachers don't pay much attention to accuracy or neatness until a child is well on in his writing. They introduce grammar and spelling after a time, but not as separate subjects or ends in themselves. They are simply ways to say what you want more efficiently. Under these methods, where the children choose the content of their writing, more at-tention is paid to content than externals such as punctuation, spelling, and grammar. In good schools these are presented as what they are: living ways to get a meaning across, to be understood. Even unimaginative teachers, who quibble with children about other work, can learn to respect the con-tent of the free-writing books and take it seriously. This emphasis on self-chosen content has produced a flowering of young children's literature in schools working with many kinds of teachers and children. There is grow-ing recognition that different people flourish on different kinds of writing; storytellers and poets are not necessarily the same as those who can do elegant and graceful writing about mathematics. Books made and illus-trated by the children are coming to be a regular part of the curriculum in some schools.

I've focused on reading, although of course children spend their time doing other things, and the teachers in the schools we saw would be annoyed at the manner in which I've singled out one academic subject. The very best often argue that art is the key. The head of Sea Mills School in Bristol be-lieves firmly that if the art is good, all else follows. All else does follow, richly, at Sea Mills, where the infants sat us down and performed a concert of skill-ful poetry and songs they had made up on musical instruments.

But my purpose was to show not reading but the changed role of the teacher. Formal classroom teaching—the instructor standing up front, talk-ing to the group, or even the first-grade room divided up into reading groups that the teacher listens to separately as she tries desperately to keep order—has disappeared from many infant and a number of junior schools. It has disappeared because it imposes a single pattern of learning on a whole group of children—thus forcing the schools to "track," or to group classes by ability—because it ignores the extent to which children teach each other, and because in many workaday schools other methods are working bet-ter. Ordinary teachers, trained formally, take to the new role when they can see with their own eyes that the result is not chaos.

INFORMALITY IS HARD WORK

These methods mean more work for the teacher, not less. In informal con-ditions, it is essential for the teacher to keep detailed and accurate accounts of what a child is learning, even though at any given moment she might not know what he's up to. Children help by keeping their own records: In some schools they have private shelves where they store writing books, accounts of experiments and work in "maths," lists of the books they've read, and dates when they checked in with the teacher to read aloud. If

American parents could see some of the detailed folders of each child's work, including samples of his art work, they would feel, quite rightly, that a report card is a swindle.

When the class seldom meets as a unit, when children work independently, discipline is less of a problem. It does not disappear as a problem, but it becomes less paramount. The purposeful self-discipline of these children is, we were told, just as surprising to middle-aged Englishmen as it is to Americans. It is a recent development, and by no means the product of luck; much hard work and thought go into the arrangement of these classrooms and their rich materials. When they work at it, teachers find they can make time during the day for children who need it. "I can give all my attention to a child for 5 minutes, and that's worth more to him than being part of a sea of faces all day," said a teacher in an East London school overlooking the docks. Other teachers say they can watch children as they work and ask them questions; there is a better chance of finding out what children really understand.

What we saw is no statistical sample. The practices of the good schools we visited in different kinds of communities are not universal; but there are reasons for thinking they are no longer strikingly exceptional. The schools we saw are, for the most part, staffed by ordinary teachers; they are not isolated experiments run by cranks or geniuses. A government advisory body—the Plowden Committee—published a massive, and to American eyes, radical report in 1967 in which it indicated that about one third of England's 23,000 primary schools had been deeply influenced by the new ideas and methods, that another third were stirring under their impact, and that the remaining third were still teaching along the formal lines of British schools in the 1930s, and of American schools now.

The change is most widespread and impressive in the infant schools, and becomes more scattered on the junior level. Junior schools in some authorities are playing stunning variations on the free themes developed by the infant schools; but, in general, change in the junior schools is slower, more diffident, and faces more problems.

Many formal schools—English and American—are probably doing a more effective job, in conventional terms, than these schools. It doesn't do to dogmatize. For example, by and large, in terms of measurable achievement on conventional tests, children in traditional, formal classes in England do slightly better than children from the freer classes. (The survey is submitted by the Plowden Report.) The difference is greatest in mechanical arithmetic, and least in reading. These are facts, but there are reasons for discounting them apart from evidence that the differences disappear in later school years. Formal schools teach children to take conventional tests; that is their function, and it would be surprising if all their efforts didn't produce some results. In view of the lack of test training in the freer schools, the students' results seem to me surprisingly high. It is perfectly clear that the mathematics taught in the informal schools—mathematical relationships in which process of thought counts for more than arithmetical skill—and the English—free writing, rather than grammar and so on—put their students at a disadvantage on achievement tests, whose authors would probably be the first to admit this. England and America badly need new kinds of tests. My own strong impression is that in areas easy to define and probably not hard to test—ability to write, for example, or understanding of the math they were doing—the children in the good schools I saw, including slum schools, were far ahead of students in good formal schools in this country.

The external motions teachers go through in the schools matter less than what the teachers are and what they think. An organizational change—the free day, for example, or simply rearranging classroom space—is unlikely to make much difference unless teachers are really prepared to act on the belief that in a rich environment young children can learn a great deal by themselves and that most often their own choices reflect their needs. But when you see schools where teachers do believe in them, it is easy to share the Plowden Report's enthusiasm for informal, individual learning in the early years of school. The infant schools are a historical accident—nobody years ago gave much thought to why children should begin school at 5—but British teachers are now realizing their advantages. With kindergarten and the first few years of school fused, children have an extended time in which to learn to read and write and work with numbers. This is especially effective if the pattern of learning is largely individual, if the teacher is important but doesn't stand in the way or try to take over the whole job. Many of the difficulties that plague formal first-grade classes disappear; children aren't kept back from learning, nor are they branded as problems if they take their time.

Teaching Children to Think

DISCONTENTED PEOPLE in Britain sometimes make polemical use of an imaginary land called America, where everything is democratic and efficient. My purpose is not to create another equally useless myth for the comfort of disheartened educators on this side of the Atlantic. There is nothing utopian about the good British schools I am describing. Teachers are, by American standards, underpaid (salaries start at $30 a week). The turnover in staff is ferocious, and schools receive pittances for buying equipment and books. All over, teaching is often a flat business and always a tough one. It is of immense practical significance that in the flat, tough world of overworked teachers and daily routines, substantial numbers of British primary teachers are organizing their classrooms in a way that really does promote individual learning, that allows children to develop at their own pace in the early years of school.

As samples of this kind of approach, I've described how children learn to read and write, and the careful way in which they are introduced to mathematics. These methods, I've indicated, are successful in fairly measurable, as well as other, terms. They are not guaranteed to make bad teachers, or people who dislike children, into good teachers. But they are more suited than formal methods to the nature of small children and to the kinds of subjects that should be taught in primary school; and they encourage many ordinary teachers, who find that they are happier using them and less likely to spend all their time worrying about keeping order. Such methods assume that children can respond to courteous treatment by adults, and that to a great extent they can be trained to take the initiative in learning, if choices are real, and if a rich variety of material is offered them. As the Plowden Report concedes, these assumptions are not true for all children (some will probably always benefit more from formal teaching) or for every child all of the time. But the Plowden Report is itself testimony to a growing conviction in Britain that these assumptions can provide a workable basis for an entire nation's schools.

Are they a workable basis for American schools? The task of creating American schools along these lines will be formidable, to say the very least. This isn't the place to rehearse the institutional and cultural obstacles to change in American education, but I do want to anticipate some of the most serious questions that may be raised about the kinds of schools I've described. In reform, as in anything else, there must be priorities, and the first priority is simply to see clearly.

One thing that troubles some Americans about these schools is discipline. They may acknowledge that good British schools are doing better work than good American schools, but they are reluctant to admit that this is because, among other things, children are given freedom to choose from among selected activities in the classroom and to move around the room talking to each other. If they are teachers, they may react to such a proposition with contempt, because they know how hard it is to maintain discipline in many American classrooms. Where the class is taught as a unit, and every child is supposed to pay attention as the teacher talks, discipline can be a serious matter; it is even more so when the class splits into groups for reading aloud, as any first-grade teacher knows. Quick children get restless; slow children dread the ordeal, and act accordingly. Any teacher who can keep order under the circumstances has a certain amount of talent, however wasted. Tony Kallet, a perceptive American who worked as an advisor in Leicestershire, has written of the difficulties in maintaining control of the class in the good, but very formal, American school in which he apprenticed. Some children managed quite well, he recalls, but others, especially the "problem children," found the discipline too much, too little was permitted them, and "their problems were, in part, being created, rather than mitigated by control." After working with English classes, he felt very different about the problem, but, for all the time he was in an American classroom, "it did truly seem that every single control imposed was necessary if anything was to be accomplished," a view many American teachers will understand.

Some American teachers who have seen the spectacle of children in British classes working diligently on their own have raised another question: They have wondered whether British children are fundamentally different from American children. Certainly British grown-ups are different from Americans and there may be important differences in national character. Yet middle-aged English visitors to the informal schools often react with the same disbelief as Americans; they find it hard to credit British children with so much initiative and so much responsibility. Also, formal schools in Britain suffer from discipline problems, so it is hard to know how to speculate intelligently on the question. American teachers working on their own—and how lonely they seem—have often succeeded with methods similar to those of good British primary schools: A forthcoming book by Herbert Kohl describes a sixth-grade class in Harlem run along fairly free lines—Kohl's *36 Children* includes some extraordinarily powerful samples of the children's free writing. A British teacher from one of the good local authorities came to a large American city to teach a demonstration class of 8- to 11-year-olds in a slum school. Before he went, he was assured—by Americans—that he would find American children as different from British as day is from night. Yet, he reported, the children reacted exactly as English children to a classroom thoughtfully laid out to permit choices. At first they couldn't believe he meant what he said. After a timid start, they began rushing around the room, trying to sample everything fast, as though time were going to run out on them. Then they "settled remarkably quickly to study in more depth and to explore their environment with interest and enthusiasm." The teacher noticed that for the first 2 weeks no one did any written English or math, and when he asked them why, they said they hated those subjects. Eventually he got more and more of the class interested in free writing, but he never could get them interested in mathematics.

Another, more serious, argument that one hears against this kind of education is that it won't prepare children for life. The answer the Plowden Report makes to this seems to me remarkably sensible: The best preparation for life is to live fully as a child. Sometimes this fear takes the reasonable form of a parent's question: Will these informal methods handicap a child if he moves on to a school run on formal lines? This problem is now fairly common in Britain as children move from good infant schools to old-fashioned junior schools, or from informal primary school to rigid secondary school. I went to a parents' meeting at one superb infant school; the parents, who clearly were completely won over by the methods of the school, were nonetheless apprehensive of what could become of their children in a new situation. The head of the school said—which was true—that the children did in fact do well in the very formal junior school. There was only one repeated complaint about them: They were not very good at sitting still for long periods of time. In general, it seemed clear that an ability to write and to really understand mathematics—to say nothing of an ability to work on their own—stands children in good stead, whatever school they later attend. Heads of good schools argue that children are more adaptable than most parents imagine—and one indication that the problem of switching from one school to another is not crucial is that most heads agree with the Plowden Report's recommendation for another year of the informal methods of infant school; with an extra year, most of them think, they could lick their remaining reading problems, and the transfers will be even easier.

Another pressing question Americans ask about these methods is, oddly enough, historical in nature. It is said that these kinds of classes were tried in the progressive era of American education, and found wanting.

This is an example of a lesson drawn from history, one of those lessons we cling to tenaciously, and since nothing is as treacherous as our sense of recent history, it bears looking into. Progressive education, like the progressive movements in thought and politics, was woven from many different, often contradictory threads. It took place against a background of the great shift in the function of American secondary schools, which were changing from elite preparatory institutions to mass terminal institutions; just as in the 1950s, when our present picture of progressive education was firmly etched in the popular mind, many high schools were turning into mass college preparatory institutions. The radical attempt to give secondary education to the whole American population was an important aspect of progressive education, just as the reaction against it was appropriate to an era when nearly half the students in secondary school would go on to college.

As a movement, progressive education reflected a new concern for science brought to bear on society—in the schools this meant educational psychology, tests, and the cult of research. Another element was the characteristic progressive concern with social reform: John Dewey's vain hope that the schools could in some way become centers for the continuous reconstruction of society. Another distinct, if sometimes related, strand was an emphasis on individual growth and development of the child. This last, in particular, was reflected in the practices of a number of American private schools in the 1920s and 1930s. Good and bad, these schools tended to see children through ideological lenses: They were followers of Freud, at least to the extent that they thought repression wicked, and some idealized children as participants in the artist's historic struggle against bourgeois society. The best of the "child-centered" private schools based much of their teaching on the idea that children come to understand the world through play; they tried to get students to take part in the running of the school, and they broke down barriers dividing one subject from another, often making the community around them and its life part of the curriculum. These seem today the sound aspects of their work. The ideological emphasis on liberating the child seems, from today's perspective, less useful. In some schools, the energies of staff and children were wasted in testing the limits of permissible behavior, a procedure that was almost forced on the children by an abdication of adult authority. It is not strange that the abdication did not always result in freedom: In practice, freeing children from adult authority can mean exposing them to the tyranny of their peers, and eliminating "external" rules can mean setting up subtle and unacknowledged rules that are just as ruthless and, even worse, vague and arbitrary.

THEY NEVER TRIED IT

It is difficult to find much evidence that the classroom practices of the private schools stressing individual growth ever spread to large numbers of the public schools. The emphasis of the private progressive schools on cooperation and adjustment to the group was shared by the public school, but it took a different turn: The public schools practicing adjustment and "Americanization" were fulfilling one of the traditional roles of the American schools, taming objectionable outsiders, making sure that immigrants and lower class people didn't make trouble. The progressive movement in public education was deeply conservative, and was mainly reflected in reform of school administration, putting the operations of the schools more in line with the principles of scientific management espoused by Frederick Taylor and his disciples. (It says much about a misunderstood period that the idea of a school run as a business was more powerful than the idea of the school as a model civic community, though of course social science, civics, and other shattered fragments of John Dewey's dream did enter the curriculum, for better or worse.)

Thus in American public schools, with a few notable exceptions, what we call progressive education was never tried. Progressive education in practice meant secondary education for all, and, perhaps, more educational opportunity; more courses, especially in high school, of the life-adjustment variety; more emphasis on extracurricular activities; more grouping by ability and emphasis on testing; some "project work" that was no doubt a welcome relief from the textbooks; some more or less important changes in the textbooks themselves; reform in the management of the schools, often based on inappropriate models from the world of business.

What wisps of the vision of education as individual growth trailed into the public schools were largely rhetorical. In their famous study of "Middletown" (Muncie, Indiana) in 1925, Robert and Helen Merrell Lynd (1929) described the classrooms: "Immovable seats in orderly rows fix the sphere of activity to each child. For all from the timid six-year-old . . . to the . . . high school senior . . . the general routine is much the same." When they returned to Middletown 10 years later, in 1935, "progressive education" had arrived. There was talk of growth, personality development, and creative self-expression: "The aim of education should be to enable every child to become a useful citizen, to develop his individual powers to the fullest extent of which he is capable, while at the same time engaged in useful and lifelike activities." Along with the new rhetoric, the Lynds noted, went increased emphasis on administration; there was no basic change in methods of teaching or classroom organization. Their report can stand as a paradigm of what progressive education amounted to in most American schools. Education that treats people as individuals had become a cliche without ever being reality.

There are clear parallels here with the primary school revolution in Britain. It, too, is distantly tied to the changing role of the secondary schools, and certainly much of its rhetoric is reminiscent of the progressive education movement. British schools certainly share the concern with individual development of the good progressive schools. And yet the differences in the two movements are profound. Although there is an emphasis on co-operation in British school and the children are encouraged to teach each other, there is no abdication of adult authority and no belief that this would be desirable. The idea of giving children choices reflects ideology less than a considered judgment as to how they best learn. The teaching of mathematics[1] illustrates how intent these schools are on teaching children to think; they have no particular ideological interest in making children into social saviors or artistic rebels against bourgeois conventions, or whatever. It is this deep pedagogical seriousness, the attention paid to learning in the classroom, that makes the British primary school revolution so different from American progressive education, which was all too often unconcerned with pedagogy.

This pedagogical focus and what it means can be seen in the way informal British schools are solving the problem of grouping children into classes according to abilities—what the British call "streaming," and what we call "tracking." In both countries it is customary for larger schools to track students so that there are A, B, C, and sometimes D or E classes in a supposed order of ability and intelligence. (And within a class there are slow, average, and fast reading groups.) On the whole, teachers in Britain and America favor the practice, and it is easy to see why. When you deal with the class as a unit, when learning is done by groups, it is less grueling if the group is of roughly similar abilities, and, within limits of conventional instruction, tracking does enable children to go at something closer to their own pace. Tracking, or streaming, is a heated subject now in Britain, as it is in this country. The spread of informal methods of teaching is calling its utility into question, and many of the schools run on freer lines are abandoning the practice. The Plowden Report, which clearly favors "unstreaming," cites a survey—the same survey I mentioned in my first report, discussing tested differences between formal and informal schools—suggesting that in terms of measurable achievement, children in tracked schools do slightly, but not much, better than children in informal schools where tracking has been abandoned. There are, as I have suggested, reasons for discounting this—the fact that formal schools train children to take achievement tests, whereas informal ones teach more important things, and the evidence that the differences in test scores wane as the children grow older.

BRANDED AS STUPID

In England, as in America, there are many reasons why a practical alternative to tracking would be desirable. Tracking in a primary school brands children as stupid at an early age, with profound and unhappy effects on them.

"I'll never forget the look on the faces of the boys in the lower stream," an East London junior school head told me. His school has successfully abolished the practice, but he is unable to forget the look: "I still see it when my boys in the lower streams of secondary modern school come back to visit." Tracking has a profound effect on teachers, too: It tempts them to think that a single pattern of instruction can be applied to a whole class, and it increases the odds that they will deal with their children in terms of abstract categories, IQ, or whatever. In England, as here, the upper tracks of a school tend to be middle class, which makes the school even more an instrument for reinforcing social inequity. In America, of course, tracking is commonly a means of maintaining racial segregation within a supposedly integrated school.

After watching British classes, another argument against tracking occurs to you: It ignores the extent to which children learn from each other, slow children learning from the quick, and the bright ones, in turn, learning from the role of teacher they must adopt with the slow. This is most evident in the small number of schools that have adopted family, or vertical, grouping: Where there is not only no grouping by ability but no grouping by age, and every class is a mixed bag of older and younger children. Yet while all this is true, it makes little sense to condemn tracking unless you can show teachers alternatives to formal classroom teaching. This is where the pedagogical bite of the primary school revolution is so impressive: When a British school stops tracking, it is not simply returning to the past, it is shifting to a different definition of the roles of teacher and student, and setting up a new kind of classroom in which students are trained to work independently. With the blessing of the Plowden Report, fewer and fewer infant schools track and it is increasingly common for junior schools to abandon tracking in the first 2 years, and in some cases in the third. How far this trend will go depends on the impact the primary school revolution makes on the secondary schools. One survey in the Plowden

Report shows that English teachers, who used to be overwhelmingly in favor of streaming as a general policy for primary schools, are coming to approve of unstreaming. The reason, clearly, is that they are beginning to see workable alternatives.

Tracking is regarded as a necessary evil in America, as are IQ and standardized achievement tests, formal class teaching, specified curriculum materials, set hours for set subjects, and so on. Teachers and administrators realize that children's intellectual and emotional growth varies just as widely as their physical growth, yet they seldom feel able to act on their understanding, to treat each child differently. The good British schools raise serious doubts as to whether these evils are in fact necessary. In this country, as in England, there is a growing, and on the whole healthy, skepticism about education: People are questioning the standard methods, and they are becoming realistic about the limited extent to which any school can be expected to pick up the marbles for the rest of society. No British teacher would claim that his methods could solve our deepest historical and social problems, but, as far as education can make a difference, in many communities the work of the British schools suggests working models of individual learning to those who believe, as I do, that what American education needs is definitely not more of the same.

The forces that might help bring about similar changes in American schools are few. To some extent the best of the American curriculum projects—such as the Educational Development Center—are pushing schools in the right direction. Good, open-ended materials are often in themselves a kind of retraining course for teachers, helping them become more confident of trying informal methods. Curriculum materials are by no means being abandoned in the British schools, but they are making different use of them: It is clear that any curriculum materials must give teachers and students freedom to use them in a variety of ways, and the best materials are often simply handbooks and guides to new approaches, rather than set lessons. Curriculum materials become even more important in the later years of school. Geoffrey Casten, of the Schools Council, worries that the successful methods of the infant schools, where, of course, the "curriculum" is largely generated by the students' own activities, will prove less successful when widely applied to older children by teachers of varying abilities. This may or may not be true: I saw junior schools where the free methods of the infant schools were being triumphantly vindicated, but I also saw others that were very sleepy and could have used the stimulation of good materials. It is unlikely that curriculum projects can make much difference in America until they find a way of engaging ordinary teachers in creating materials. Americans should profit from the British understanding that the valuable and enduring part of curriculum reform is the process of creation and thought; unless you let teachers in on that, the stuff is likely to be dead. The American curriculum projects and some school systems might help set up equivalents to the advisory centers in good British authorities, teams of teachers and others whose only task is to work in the field with classroom teachers, spreading new ideas. Jerrold Zacharias once proposed display centers that would act as supermarkets for teachers interested in new ideas and techniques. (One role of the advisors in England is to take over classes for teachers so they can attend courses and displays.)

THE PROSPECTS FOR CHANGE

Useful work could be done developing new kinds of tests. The IQ and standard achievement tests are not the bogies they are made out to be—I have the feeling that schools use tests as an excuse to keep from having to try out anything new. But the likelihood of change would be increased if their grip on the minds of school administrators and parents could be loosened. Tests that reflect an ability to write, or to reason mathematically, would be a great help: The problem is to persuade people to consider the relevance of standards other than the ones now used, and it is clearly a problem that new tests alone won't solve.

Techniques, particularly when devised by outsiders, are never going to be enough. It is in the schools that change has to come, and yet the prospects are dim. The private schools that once promoted progressive education are now largely formal in their methods; many are test-ridden, catering to parents who want solid evidence that a second-grade performance will lead to Harvard, and they have invited John Holt's gibe: "A conservative is someone who worships a dead radical." There are communities, where principals and teachers are confident of their relationship with parents, that could begin gradually and carefully working along individual lines. Good suburban schools able to withstand the possibility of slightly lower achievement-test scores exist, but they seem to be getting rarer. Some of the good Head Start programs may influence the schools to make the first few years more flexible. And there is a chance that some of the cities where education has reached a crisis point can be prodded into setting up some freer demonstration classes.

This is the point: We lack actual classrooms that people can see, that teachers can work in, functioning schools that demonstrate to the public and to educators the kind of learning I have described in this series. They must be institutions that develop and grow over time, not just demonstration classes. (New York City has tried out every good idea in educational history: once.) To make any impact, such schools will have to be very different from the private experiments of the 1920s and 1930s, with their ideological confusions and their indifference to public education. The temptation is to say America needs many such schools, and we do. But a tiny number of infant schools pioneered the changes in the British schools, and it is probable that careful work on a small scale is the way to start a reform worth having, whatever our grandiose educational reformers might say. In the end, you always return to a teacher in a classroom full of children. That is the proper locus of a revolution in the primary schools.

NOTE

1. Described in Featherstone's book, *Schools Where Children Learn* (1971).

Experiments in Learning

LAST YEAR IN THESE PAGES, I reported on certain classroom practices, styles of teaching and learning, now spreading throughout the better infant schools in Britain. What follows is a different sort of report, a series of reflections on attempts to continue this style of education in British junior schools dealing with older children. (Infant schools take children from 5 to 7, teaching beginning reading and math, among other things; junior schools take them from 7 to 11.) The approach I earlier described is by no means as widespread at the junior level; a handful of good schools are playing dazzling variations on the free themes worked out with younger children, but junior schools of the quality now becoming relatively common at the infant level are still rare. Why this is so is worth pursuing; I hope I can suggest some useful answers. Part of what follows will be about the work of exceptional schools; part will be about the efforts of ordinary teachers to pursue, not always successfully, a common idea of what good teaching might be.

In this report I want to focus fairly narrowly on junior schools that encourage children's free writing. The variety of writing in infant schools is not matched by many junior schools. It is depressing to go from a superb infant school to a mediocre junior school where the children's confidence in themselves crumbles under the weight of anxieties, drills, and the boredom of rote learning. But a growing number of junior schools are encouraging free writing. What they are attempting is scarcely new—able teachers have always set children to writing, and isolated American teachers right this moment are no doubt shutting the classroom door and telling the kids to write their heads off. The significance of what is happening in some British junior schools is simply that a lot of ordinary teachers are becoming convinced that it is important for primary school children to write on subjects of their own choosing. Though in many cases this hasn't carried them very far, I think it could suggest a very different set of priorities for teaching young children than those that prevail, in this country and many parts of Britain.

Everything begins at the infant level, of course. A big part of what we call the reading program is a writing and talking program. Before they can read, kids are dictating captions and stories to teachers and learning to write them, developing a written vocabulary along with their reading vocabulary. This has many advantages: A child is apt to be interested in what he has to say even though primers and beginning books bore him; there is less class or racial bias to his own material and the vocabulary will be suitable, because it's his own. Beginning writing is an excellent way to get a good background in phonics—it's becoming increasingly clear that phonics is important—and most writers also pick up a working vocabulary of sight words. Good infant teachers say that lots of reading and talking are an essential part of developing the writing: Thus, within limits, children in the schools I visited are encouraged to talk to each other, and classrooms are filled with all kinds of books, not textbooks.

When I speak of writing by 5-to-8-year-olds, I'm not talking about any great literary efforts. Some children write strings of simple sentences that are barely literate, every sentence beginning with "and . . ." like the first attempts at popular writing in the Middle Ages. Others are astonishingly precocious, using subordinate clauses, vivid images, and fairly intricate constructions. John Blackie, who has done a great deal to promote writing in British schools, collects some examples in his book *Inside the Primary School* (1971). Since they are in print and accessible, I'll quote them as typical of the ordinary infant work I've seen, not the best or the worst. Thus a 6-year-old boy: "We are going to see a film this afternoon. It is about Boys town in India. We have brought some money to see it. I gave Lewis a penny. . . ." Or a 7-year-old: "Once upon a time there was a little girl Judy who longed for a doll with long hair at Christmas she wolk up and saw a doll just as she wanted with long hair She played with it all day then at night she put it in a shoe box and forgot to take it upstairs with her in the morning. . . ." Readers will note how few serious spelling errors there are. What marks the writing in the better infant schools is sincerity and liveliness: The reader feels he is being told something a writer really wanted to say.

In the junior school, as in the infant school, much of the early writing is finished the same day, or even in the same period as the children start it. (Junior schools are more likely to divide the day into periods.) Gradually the time for writing can be extended. There, too, children alternate between small reports on their own experiences—including things they've done in science and math—and stories which often take their themes and heroes from television and adventure stories, and, less often, from fairy tales. Some of the 9-, 10- and 11-year-olds are more apt to show literary influences in their writing, picking up the tricks of any writer they happen to be reading. A few children, like literary hacks, get used to standard formulas. For this reason, teachers who are serious about writing try to steer children away from stories of the "once upon a time" sort, at least at the outset.

Schools that require certain themes tend to get derivative and artificial work. The Plowden Report, *Children and Their Primary Schools,* holds no brief for teachers who force children into "stock phrases and insincerity by setting them to write about the conventional subject: the autobiography of a penny, the loaf of bread, or the tree, which may culminate in 'I am happy as a table, but I was happiest as a tree.'"

Teachers concerned with quality try to make sure that writing doesn't become a chore; they are reluctant to push children to write unless they seem genuinely interested. If children are to write freely, many say, it is important to let them choose what can be read aloud; or what is only for the eyes of a teacher or a friend or what is secret, the property of the author.

When children are confident enough in their writing, teachers encourage them to make "books," with folded pieces of paper and slightly thicker covers. Some classes have a big display rack for these books, which children browse through and read according to their tastes. The books contain considerable personal writing, some poetry (usually unrhymed), stories, accounts of math and science projects, and topics of one sort or another that children choose—from cavemen to hobbies. Some of the writing on topics comes from information books in the classroom—volumes on birds, ancient Britons, or whatever. Where there is no incentive to copy, children don't. Where there is, they do.

Mr. A. B. Clegg, the chief education officer of West Riding, has gathered some work of children in his authority into a fascinating collection called *The Excitement of Writing.* Since I wish school authorities in this country would take a good long look at this book, I'll quote from a few typical selections. Here's a boy, 10:

> I remember that hour I walked on the sands by a very rough sea.
> The waves crashed down so hard I could feel the trembling of them
> on me. It sounded like bricks tumbling down from an old house
> when it is being knocked down . . .

Here's a girl, 11:

> We set out, Mummy and I, we were going into the town. I was
> delighted, for I was to have a pair of new shoes, they were to be for
> school. When we got to the town we went into a shoe shop. I saw a
> few pairs of shoes but I didn't like any of them, the woman then

brought out another pair of shoes brown and ugly. Mummy liked them. I looked at her in horror unable to speak surely, surely she wouldn't buy them. But the purchase was complete she had bought them. I pinched myself to make sure it wasn't a dream, unluckily for me it wasn't . . .

This is a 10-year-old, writing about a candle:

White polish; sour milk,
Delicate finger wrapped in cotton blanket.
Star growing bigger, bigger, bigger flickering in darkness,
A great Lord, now a humble person bowing.
Golden crystals, dark eye,
Slowly, flowing, running, milk.
Faint glimmer of hope, trying to enlarge itself.
Black Burned pie; all beauty gone.

The writing teachers get inevitably reflects their concerns. They can be impresarios, hustling formidable feats of child-writing—they inspire you with a self-righteous itch to remind them that the job is to help a kid along, not to promote an author. (As Mr. Clegg wisely points out, what gets written in any school is pretty much a by-product, the main point being the development of the child himself.) There are Miss Jean Brodies who encourage marvelous fairy tales, poetry, fantasies, and all kinds of "creative" writing, but who ignore precise and elegant math and science reporting going on right under their noses. In writing, as in other matters, it is difficult to exaggerate the extent to which schools everywhere are bearers of the genteel culture and its class biases. Still, where local authorities and principals have encouraged free writing, it is impressive to see how many teachers do learn to respect the content of children's writing without being shocked or disapproving or niggling about inessential errors. (The students of emancipated teachers produce writings about sex and life in the raw, some of which is true.)

Writing is getting across what you have to say, and the teachers in the best classes I saw tried to treat mistakes in grammar, spelling, and messiness as obstacles to communication. They let slips go by without much comment. Correcting writing is extremely difficult in classes of 40 or so, but watching good teachers, you begin to see that the priorities are clear: It is easier to help children with language if you have a basis for diagnosing what you need to know. In part, you get the raw material for a diagnosis from writing. You also find out more if the classroom routine is arranged so that you can listen and watch and, at least occasionally, talk with a child.

A lot of teachers try to correct all mistakes in sessions with a child. There is no point in scribbling red marks over somebody's personal statement. John Blackie has an ugly story of a 9-year-old whose theme, "My Father," told about his dead parent. The teacher's only written comment was: "Tenses. You keep mixing past and present."

Nowhere is it clearer than in correcting that a central part of teaching is relationships between people which are always impossible to speak of in a general way. The finest analytical nets will never land a pure example of good teaching, any more than they will deliver up pure specimens of friendship and love. We are condemned to rough impressions, which nearly always float up to the level of platitudes, about as useful as advising people not to take any wooden nickels. Still, for what it's worth, good teachers pay serious attention to the content, the subject of a piece of writing (or the painting or whatever). There is this bond of interest between them and the children. Children seem very interested in finding out if a meaning has come across and what the reader feels about it, and many are quite ready to accept criticism. If it's an unfinished story, the teacher inquires how it's going to end. He asks how the child came to choose this subject. He makes an effort to talk thoughtfully about specific details, asking when, how, why. Sometimes he'll want to know if the writer is pleased with his work, and if he answers no, the teacher might wonder if he doesn't have some ideas on how it could be better. All rules of thumb fall away before the rule that says the worst thing is to discourage future work.

There is never enough teaching to go around. Teachers try to enlist the children to do some of the correcting—many ask the class to spot errors in the "books" or other writings on display in the room and bring them to the attention of the author, who can then make the corrections himself. The work of good junior schools runs increasingly against the grain of the British educational system as the children get older. Even in very free junior schools, a visitor sometimes notices the decline of the superb work of the first few years as children are tuned up for examinations. Competition for university places is keen in England, and most of your fate still rests on getting into the right secondary school. This not the whole story, and I'll return to this point later; what I want to emphasize now is the way that what is taught comes more and more to resemble the standard fare in American schools. There are plenty of exceptions—enough to make me doubt that the process is inevitable. Most of them are in authorities where free methods have become a reigning orthodoxy. Still, it is depressing to see good schools succumbing to the idea that there is a separate subject called "English," and giving the children spelling lists, workbooks, and grammar exercises, as though anybody ever learned much that way. In a school where children's writing is well supervised there is no place for grammar and spelling as distinct subjects. It is absurd to think that if a child can take somebody else's sentences to pieces and label the parts, he will write better ones of his own. Correctness comes from using the language and hearing it used under sound guidance. People learn to write correctly through writing, not by plowing through mountains of workbooks.

There is no general formula that fits all schools that encourage good writing. Mr. Clegg makes a stab in the right direction when he says that they respect children, and that they are more concerned with how they learn than what they learn. The same attitude that led them to encourage free writing led them to stop grouping classes by ability (tracking here, "streaming" in England). Firsthand experience stimulates good written work; and for at least part of the day in most of the schools, children are given choices about what to do.

This is all vague. So is what the teachers presiding over the best classes said. They all said that children write for people they trust, and they don't write freely until they can talk with confidence; and, except for the work of certain born storytellers, most of their best writing comes from things they experience directly. I thought of asking them what their position was on wooden nickels but then decided that these truisms were in fact true. There is no getting around them. If we want the kind of schools where children write freely—which is not something separate, but only an emblem, after all, for a whole way of teaching—we had better understand that there simply are no shortcuts.

Open Schools II: Tempering a Fad

W ORD OF ENGLISH SCHOOLS reaches us at a time of cultural and political ferment, and the American vogue for British reforms must be seen as one element in a complex and many-sided movement. Within our schools, there is nearly a pedagogical vacuum. Few reformers have come forward with practical alternatives; even fewer have deigned to address themselves to working teachers. The grass-roots nature of the English reforms, with their emphasis on the central importance of good teaching, has a great appeal for people who are victims of the general staff mentality of our school reformers and managers. Blacks and other minorities are interested in new approaches simply because they reject all the workings of schools as they stand; some of the best of the community control ventures, such as the East Harlem Block Schools, have been promoting informal methods, as have some of the parent-controlled Head Start programs; and there are a growing number of middle- and upper-middle-class parents in favor of "open" and "informal" schooling, even though they are vague on the pedagogical implications of these terms.

The most cogent chapters in Charles Silberman's *Crisis in the Classroom* (1970) are a plea for American educators to consider the English example. Silberman's book is interesting as a cultural document, as well as a statement in its own right. For it registers an important shift in opinion. Silberman is arguing that too many American schools are grim and joyless for both children and teachers. What was once said only by a handful of radical critics is now very close to being official wisdom. Silberman, it should be added, distinguishes himself from many critics of the schools in that he is deeply sympathetic to ordinary classroom teachers and has a clear sense of the critical importance of the teacher's role in creating a decent setting for learning.

By now I've visited a fair number of American classrooms working along informal lines. The best are as good as anything I've seen in England; the worst are a shambles. In the efforts that look most promising, people are proceeding slowly, understanding that preparing the way for further improvements and long-term growth is more important than any single "innovation." (As I've noted, there are too few entire school environments run along informal lines.)

Understanding the need for slow growth and hard work with teachers and children, many of the informal American practitioners I've talked to are alarmed at the dimensions of the current fad for "open" schools. There are reasons for skepticism. From today's perspective, which is no doubt morbid and too disheartened, it seems that our successive waves of educational reform have been, at best, intellectual and ideological justifications for institutions whose actual workings never changed all that much. At the worst, the suspicion is that past reform movements, whatever their rhetoric, have only reinforced the role schools play in promoting social inequality. The realization that schools alone cannot save the social order—which should have been obvious all along—has prompted some to despair over ever getting decent education.

Added to these sobering reflections is a fresh sense of dismay over the outcomes of the past ten years of "innovation." For we have finished a decade of busy reform with little to show for it. Classrooms are the same. Teachers conduct monologues, or more or less forced class discussions; too much learning is still rote; textbooks, timetables, clocks set the pace; discipline is an obsession. The curriculum reform efforts of the '60s brought forth excellent materials in some cases—materials still essential for good informal classrooms—but they took the existing environment of the schools for granted. Perhaps because so many were outsiders, the reformers failed to engage teachers in continuous thought and creation, with the result that the teachers ended up teaching the new materials in the old ways. Being for the most part university people, the reformers were ignorant of classrooms and children: of pedagogy. They concentrated on content—organized in the form of the standard graduate school disciplines—and ignored the nature of children and their ways of learning. Too often children were regarded as passive recipients of good materials, and teachers as passive conduits. The reformers lacked a coherent vision of the school environment as a whole. It was characteristic of the movement that it ignored the arts and children's expressiveness.

In the philosophical chaos of the curriculum projects, the proponents of precision had a debater's advantage. They were able to state their goals in precise, measurable, often behavioral terms. For a time this false precision encouraged a false sense of security. And for a while the behaviorist and the education technology businessmen were allies: They imagined that a new era of educational hardware was dawning, promising profits commensurate with those in the advanced defense and aerospace industries. Now that the bubble has burst, it seems evident to more and more people that this curious alliance had all along been talking about training, not education. Training means imparting skills. It is an aspect of education, but not all of it. I suggest a reading example: If I teach you phonic skills, we are engaged in a kind of training. Unless you go on to use them to develop interests in books, you are not educated. This ought to be the common sense of the matter, but it isn't. Our technicians conceive of reading as a training problem on the order of training spotters to recognize airplane silhouettes. If a sixth grader in a ghetto school is reading two years below grade level, as so many are, the problem may not be reading skills at all. A fourth grade reading level often represents a grasp of the necessary skills: Part of the problem is surely that the sixth grader isn't reading books and isn't interested.

Another reason why some practitioners are dubious about "open" education reflects further skepticism about the evangelical American mode of reform, with its hunger for absolutes and its weakness for rhetoric. Our progressive education movement often neglected pedagogy—and the realities of life in classrooms—and instead concentrated on lofty abstractions. It will be essential in promoting good practice today to abandon ideological debates. Yet the English example is now part of a whole diverse American cultural mood, which means that it is already ranged on one side of an ideological debate. The American milieu is polarized culturally and politically, which conditions our responses to accounts of informal teaching. The responses tend to fall into the stereotyped categories, of a cultural cold war raging between the hip, emancipated upper middle class and the straight middle and working class. It is a class and cultural conflict, and it takes the form of battles between those who see life as essentially a matter of scarcity—and defend the virtues of a scarce order, such as thrift, discipline, hard work—and those who see life as essentially abundant—and preach newer virtues, such as openness, feelings, spontaneity. Hip people like the idea of open classrooms, because they seem to give children freedom; straight people fear the supposed absence of order, discipline, and adult authority.

If I portray this conflict in highly abstract terms, it is because it seems to me remote from the concerns of good American and British practitioners actually teaching in informal settings. Take the issue of freedom, for example. Letting children talk and move about is helpful in establishing a setting in which a teacher can find out about students; it helps children learn actively to get the habit of framing purposes independently using their own judgment. But this freedom is a means to an end, not a goal in itself: As a goal, freedom is empty and meaningless—"a breakfast food," as e. e. cummings once put it.

There are always those who argue that freedom is something negative—freedom from—and those who argue that freedom is positive. From authoritarians like Plato to libertarians like Kant and Dewey, the second line of argument has linked freedom with knowledge—the free use of reason or intelligence (and sometimes action) with knowledge. Whatever the merits of the positions in this fascinating perpetual debate, it is surely more appropriate for educators of the young to conceive of freedom in the second sense, not a momentary thing at all, but the result of a process of discipline and learning. Informality is pointless unless it leads to intellectual stimulation. Many children in our "free" schools are not happy, and one suspects that part of the reason is that they are bored with their own lack of intellectual progress. As William Hull remarks in a trenchant critique of the current fad for "open" education: "Children are not going to be happy for very long in schools in which they realize they are not accomplishing very much."

Or take the problem of authority. The fact that it is an issue in schools reflects deep cultural confusion, and is a measure of the frequent misuse of legitimate authority in America. Whatever their politics, good practitioners assume as a matter of course that teachers have a responsibility to create an environment hospitable to learning, that there is what might be called a natural, legitimate bases for the authority of an adult working with children. In his superb little book, *The Lives of Children*, George Dennison (1969) outlines some aspects of this legitimate authority: "Its attributes are obvious: Adults are larger, more experienced, possess more words, have entered into prior agreements with themselves. When all this takes on a positive instead of a merely negative character, the children see the adults as protectors and as sources of certitude, approval, novelty, skills. In the fact that adults have entered into prior agreements, children intuit seriousness and a web of relations in the life that surrounds them. It is a bit mysterious, it is also impressive and somewhat attractive; they see it quite correctly as the way of the world, and they are not indifferent to its benefits and demands.... [For a child] the adult is his ally, his model—and his obstacle [for there are natural conflicts, too, and they must be given their due]."

Disciplinary matters and the rest of the structure of authority in American schools work against the exercise of legitimate authority. And thus, in reaction to the schools, the education opposition movement foolishly assumes that all adult guidance is an invasion of children's freedom. Actually, in a proper informal setting, as John Dewey pointed out, adults ought to become more important: "Basing education upon personal experience may mean more multiplied and more intimate contacts between the mature and the immature than ever existed in the traditional schools, *and consequently more rather than less guidance.*"

If you remove adult authority from a given group of children, you are not necessarily freeing them. Instead, as David Riesman and his colleagues noted in *The Lonely Crowd*'s (1950) critique of "progressive" education, you are often sentencing them to the tyranny of their peers. And unacknowledged adult authority has a way of creeping back in subtle and manipulative ways that can be more arbitrary than its formal exercise.

Another fake issue in the debate on open education is the old, boring question of whether to have, as they say, a child-centered or an adult-directed classroom. There are, to be sure, certain respects in which the best informal practice is child-centered. The basic conception of learning, after all, reflects the image of Piaget's child-inventor, fashioning an orderly model of the universe from his varied encounters with experience. The child's experience is the starting point of all good informal teaching. But passive teaching has no place in a good informal setting, any more than passive children do. Active teaching is essential, and one of the appeals of this approach to experienced teachers is that it transforms the teacher's role. From enacting somebody else's text of curriculum, the teacher moves toward working out his own responses to children's learning. The teacher is responsible for creating the learning environment.

Still another confusion on the American scene lies in the notion that liberalizing the repressive atmosphere of our schools—which is worth doing for its own sake—will automatically promote intellectual development. It won't. We need more humane schools, but we also need a steady concern for intellectual progress and workmanship. Without this it is unlikely that we will get any sort of cumulative development, and we will never establish practical standards by which to judge good and bad work.

Some American practitioners question the utility of slogans such as the "open school," or "informal education." The terms are suspect because they become clichés, because they don't convey the necessary values underlying this kind of teaching, because they suggest a hucksterized package, and because they divide teaching staffs into the "we" doing the open approach and the "they" who are not. Some imitate the philosopher Charles Saunders Pierce, who changed his "pragmatism" to the much uglier-sounding "pragmaticism"—in order, he said, to keep ideas safe from kidnappers. They prefer an awkward and reasonably neutral turn like "less formal." A brave few are modestly willing to march under a banner inscribed "decent schools."

This suspicion of slogans can be carried to ludicrous extremes. But at the heart of the evasiveness is an important point: Educating children or working with teachers is an entire process. A good informal setting should not be thought of as a "model" or as an "experiment," but as an environment in which to support educational growth, in directions that have already proved sound.

Some observers fear that the manner in which our schools implement reforms destroys the possibility for development of teachers. (There, are already instances where principals have dictated "open education" to their staffs.) There is a deep—and I think altogether justified—mistrust of the conventional channels of reform from the top down: *pronunciamentos* by educational statesmen, the roll of ceremonial drums, the swishing sound of entrepreneurs shaking the money tree. Most of the serious American informal practitioners are self-consciously local in their orientation. They are interested in planting themselves in Vermont, Philadelphia, New York City, North Dakota, or wherever, and working at the grass roots. They imagine that it will take a very long time to get good schools, and they do not believe that big-wig oratory or White House Conferences on Education are any substitute for direct engagement with teachers and children in classrooms.

The changes they are starting are small, but they have large implications. All teachers, no matter how they teach, suffer from the climate of our schools, and every serious attempt at reform will soon find itself talking about lunchrooms, toilet passes, the whole internal control structure of the schools; relationships to parents, relationships to supervisory staff, the ways in which supplies are ordered, the link between an individual school and the central bureaucracies; all, ultimately, issues of politics, power and money.

As schools move in informal directions, there will be an increasing criticism of our system of training and credentialing teachers and administrators. (Here, with the exception of outstanding institutions like London's Froebel Institute, the English do not have examples to emulate: Their teachers colleges are improving, but they have trailed behind the work of the country's best infant and junior schools.) The training of administrators will come under attack, and in some places separate training programs for administrators will be abolished. The inadequacy of teacher training will also become more evident, although it is far from clear how to improve it. What we do know is that theory has to be reunited with practice. Without a solid grounding in child development, much of our informal teaching will be gimmicky; and without a sound base in actual practice in classrooms, theory will remain useless.

The enormous variety of the American educational landscape makes it difficult to speak in general terms. In certain areas, education schools willing to restore an emphasis on classroom practice may unite with school systems ready to move in informal directions. In other areas, where the education schools are unable to change their mandarin ways, school systems will have to assume more and more of the responsibility for training and credentialing teachers. Whichever the pattern, a central feature of successful programs will be periods of work in good informal settings. Thus a prerequisite to any scheme of training will be the existence of good schools and classrooms to work in. The single most important task is the reform of schools and classrooms, for good informal classrooms provide the best teacher training sites.

Whether the current interest in informal teaching leads to cumulative change will depend on many things. Two are worth repeating: whether enough people can understand the essentially different outlook on children's intellectual development which good informal work must be based on, and whether our schools can be reorganized to give teachers sustained on-the-job support. I'm somewhat optimistic about the first: The ideas are in the air, and many teachers, on their own, are already questioning the assumptions behind the traditional classroom. The second question will be much harder to answer satisfactorily. In some places, the schools are ripe for change; in others change will come slowly and painfully, if at all; and in others the chances for growth are almost zero. Those promoting informal teaching ought to be wary of suggesting good practices to teachers who are working in institutional settings where real professional growth is out of the question. In such a setting, all obstacles mesh together to join what people rightly call the System. Right now it seems unlikely that the System—in our worst school systems—will ever permit teachers to teach and children to learn. But things may have looked that way to some British educational authorities in the '30s, too.

A final word on the faddishness of our educational concerns. The appearance of new ideas such as the clamor for open, informal schools does not cancel out old ideas. "Open education" will be a sham unless those supporting it also address themselves to recurring, fundamental problems, such as the basic inequality and racism of our society. The most pressing American educational dilemma is not the lack of informality in classrooms: It is whether we can build a, more equal, multiracial society. Issues like school integration and community control have not disappeared, to be replaced by issues like open education. The agenda simply gets more crowded. It will be all the more essential, however, to keep alive in bad times a vision of the kind of education that all wise parents want for their children.

Ghetto Classroom

36 *CHILDREN* is a simple and direct narrative of Mr. Kohl's experiences with a sixth-grade class in a Harlem school, and it is one of the best books by a teacher I've read. It gives an honest and illuminating description of how a teacher works, and it explores the process of change he has to undergo as he and his children respond to each other and he begins to gather his nerve to alter his way of teaching. He shows, for example, the complicated private war he waged with himself over the matter of discipline. The class was the top sixth-grade class in the school; but only five or six out of the *36 Children* could read a sixth-grade book, and more than half were reading at fourth grade level. As an inexperienced teacher, he stuck to the assigned texts and tried hard to maintain a strict schedule, with separate periods for different subjects. Looking back, he suggests that this tightness with time and material had nothing to do with the quantity of things to be learned in a school year, or the amount of ground the class had to cover, for the truth was that the children had learned very little anyway after 5 full years of school. It stemmed, he admits, from his own fear of loss of control. Gradually building up his own confidence he made his own accommodation to discipline, and so did the children. He tells how he started letting them take 10-minute breaks between subjects, when they could play the piano, read books, and play chess and checkers. At the end of the second day's break, the class resisted going back to work, but he insisted, and believes that a failure at this point would have been disastrous, because the children had made a bargain and had to keep it. (Perhaps it was important for him to know that the class *could* keep bargains.)

Things worked out, painfully:

> I remember days getting home from school angry at myself, confused by my behavior in the classroom, my ranting and carping, my inability to let the children alone. I kept saying "That's not me, that's not me." For a while, as I learned to teach, the me in the classroom was an alien and hostile being.

He overcame his conviction that if one child got out of control the whole class would follow and chaos would result:

I let an insult pass and discovered that the rest of the class didn't take up the insult; I learned to say nothing when Ralph returned from pacing the halls or when Alvin refused to do arithmetic. The children did not want to be defiant, insulting, idle; nor were they any less afraid of chaos than I was.

He never completely solved the problem of discipline. He never was able to line everybody up at 3 o'clock. Sadly, he reports that one boy he couldn't reach left the class. He and the other children learned to live with each other, which is as close as anybody comes to solving the discipline problem.

There are many profound reflections on teaching scattered through *36 Children*, but one small and almost peripheral illustration of Mr. Kohl's awareness of the complexities will have to suffice. This concerns a teacher's need for privacy, a separate existence outside the classroom, even sometimes, for a year or two away from teaching. At one point he began having children over to his apartment after school. (To some teachers and administrators this is the same thing as deserting the trenches to fraternize with the enemy in no-man's-land.) The visits were a success, but he found, finally, that he had to restrict them to just one day in the week. The children were angry when he told them he needed his own life. I've met good teachers who never appreciated this, or if they did, were unable to do anything about it. They never set apart any aspect of themselves, they gave their classes everything, and you sensed that somehow in the long process they were being scooped hollow. In the end they were left trying to live vicariously through the children, which was not enough.

So much for the complexities, which fill Mr. Kohl's account. *36 Children* is an important book because it shows how a teacher abandoned the usual classroom methods and developed an informal class where children could work on their own, where they were offered choices about what to do, and where in fact they generated a good deal of the curriculum themselves, including an extraordinary outpouring of free writing. It reports all this convincingly, with the kind of specific detail necessary for understanding and yet so often absent from discussions of teaching. He includes many samples of the children's work, so that *36 Children* becomes, in parts, an eloquent anthology testifying to the creative energy of these Harlem students. He shows us their poems, myths, sly fables, comic strips, autobiographies, essays, and wildly inventive science fiction novels.

Mr. Kohl's book and his pamphlet, *Teaching the Unteachable*, provide American teachers, parents, and the public with the kind of thing they desperately lack: concrete examples of what a really good job of teaching might look like. There is a big difference between a class in which the teacher simply likes the children and a class where the children are stimulated to do first-rate work. *36 Children* sheds some light on the difference. Its lessons apply to suburbs, as well as slums, for very few schools of any sort in this country regularly permit children to choose the content of their writing, and children's literature is rarely read with the respect and attention it needs in order to flourish. Mr. Kohl claims no great originality for his discovery that children can write. Other teachers have discovered the same thing. People learn to use words—to want to use words well—by trying to get across something they want to say to an audience they wish to reach and move. Children learn to write by writing. (But it is true, as he says, that children will not write if they are afraid to talk.) His example is relevant to every level of education from first grade through graduate school, but of course it hits with all the more force because his class was composed of Black and Puerto Rican children, who, we are so often told, lack any vocabulary, are unable to handle abstractions, learn mainly from physical, rather than mental, activity, and so on and so on. In fact his children liked to write and had a lot to say. Not all were gifted writers, though some clearly were, and many, like many adults, had only a single important story to tell, to write and rewrite. Yet, "all of them . . . seemed to become more alive through their writing."

In making the change from a formal class to a freer one, he was driven by desperation, not by any particular vision of good teaching. For 6 or 7 weeks he struggled with the assigned books, but it was hopeless. He was bored and so were the children. A few times the class came to life: They had an intricate discussion of the Patterson–Liston fight, and a conversation about the word "psyche" that led the astonished children to consider the idea that language and words changed over time, had a history. "You mean words change?" "You mean one day the way we talk—you know with words like cool and dig and soul—may be all right?" They were fascinated by the myth of Cupid and Psyche, and became hungry for words and myths. He dropped the dreary social studies texts (*How We Became Modern America*) and started teaching them about words, myths, and periods of history that interested him. Social studies became a free period, a long break in which the teacher overwhelmed the class with books and projects, and let them discover what they liked. There were books on architecture, the Greeks, mythology, Mesopotamia, early man, books on World War II for a set of war buffs, art books for a boy who drew all the time, the

Bobbsey Twins, and novels like Dorothy Sterling's *Mary Jane*, the story of
a Negro girl who integrates a White school.

As they began making choices, the teacher found that he could take
the time to watch and listen and get some idea of what intrigued them. A
few boys got interested in science, and they told him of an unused cache of
science equipment somewhere in the school. Others knew where they could
lay hands on a record player. He brought in his records and the class introduced him to Moms Mabley. By the end of October, they were telling him
about the neighborhood, and then they began to write about it. The papers
weren't marked, and no one had to write. This was, he says, probably the
first time they had ever written to say something that mattered:

> I live 62 E. 120st My neighborhood is not so bad. Everyone has
> children in the block. Many of the children are Spanish. Some
> of them run around nude and dirty. Some of the houses are so dirty
> you would be sacre to come in the door. Sometimes the drunks
> come out and fight. . . . Many of the people in the block drink so
> much they don't have time for the children. The children have no
> place to play they have the park but the parents don't care enough
> to take them. Now you have a idea of what my block is like.

He found himself running a very different kind of class from the one
he had begun with. The free social studies period expanded to a free day.
Each morning he put an assignment on the board and the class had a choice
of reading and writing or else doing the assignment. Writing was private,
unless the author chose to make it public, and the children were encouraged to work at one task until the momentum was lost. Some were upset
by the absence of routine, and missed the comfort of doing things by rote.
Their teacher often wavered, too, and thought about going back to formal
teaching. The slow result was a flowering of free writing.

The first book he was allowed to see was an autobiography by Maurice,
11 years old:

> This story is about a boy named Maurice and his life as it is and
> how it will be. Maurice is in the sixth grade now, but this story will
> tell you about his past, present, and future. . . . When I was born I
> couldn't see at first, but like all families my father was waiting
> outside after a hour or so I could see shadows.

Robert Jackson, the artist, began an astonishing literary output with a
book clearly influenced by his readings about Greece. *A Barbarian Becomes*

a Greek Warrior is a violent adventure story about a weakling with "the strength of luck" who grows into a great hero: "One day in Ancient Germany, a boy was growing up. His name was Pathos. He was named after this Latin word because he had sensitive feelings. In Ancient Germany the Romans had their vast empire . . ."

The teacher found that different children respond to different kinds of writing, trying out new voices and modes. After hearing fables from Aesop and Thurber, some took to the fable:

> Once upon a time there was a pig and a cat. The cat kept saying you old dirty pig who want to eat you. And the pig replied when I die I'll be made use of, but when you die you'll just rot. The cat always thought he was better than the pig. When the pig died he was used as food for the people to eat. When the cat died he was buried in old dirt.
>
> Moral: Live dirty die clean.

Some children fashioned myths, mingling Cyclops and Zeus with Superman and Wonder Woman. The most impressive—"awesome" is, quite properly, the word his teacher uses—is a long unfinished fragment of the Elektra myth by Alvin Curry, Jr., which begins: "This story called Elektra is of the deepest passion and the deepest hope of vengeance of her father's death . . ." The children produced a magazine, *And*, the two issues of which appear in *36 Children*. *And* has many fine things, including illustrated mythologies by Robert Jackson, and Marie Ford's poem, "The Junkies":

> *When they are*
> *in the street*
> *they pass it*
> *along to each*
> *other but when*
> *they see the*
> *police they would*
> *just stand still*
> *and be beat*
> *so pity ful*
> *that they want*
> *to cry.*

The school's authorities, who in most respects seem to have left Mr. Kohl to his own devices, thought that *And* contained too much terror and violence, and recommended that the class study a fifth grader's sticky little poem on shopping with Mom. The assistant principal's only reaction to *And* was an offer to give its creators a lesson in proofreading.

Mr. Kohl's cumulative portrait of the New York City schools is devastating, but the portrait emerges slowly, and it is done with justice and a certain amount of pity, as well as rage. For instance, "It was difficult not to feel the general chaos—to observe the classes without teachers, the children wandering aimlessly, sometimes wantonly through the halls, disrupting classes, intimidating, extorting, yet being courted by the administration: 'Please don't make trouble, anything you want, but no trouble.'" In April, he demonstrated what he thought of the system by doing something that radically contradicted its premises, something that many teachers in slum schools would regard as unprofessional. (If teachers really were professionals, of course, they would be loyal to their immediate students and not to their superiors or the school system.) He explained to his children that they were going to have to take reading and (at that time in New York) IQ tests that determined placement in junior high school and thus their whole future. He took out their records and told them their past scores. They were angry and shocked, for no one in all their years in school had ever told them frankly how low they stood. In this, the top sixth-grade class in the school, only two children had IQ scores above 100; the majority had scores in the 80 to 90 range. The class asked what could be done, and he did what teachers of middle-class children often do and teachers of slum children almost never do: He taught them how to take tests. (As he explains, many teachers in slum schools feel that their own failures with the children are excused if objective tests can establish that the children are failures.) He got old tests and drilled the class for several weeks in the tricky art of following instructions. The children objected to the boring drill, but he made them be realistic. Their superb sixth-grade work didn't matter; they would go nowhere in junior high school unless the test scores were satisfactory. He taught them the different kinds of test questions and got them to see that they mustn't be too clever and outsmart tests. Children sometimes have trouble learning that a test has only one right answer, and that the task is to figure out what the man who made the test expects and not simply what seems like a reasonable answer. They have to be trained to think on the test's level, not on their level. The children learned. As their teacher put it, "they agreed to be dull for the sake of their future."

There was too little time to prepare for the IQ tests, and only 10 in the class scored over 100, one girl getting 135. But the reading tests later on in the year showed the results of determined coaching. Most of the class jumped 1 to 3 years, a few were at a fifth-grade level, 12 were on the seventh-grade level, and 8 read on levels between eighth and twelfth grades.

The reading tests were a victory of sorts. The year was most certainly a victory for Mr. Kohl and his children. He hadn't created the visionary social studies course he once imagined teaching, which would instruct children "to be able to persist, revolt, and change things in our society and yet not lose their souls in the process." But he had done wonderful things. The children had learned to read widely and to like reading, and they had discovered that they could write—to touch on the more obvious and perhaps less important aspects of their encounter with a gifted and warm teacher. The first and longest section of *36 Children* is written in a tone of quiet pride. This, it seems to say, is how it's done. This is being a successful teacher.

A short second section makes *36 Children* a tragic book, as well as the story of a success. It follows the careers of the children in the years after leaving sixth grade in 1963. While the returns are far from being complete, there is enough evidence to justify one child's mournful observation, "Mr. Kohl, one good year isn't enough." Despite the children's tenacious desire to finish school, and the foolish hopes and dreams that kept them going long after the pointlessness of school was evident, they began coming back, bewildered, to their sixth-grade teacher to report discouragement and steady demoralization. One girl made it to a prep school in New England, paying a heavy psychic price for making it in the White world. A handful of other girls endured because they were strong. The attrition rate among the boys was sickening. Robert Jackson, whose drawings and writings adorn *36 Children*, quit the High School of Music and Art. (When Mr. Kohl went to discover why, he met a guidance counselor whose office was full of Black students. "You know we're very good to . . . here," she whispered, writing the word "Negroes" on a pad.) Michael, who once worked on a novel, *Frankenstein Meets Cyclops and Psyche*, still dreamed of becoming a writer. He wanted to master the craft, but school was irrelevant, and he was selling newspapers for a living. Another boy, Ralph, was "beginning to look like those permanent dwellers in junkies' paradise." In a series of letters and writings to his teacher, Alvin Curry records the downward path to wisdom. Subsequent teachers have treated him as an illiterate, and yet gloomily he continues to write. This is from "The Condemned Building."

> There is a leaky faucet, going with a steady drip of water, there is no recreation whatsoever where a person can spend his leisure time, but there is something to look at, the walls which have plaster peeling, which suggests different moods that a person may be in, the walls are so arranged that they suggest different scenes like maybe a scene of you gradually graduating from boyhood to man when the mirage has passed you notice that the windows

are uneasily pitch black suggesting for you maybe a private hell where you can satisfy your own desires ... you step into the outside where you ask yourself why is this building condemned, where a person can find his inner self. Why do they condemn this building where man can find out what he is or will be.

Why do they condemn Life.

As the toll mounts, their teacher is forced to ask himself whether he did his children a favor by teaching them to write and think, whether it was good to create expectations that the schools did not live up to. His answer is troubled. He will not teach again in the public school system as it stands. He hopes he can find a way to continue teaching children, but it is clear that he will be less certain that he can save them next time. What he will be able to do, at least, is add his weight to "easing the burden of being alive in the United States today."

36 Children presents an aspect of the social tragedy now engulfing this country, but it is much more than simply another book with the same message we have heard and ignored often before. Each child has signed his teacher's memory with a characteristic kind of wit, a way of talking or writing, a special bravado. The book is tragic, but it is its triumph to demonstrate the stubborn individuality of these children, who, with their intelligence and their promise, are so much bigger than the small, mean fates stalking them. In Harlem iron traps are set and waiting for the young flesh, but there is gaiety in their lives, and there are gestures of deep courtesy, too, and these are also part of the rich, increasingly bitter truth 36 Children tells us.

Teaching Teacher: A Utopian Bulletin

I HAVE COME ACROSS a rare example of the kind of classroom record we almost never get—a full, intelligent account by a teacher of the experience of teaching informally over a period of time.

Elwyn S. Richardson's *In the Early World* (Random House, 1964) is a utopian bulletin on 12 years of work in one tiny country school in northern New Zealand. It may be the best book about teaching ever written; certainly it's the most beautifully designed. Reproductions of children's art of an astonishing quality fill its pages—examples of writing, as well as wood and linoleum cuts, pottery, and fabrics. It is a densely constructed work, not at all easy to read. In different puzzling contexts, Richardson thinks and rethinks his ideas. The reader seems to be sitting with him, listening in on the effort of recollection as he turns an accumulation of children's work over in his hands, trying to figure out what went into its making.

It takes time for the reader to see that a long account of how the class took up pottery is meant to be emblematic of a whole style of teaching. Clay in various grades lay in deposits near the school, and Richardson and the children tested samples to see which kinds were good to work with. They built a small brick kiln and pottery became a standard activity in the school. Messing around, the children slowly learned the limits of the material— you couldn't build wet clay too high or it would collapse. They tended toward fussy over-decoration of pots, producing a mass of derivative and cliched work. His tactic when they showed him their poor early efforts was to find small aspects to praise, little virtues to single out. The important thing that was emerging, Richardson saw only in retrospect, was a sense of values, the idea that some work was better than other work and that children could learn to make judgments of this sort. He tried to get them to examine why a pot was better, but the children at first were content to decide that it just was, and deserved to be put in a special display area that in time enveloped the whole classroom. In discussions, many contributed to setting a standard of values. (Later, Richardson says he worried about this procedure, but "that was after I saw that there were different standards of values developing among the children.") They began to take each other's work seriously, in a critical spirit. This pot was too heavy and not as good as your last one; one boy told another the lips weren't drawn in enough, but certain strokes were lovely. Quality improved: "As soon as judgment begins, as in the selection of some better pots from the mass of work, the influences of the inferior are no longer felt so much and there is a need . . . to re-order . . . thinking." Looking back, Richardson felt that a great deal of his early teaching was ineffective, because he did not know how to discriminate between good work and bad (he knew nothing about pottery to start with), and because he failed to see the process of learning to discriminate as one of the points of the whole enterprise.

With the smaller and less confident children (the school took students from 5 to 15 years of age) he found he had to arrange matters more carefully. Plaster molds into which clay could be pressed to make pottery were useful because they enabled kids to make adequate pottery right away without first having to master the tricky art of laying down coils of clay to form the foundation of a pot. On their own, the children experimented with textures, pressing wood, bark, and seashells into the clay to form designs. They discovered that a few bold strokes were often more effective than fussy decoration, and increasingly they were confident enough to use line, mass, and color, in abstract ways. A dozen or so children became real potters; their work is handsomely displayed in the book's illustrations.

Pottery was where Richardson began. The most sustained account of his teaching, however, comes in a number of detailed chapters on children's writing. After a time, the work in pottery influenced other work, especially in crafts. But not writing, which the children regarded as a chore. Once in a while there would be an apt caption for a picture, but Richardson was appalled by what the children produced when they tried their hand at "poetry." Their whole notion of written expression was stunted: What writing they had been exposed to was unrelated to any of their experiences, and totally alien to the way they talked. Fine writing was poetry, which was about certain set, usually esoteric or fey subjects. It had to be rhymed: "The thrush sings all day. / But it doesn't have any pay."

With poetry and crafts, discussions had rapidly helped the work, but not with writing. There was little promising new material to begin with. A small piece of a small lino cut could be singled out for praise, but Richardson found little to note in the children's first labored literary efforts. A few children, misinterpreting his anxiety over quality, attempted to please him by writing up storms of turgid poetry. He started picking out one good sentence from these lengthy efforts, trying to encourage much shorter pieces of writing.

He took to collecting vivid sentences and even single images from things the children said or wrote, copying them for display. (The smaller children were a fund of images—they looked at puddles and found "the upside down world.") He read the class translations of short poems, Japanese haiku. Working small, in bits of prose, each child could have the sense of doing something well. And, as with the pottery, there came to be a basis for discussing the quality of the work. A whole genre of short poems evolved, which the children called "picture-poems," unrhymed lyrical statements expressing one or two thoughts at most. Irene, 13, wrote: "The pine tree stands/With cracked sooted arms/ With stumped branches/ Rotted into the ground."

These formed a starting point for talking about longer efforts, which began to reappear in many forms. When the class read—

Under the blind seawater
The bubble fingered seaweeds
Dance and run around in airy water

They never seem to sleep
And never seem to break the surface
Or dance too heavily.

The sun does never beat upon them
And they are never afraid of a drop of water
Because it is well and truly wet down there.

And on the darkly shaded rocks,
The limpets spit and cling.

—they selected the first two verses as poems in themselves, rejected the third as weak (among other faults it talked of matters about which the poet was ignorant), and suggested that the last verse stand on its own as a brief statement.

It was not enough to consider the value of a finished piece of prose or pottery. It was more helpful if the children talked as they worked. "Why no leaves?" somebody would ask. "I don't like your two figures. They're better than the ones in your last painting, David." "I like your story, but I was disappointed you didn't say more about things you people were talking about after lights went out." . . . "I like that (a poem on moths) very much. . . . Stuart knows a lot about moths. He writes as if he *is* a moth." Richards found himself impressed by their ability to judge work dispassionately. Now and then something one of them considered important was rejected, but usually "they were kind to children who rarely shone in their expression and saw that what was 'good' for one person was not the same 'good' for another . . ."

Sometimes he set the class exercises, which produced effective, if contrived, writing: Describe water going down a drain, put your chin on a level with the grass and tell how things look, characterize a visitor to the school, or write down, as fast as possible, all the thoughts that run through your head in 10 minutes. (This last produced raw material, ideas and images the children could later work on.)

As writing of all sorts—nature studies, stories, narratives, poems, autobiographical fragments, fantasies—developed, the class perfected a system. A child could decide which of his works were to be read out loud and discussed. The class then selected the best, which were gathered and bound into a series of school magazines, each bearing a new title. Richardson says he seldom tried to get the whole class interested in the same thing; the idea was to interest a child in something and then encourage him to pursue it. As time went on, children's topics encroached on his formal class lessons, but he still gave lessons for the whole class when he felt there was something they all needed to know. Some days he left school feeling he had taught too much; other days he thought the kids needed more direction than he had provided. (He kept notes on errors that individual children kept making.)

Children's topics overrode subjects, as well as the timetable. He found stories and picture-poems would suggest ideas for paintings and cuts— sometimes he suggested that a child paint what he hadn't said so much about in a story. With many, and particularly some of the Maori children, the development of art led to much better work in other areas. A few children flourished by an almost obsessive concentration on a single theme: One painted darkness and wrote about night, and another worked and reworked, in prose, cuts, poems, and paintings, the discovery of a dead bird.

In the Early World is an extraordinary anthology of children's writing, but Richardson is careful to emphasize the time it took for many children to write anything of value; only a few, he says, ever developed a distinctive style. What was missing for many—and he recurs to this notion all through the book—was simply stimulation: something to write about. The best work arose from chance encounters—some starlings nesting near the school led to a particularly rich harvest of writing and painting, and once a boy's clay portrait led to an impressive series of heads and masks. Work of true quality was rare even in his school, Richardson felt, because so little school work ever captured real experience on the wing.

His country school never offered what could be called a balanced curriculum—his own absorption with nature studies, crafts, and writing clearly predominated, although there are some interesting chapters on mathematics and drama. But *In the Early World* is the most thoughtful, serious portrait I've come across of a school in which children were writing, thinking, and talking, and not simply going through a set of motions called education. The temptation never to believe what anybody says about schools is very strong, yet this account is convincing. Its few ideas are densely wound around examples of actual work on the part of children who seem very alive. You are inclined to accept the spirit of Richardson's testimony when, at the end, he struggles to put matters into words and finishes with some very old, tired, and much-abused formulas:

> I saw that I had to teach as much as I could when opportunities arose, and that this was a better kind of teaching than I had known when I was following through topic after topic. If I did not teach at such times, the work became poor and lifeless. . . . The series of developments taught me too that I must use environment to the full and encourage individual expression rather than class. This meant more individual and small group observation. . . .

The Real Thing in Teaching

SEPTEMBER 27, 1969

FRANCES POCKMAN HAWKINS is a gifted teacher who spent every Thursday of a spring semester with six deaf nursery school children in a Colorado public school. This was a special program, bristling with designs and elaborate purposes, but the authorities were wise enough to give Mrs. Hawkins a pretty free rein. (They must have wondered about all the things she kept trucking into the school: equipment for making bubbles, tire pumps, plastic tubes, a hamster, food coloring, water trays, balances, and hundreds of other items to stock an informal classroom.) *The Logic of Action: From a Teacher's Notebook* is a series of notes, photographs, and reflections in the form of a running daily log of each class session—how it went, what particular children spent their time doing, what Mrs. Hawkins did—as well as what she refrained from doing—and what was in her mind as she taught. Each entry starts off with a list of new equipment introduced—there's an appendix with useful notes about it all—and then a narrative of the day's teaching and learning follows.

Almost any attempt to describe what goes on in a good classroom fails, and every reader will face points in this log when he is not being told enough, or when he is being told too much. Nonetheless, Mrs. Hawkins is an extremely shrewd observer, and her individual sketches of the children are delightful. She is keen to distill an occasional abstract principle from her experiences, and passages in these notes have the muffled, occasionally dense quality that nearly always marks the efforts of good teachers to pin down their art in words and general terms: The brilliance poises on the edge of portentousness, and only her massive common sense and her instinct for detail keep her upright. The reader is standing on a heaving deck that is likely to pitch him from soap bubbles and giggles to very different levels of discourse: "Attention is a close cousin of love, and one does not speak of training someone to love, but rather of providing the right setting."

What emerges is an original and fascinating sketch of what one experienced teacher is thinking about as she teaches. Mrs. Hawkins has illuminating things to say about her deaf charges, but this is really a book about teaching all children, rich or poor, wounded or whole. Those likely to read

139

it with the greatest interest are the growing number of teachers and parents concerned with developing alternatives to formal teaching. They will find that it has one virtue that few books about free schools and classrooms possess: It really is about what an adult has to contribute to children's learning. While she believes as passionately as anyone in environments where children are free to pursue their own learning independently, Mrs. Hawkins does not believe that such environments come about by accident. In the beginning, at least, a teacher has the responsibility for creating a setting, choosing the materials, arranging the stage. And as the children learn, as they choose, the teacher still has further decisions to make: when to step in, when to keep quiet, what kind of help to give. It is an elusive, complex process.

At first, for example, she saw that her children, perhaps because they were deaf, clung to routine more than most 4-year-olds she had met; they reminded her of older children, trained by the schools to rely less and less on their own experiences. So her tactics included deliberate small interruptions of routine, to wean them from the ordinary and get them used to novelties:

> Whatever I did was immediately copied, and, as one must when
> this happens, I had to change what I started as quickly as possible,
> providing more than one way to copy, thus sanctioning and inviting
> variety. . . . When a group of fives produces replica upon replica of
> one paper ornament, it's time to watch for and dignify, perhaps
> hanging from a mobile, one child's "mistake"—one hard to copy
> and thus conducive to the production of still more mistakes.

The point of the enterprise is, as she says, to help a child "regain and develop this capacity to probe and test, to summon his sleeping resources of imagery, control, and understanding—in short, to learn, and not to memorize." One avenue to a classroom where this is likely to happen is the teacher's own interests. If she herself is exploring the material and not just watching it being used, the odds of engaging a child's mind increase. There are, as Mrs. Hawkins demonstrates, innumerable things that adults and 4-year-olds can pursue together. Mrs. Hawkins enjoyed watching water bubbles in the plastic tubes "falling upward," and argues convincingly that this shared interest was more valuable to the children than any amount of mere adult praise for their inventions. Her class suggests some of the richness inherent in good, open-ended science materials.

She is always conscious of herself as stage manager and catalyst. Sometimes the role is straightforward and simple, as when Patty takes up the attribute blocks to get away from the crowd and work on her own: "I protected her right to work there alone." Other times, as in planning to introduce new materials, there are many things to consider. Two long soundings from Mrs. Hawkins's flow of thought will have to suffice. Here she is thinking about artificial food coloring:

> [The materials here are] still inherently new to most children, and esthetically vivid. It has been my experience that there is more enjoyment and exploration if the introduction of food color is "structured." On this particular morning . . . I made another judgement. A time for quieter activity with teacher involved was needed. Had the early part of morning followed another kind of pattern, I might have cancelled these plans. On a Monday morning, for example, after a cold and confining weekend, I have found children so deeply in need of self-direction in familiar paths, with adults far in the background, that I have put away "structured" plans. Guidance at such times courts trouble . . .

And here she is thinking about setting up balances:

> I wanted to introduce them, not head-on, but tangentially and in sequence with enough sure-fire old stuff so that the children would not rush all at once to the balances just *because* they were new. Such structuring has at least two justifications: it allows a child sufficient time to use a new piece of equipment without having at once to share or wait turns. Materials such as this yardstick-cum-weights-on-upright are more likely to "speak" to a child when there is time for continued experimentation. In addition . . . [this] approach provides a teacher the luxury of observation. In time, most of the children followed their separate paths to the realization that not all things had to be demonstrated. Some, perhaps, knew this all along but were not used to acting on it in practice.

Mrs. Hawkins makes no attempt to sum up the significance of her role, and that is probably wise, for it is built up from thousands of such small specific concerns: ranging from making sure to take great pains in presenting the delicate acetate gels—colored sheets to look through—to the children, so they treat them with proper care, to remembering to start cleaning up early enough so the children have time to unwind. Most people who read these notes may be inclined to say that all this simply reflects the fact that Mrs. Hawkins is a remarkable person. That goes without saying. Yet many of the concerns she touches on are to some extent those of all good teachers of children of all ages. They come naturally to some, and by experience to others; each would certainly describe how he works in a different way. This is only a notebook; the sketches leave you with an unfinished feeling. It doesn't pretend to tell teachers what to teach, although it is full of good suggestions. It merely presents a series of working illustrations of principles in practice. Through it, a philosophy of education is struggling to be heard, although in the absence of many more such classrooms and firsthand teachers' accounts, we will never be able to articulate it realistically, without dogma or cant.

To Touch More Life

JUNE 8, 1980

JOSEPH LASH'S *Helen and Teacher* is part of the Radcliffe biography series about distinguished American women. It's a risky book in two respects. First of all, the lives of Helen Keller and her teacher Anne Sullivan Macy have already been told. Helen Keller wrote *The Story of My Life* and *Teacher: Anne Sullivan Macy*, and Nella Braddy did a good biography of Mrs. Macy in the 1930s. And William Gibson dramatized the story in his wonderful play, "The Miracle Worker." A second risk is that any book this long—811 pages, to be exact—is bound to be put in the company of all those fat and mindless biographies we've been getting recently. It is to Mr. Lash's credit that he surmounts both risks. This book is not as finely wrought as Mr. Lash's *Eleanor and Franklin*—the best American biography in the last 20 years—but it is a deeply absorbing portrait of two intertwined lives whose meanings can't be understood separately. There is a great deal of new material—the portrait now has a few more warts, as well as a depth and texture it never had before. And the length is not that much of a problem. There are clearly many things that could have been cut. We don't need all the details of every triumphant world tour. We could do without at least half of the expert flattery that Helen Keller ladled so successfully into the delighted ears of the great and the rich. But there is something fascinating on every page, and the cumulative effect of all the details is so rich and complex and intimate as to make the book an event in the life of this reader.

The basic story is well known. Helen Keller was born in Tuscumbia, Alabama, in 1880. When she was 19 months old, a raging fever robbed her of both sight and hearing. Anne Sullivan was born 14 years earlier in desperate poverty near Springfield, Massachusetts. She was orphaned and contracted trachoma at the age of 5, losing half her sight. She lived in the horrible squalor of the state poorhouse at Tewksbury—where her brother Jimmie, her last relative, died of tuberculosis. With luck she landed in Boston's Perkins Institute, which gave her a good education. She also recovered much of her sight, although she fought blindness off and on throughout the rest of her life. At the age of 21, Anne Sullivan was hired to teach 7-year-old Helen. With celebrated results—Teacher and Helen began a love and a collaboration that lasted nearly 50 years, taking them through the world of the blind and disabled to Radcliffe College, friendships with the high and mighty, authorship, and world fame.

There are a number of ways to read this basic story. You can look at this pair of extraordinary women as a window on the culture. With Mr. Lash's book in hand, it's easy to recognize Anne Sullivan as one of the great progressives, a practitioner, not an intellectual, but characteristically in revolt against formalism and convention in the name of those three sacred progressive passions: life, growth, and friendship. Her blend of child-centered pedagogy, a revived romanticism, and social reform expresses her generation and her time.

Helen, more of a feminist and certainly much more of a lifelong radical than Teacher, emerges as one of the most articulate of the group of middle-class cultural radicals who fused a version of romanticism with radical politics. She was, for example, an ardent supporter of the IWW, the radical labor union, known as the "Wobblies." Mr. Lash allows us to see her as in some sense an intellectual cousin of Randolph Bourne, the great radical critic in the early days of the *New Republic* just before World War I. Both Bourne and Helen shared a romantic religion of life, a fascination with growth and development, a deep faith in education, and a desire to fuse personal issues with the wider issues of politics. They had something else in common: a radicalism that grew out of the experience of disability. Bourne's hunchback and twisted face gave him a sympathy for outsiders and the oppressed, as did Keller's blindness and deafness.

Helen Keller also enjoyed the kind of celebrity that says something about the temper of this country in the first half of the century. Like Mark Twain and Jane Addams—and, to a certain extent, Eleanor Roosevelt—she created herself as a public figure and was in turn shaped by her audience. She basked in all the attention, yet struggled hard to live a life of her own, a struggle that was all the more poignant because she really did need a great deal of help from Teacher and many others. The help was forthcoming, but it came at a price, as it always does. Mr. Lash's account of the grand reckoning of the help she got and the price she paid for it is subtle and intricate.

There is a less pleasant side to the story. Helen Keller played the role of what Erving Goffman (1959) calls a hero of adjustment, the handicapped person who lives up to the standards of the culture and therefore in some sense reassures everyone else that a fixed game is fair. A career as a sightless angel had its drawbacks. As a public figure she did an enormous amount to make Americans aware of the problems of the blind and the deaf, but she also found herself acting a part in the culture's sentimental and sometimes vicious melodramas about the handicapped. As a kind of secular saint, she reassured normal people that the blind compensate, that they are gentle and kind and that they bear no hard feelings.

Just as we start choking on the pink clouds billowing around the culture heroine, Mr. Lash introduces a Brechtian theme: In need of money, Teacher and Helen sign on as a vaudeville act, touring the country, enchanting audiences with Helen's story and making big bucks. Teacher is mortified and hates every minute of it. Helen loves show business and the traveling. It's like being exhibited as a talking dog, yet her hunger for life consumes even this experience. The reader is left wondering at the tremendous, stupid, yet goodhearted sentimentality of America in the 1920s and 1930s.

Mr. Lash's book is also a magisterial exploration of a neglected and fascinating subject: the relationship between the teacher and the student. Anne Sullivan was a genius not only as a practitioner but also, as Mr. Lash demonstrates, as an articulate theorist of education. Like the great Jean-Marc Itard, who taught Victor, the famous Wild Boy of Aveyron in pre-Revolutionary France, she certainly made the most of her encounter with her one pupil. Her practice was eclectic. She stole ideas from William James and everyone else, including Samuel Gridley Howe's work with Laura Bridgman. She worked from experience; the great example of her approach was the famous moment when she hand-spelled "water" into Helen's palm through running water, and Helen began to understand that there was such a thing as language. Yet as Mr. Lash notes, this amazing illumination was preceded by something even more basic: Teacher's gaining entry into Helen's heart.

As Mr. Lash notes, Helen gave different accounts of her early education. Some stress her own developing powers and the others strike another note: "Before my teacher came to me, I did not know that I am. I lived in a world that was a no-world." Yet she was the adored first-born child of her family, and, before blindness struck, she had already learned to toddle, to speak, to eat, to love and be loved. After her blindness and deafness but before Teacher, she had also learned to make signs for what she needed—over 60, she once calculated. Above all, most accounts, including Teacher's, stress Helen's astounding vitality.

Some critics think that Teacher tried to make Helen as much like a normal person as possible, rather than developing her distinctive potential. There's certainly something to such charges: There's a bookishness to Helen; her responses often do seem second-hand, as though her primary reality was the world of words that she had constructed out of other people's phrases. Still, on balance, the interaction between Helen, Teacher, and the world opened up many more experiences than it foreclosed, and Helen's universe surely included much more than words. She also had an amazing sense of touch, which Teacher had been at pains to help her develop by getting her to handle everything from bark to flower petals to animal fur. Words and touch did connect in her life. She felt the mouth of the child in Michelangelo's statue, "Madonna and Child," and murmured "innocent greed."

Helen's psychological development can also be understood as a study in creativity and the development of a writer. It's true that Helen's creativity has been a matter of some dispute ever since she wrote a story that turned out to be a version of something someone else had published. Her phenomenal memory may have been part of the problem. Again, many readers were bothered when Helen described colors or the "muted hoof of wild deer." Others have claimed that such criticisms are "sense arrogant," and that the word and sound imagery did mean something to her.

How much she wrote from her own experience is an intriguing question. My own guess is that the answer lies waiting to be developed out of two letters that America's greatest psychologist William James wrote to Helen:

> Evidently sensations as such form the relatively smaller part of
> the world we mentally live in, relations being the things of most
> interest there, and the whole spread and extent and interest con-
> sisting of material suggested and treated analogically, and being
> practically quite as vast in one person as another, and similar in
> effects of contrast . . . and in esthetic and moral appeal in us all. . . .
> It is no paradox you live in a world so indistinguishable from
> ours. The great world of the background in all of us is the world
> of our beliefs. That is the world of the permanencies and the im-
> mensities, and our relations with it are mostly verbal . . . it makes
> no difference in what shape the content of our verbal material
> may come. In some it is more optical, in others more motor . . . in
> you it is motor and tactile, but its functions are the same as ours,
> the relations meant by the words symbolizing the relations existing
> between the things.

An allied issue that dogged Teacher and Helen was the accusation that Teacher was in reality a fraud, that Helen's accomplishments were in fact Teacher's. On an obvious level this charge was plainly false; Helen's talents were her own. She did well on her exams at Radcliffe when the school forced Teacher to stay out of the room. On another level though, as Mr. Lash notes, Helen's work was essentially collaborative. She needed editors and ideas and people to give her information about the world from which she was blocked. In fact, some of her best work was done round-robin, with Helen writing and Teacher and her husband, John Macy, editing and improving. The suspicious will regard this as a species of fraud. I agree with Mr. Lash that matters are more complex—that, as we all know and seldom admit, the conditions for creativity are, among other things, social in nature. Teacher may have opened Helen's soul, but the soul was there first. With Teacher and Macy gone, Helen wrote less easily and well.

In the end, though, most people will want to read *Helen and Teacher* mainly as the detailed record of a lifelong relationship between two extraordinary women. We will never understand ourselves without more such accounts of friendships and marriages over time. This friendship was like a marriage in being a complex and intricate dance of dependence and independence. It also preempted other ties, taking precedence over the claims of Helen's parents and over Anne Sullivan's own marriage, which ended in divorce. And it put an end to what may have been Helen's single romance with a man. In this shocking episode, Helen Keller's whole circle, but especially her mother and Teacher, prevented her—a famous author and all of 36 years old—from marrying the suitor whom she loved, who loved her in return, and who was suitable in every respect.

Teacher was full of wit and mistrust and despair; jealous for Helen, a brutal realist, so realistic at times she missed the point. Early on, for example, Teacher speaks, without whining, of Helen's stunted emotional life. Yet all her life, Teacher was subject to black Irish furies that Helen alone could bring her out of. She hid even from Helen the great shame of her life—that she once lived in the poorhouse. She carried a permanent chip on her shoulder about the Yankees and the rich. She resented it when the world made a fuss over Helen and ignored her. At one point, her jealousy made her reluctant to see Helen taught how to talk. She was a cruel, on occasion violent, and deeply devoted woman.

Helen exceeded her in vigor and appetite for life. With her wild excitements and her odd bookish eloquence, she was like a child who has read too much and played too little, although the spirit of play remained strong. Helen was always open to new friends and new experience, always trusting. Any time she could reach out to touch more life, she did, groping for the human faces and the statues. It was in character for her to stand outside on the heaving deck of a ship during a terrifying storm. Yet Helen is the one who nurses grudges for years—especially against anyone who has slighted Teacher. Both of them are romantics, but Helen is one in both the bad and the good sense of the word. The good side is her permanent sense of wonder, a deep strain of Swedenborgian mysticism. The bad side is her penchant for living in fantasy and worlds made up of words, all those sentimental phrases that fail to do justice to what was, after all, a profoundly unsentimental life.

The dance between the two remains touched with mystery. We never completely understand other people's friendships and marriages. Reading through this book, I needed to look again and again at the photographs of Helen Keller's lovely face. We're drawn to her, as so many have been, not just for her remarkable courage and grace, but also because she's so like us all and yet so unlike us. There's little difference between one person and another, William James once said, but what difference there is is very important. Watching her, alone and yet dependent, we start to feel the mystery of this profound truth. For this and so much else in this wonderful book, I'm grateful to Joseph Lash.

The Living Classroom

L ET'S BEGIN WITH A kid's drawing. The sun in person, wearing its
lucky hair ribbon, is pouring a big syrupy rainbow down on boats,
human figures, and the creatures of the sea. The picture captures a
moment of high life on our beautiful green and blue globe—a planetary
party, really. It's gorgeous, the product of an artistic imagination with nerve
to eat a world like an apple. Next, let's read a sentence in a book written
by young Billy, whose father has died of cancer: "I wrote this book because
I think a lot of people have a lot of pain—and that's the truth."

Do you have children? Do you wish other people's kids well? If so, I
think you would like them to be part of a first-grade classroom like Jeanette
Amidon's in Belmont, Massachusetts. Room 101 is a place where first graders feel encouraged to speak and paint and write powerfully and for real
purposes, to be skilled at creating certain tangible products—this wonderful
rainbow picture, Billy's understated *Book of Pain*. A deeper skill is involved;
these children are mastering the further conditions of growth. They are
helping to create an intricate curriculum grounded in a profound reflec-
tiveness about a world they have a hand in making. With luck, this mastery—these habits of mind—will be theirs for the long run.

The Living Classroom is a book about how one teacher is able to enact—
to make manifest—a value. The value could be called love or respect,
except I'm afraid that to do so would be to lead readers into a familiar haze
of anti-intellectual sentimentality. This anti-intellectual haze is one barrier
to rethinking education. Let's be precise, intellectual. This book documents
an approach to children's thinking; the root value in Room 101 is in fact
respect for children's ideas. The children's works are the outward and visible signs of a teacher's respect for their thinking.

In the words of one observer, Ms. Amidon pays attention to what the
kids are paying attention to. She does this so thoroughly and insistently
and in such a well-organized classroom—a place arranged to capitalize on
the luck of the day—that ordinary first graders find their intellectual power
deepening in a hundred ways, including many that most schools and parents prize highly: the command of written expression, for example.

By paying passionate attention—by figuring out ways both to see and to help—Ms. Amidon makes enacting humane intellectual values the center of teaching. Her vivid example argues the case for what might be called a broad, cultural view of teaching. In this view, teaching children is not only or mainly the challenge of imparting specific skills but rather a whole approach to living together as a small provisional classroom community dedicated to the development of ideas. Jeanette Amidon's version of teaching involves a joint commitment on the part of teacher and kids to "activity of thought and receptiveness to beauty and humane feeling" that Alfred North Whitehead years ago packed like a dynamite stick into a single word: culture.

This is a first-grade classroom in which kids are learning to make, criticize, and renew humane intellectual culture. On this account alone it ought to be a very big story for a nation locked in uneasy cycles of confused and often trivial school reform. It confidently answers the biggest, usually unasked, question about school reform: What's the point? *The Living Classroom* answers by showing, not just telling. It is an all too rare opportunity to listen to a gifted practitioner thinking out loud in the company of David and Rosemary Armington.

The focus here is, however, Jeanette Amidon and the work she and the children do together. It's fascinating to see Ms. Amidon stepping on and off her high horse every few minutes, performing like some zany mixture of cook, janitor, and poet: She moves from the costumes for a class play to a hurt feeling to the fate of the human race, and then back to the felt-tip pen on which the universe balances.

I mention the pens again. They are no small matter. Felt-tip pens, Ms. Amidon argues in one revealing aside, make writing and drawing so much easier for first graders. They permit the stuff to flow—a key word—from fingertips and hands. They might be a good symbol for this whole operation. Kids don't learn from experience alone—that is a cliche, an educational bumper sticker. Raw experience often teaches nothing but confusion. Like the rest of us, kids really learn by reflecting on experience. Helping them reflect should be the basic job of teaching.

The way to do this best is by some teetering mix: a chance to do, to mess around, to experiment, and then reflect, either in talk or on paper or some other medium. Then back again for more experience to interrogate. Not one thing, but more than one thing, constantly reblended: the collision of raw material and reflection in the form of talk and writing and representation. It's important to keep this flow flowing—a teacher is performing when this happens, and managing the flow well from hour to hour may be the real heart of Jeanette Amidon's skill. The result of living in such a flow is a habit of mind, the confident capacity to interrogate experience constantly. Its possession is worth more than pearls and rubies. For first graders, as well as sophomores in college, the critical flow—the flow that swims to the top of all the other flowing things—is the flow of ideas.

Pens are means and metaphor for the ongoing river of reflection that makes Room 101 a fine place for children's minds. The pens are accessible to little kids, like phonetic spelling itself, which also allows their existing power over language to flow readily into ideas and reflection and a new skill: writing. Hard intellectual work, under such conditions, comes easy. You might even say it flows. This handsomely illustrated book must surely be the finest tribute to the felt-tip pen industry in the entire English language.

The children's works this book displays so beautifully are only the tip of a vast iceberg. One part of the iceberg you can't see is a developmental philosophy about children and the best conditions for their growth. The real hero in this classroom is not the *Book of Pain*, or even Billy or Celeste, but the power of growth itself, which, with thoughtful guidance, takes the kids along on its strong current past even the death of a father on into the life of the imagination. Throughout this book there is a focus on an approach to children that constantly builds a bridge from existing strengths to new learning. Ms. Amidon has faith in kids' power to generate serious ideas and worthy art. She conveys to kids that with her help they will take the next step and then the next after that.

And they do, even when the range is narrow and the stories are obsessional. The writing and art show the deep truth that Sigmund Freud stumbled on before he went on to more debatable conclusions: We are each of us the poet and artist of our own stories. Teaching that doesn't capitalize on this basic human fact is less powerful than teaching that taps into people's stories—in first grade, or in graduate seminars.

"Teaching children to think," like "teaching for understanding," is one of the earnest goals of today's earnest school reformers, especially those based in the universities. Jeanette Amidon is here to remind them that children are already thinking, thank you very much. It's the job of teachers to tap into this great and renewable—potentially infinite—resource.

How she does this is, of course, the question, to which there can be no single answer. This in itself is an important point: There is no one best system. The pursuit of the one best system is part of the traditional pathology of U.S. schools. What counts is not any one activity or thing but rather a developmental philosophy, an approach to working with kids, daily routines that respect mind and feelings through the exercise of what Frances Hawkins calls the logic of action.

No ideas but in things, William Carlos Williams once said about poetry—meaning that the concrete things energize a poem, whereas abstractions weaken its magnetic field. This holds for classroom teaching too. Take the abstraction, respect, for example, so central to the creation of a good intellectual community. A lot of adults respect children, but they are baffled at how to make respect manifest on a daily basis and even more baffled at how to enact a respect for children's minds as a routine matter.

Intangible respect hovers in the air of our schoolrooms like an unfulfilled romance or an unsent letter. Meanwhile too many of our schools continue as profoundly disrespectful environments for everybody involved—grown-ups as well as kids. We could all take lessons from Ms. Amidon. When the guppy dies, the response is swift: "We need a meeting." There is discussion, reflection, and then action. Language has direct purposes and concrete uses. No respect, Dr. Williams might say, but in visible acts of respect.

Pedagogically, Ms. Amidon's work represents a variation on a classic tradition that is sometimes called progressive education. I myself am still looking for the right label. "Progressive education" sounds dated, and besides, it always has a whiff of the unintended comedy captured by the famous *New Yorker* cartoon: "Teacher, do we have to do what we want to do again today?"

In the 1960s and 1970s, when "open education" was much to the fore— generating a body of remarkable creative work that is still part of the working pedagogical capital in many schools—I tried to get people to march under a banner I labeled "decent schools." I had no luck at all.

Maybe the truth is that if you deal in labels too much you end up in the gumming business. Whatever the labels, certain classic ideas are present here, made alive all over again as though rinsed by the fresh start that is young children's ongoing gift to a tired world.

One is the idea that a child learns well from experiences in which she has a vital stake, some genuine interest. Another is that much quality learning—learning that you can build on, that sticks to your bones—involves authentic performance: doing something real. Writing, for example, should be a means of saying something you want or need to say to some audience. It works less well as a school exercise you are doing because a large credentialed person orders you to do so. A third is the idea that a certain amount of the curriculum—a very great deal in Jeanette Amidon's case— can arise from a continuous reconstruction of experience generated by the ongoing activities of children. This doesn't just happen; it results from careful teaching: The teacher has to be organizer, catalyst, curriculum developer, and conductor.

A fourth idea is the importance of capitalizing on individual differences—not just accepting the intractable billiness of Billy, but taking advantage of it in a way that advances Billy's mind and his powers by tapping into his interests and his big stories—helping Billy make an education in which he can see his stories nested in wider stories about the world. A fifth idea is the collective power of common learning: the capacity of groups of children, under a teacher's guidance, to turn their shared conversation and insight and activities into a social medium of learning, so that a classroom becomes more than the sum of its individual parts, and children teach each other in an ongoing dialogue, creating a common classroom culture of ideas.

Every one of these ambitious ideas is in effect a large criticism of conventional schooling. Every single one has been enacted in some time and place by ordinary teachers—with the right support—in classrooms with all kinds of kids. People like me and Jeanette Amidon and the authors of this book have been pushing them for some years, and we are relative newcomers. Teaching this way is definitely not something new. It's actually one version of traditional education—going back at least as far as the founding of public education. Educational talk usually pits each new round of the New Education (this generation's version of progressive practice) against something called traditional education. It would be more accurate to say that the varieties of progressive practice from the 1820s on are a cumulative, dissenting tradition that stands in contrast to the lockstep and factory style that has won out in much public schooling.

This is traditional education too. In each generation since roughly the 1820s, thoughtful teachers in both public and private settings in many countries have discovered ways of working with children that are better than batch-processing and organized boredom. Often their work has been part of a dialogue with parents who were slowly democratizing child-rearing and making family life more of a conversation. This tradition of conversational practice and children's active learning—what we might call the democracy of experience—has not failed, though many obituaries have been printed. Although difficult to do, and making great demands on teachers, this style of teaching has often succeeded, and in fact has influenced schools a good deal—especially practice with younger children. And of course it has had an effect on families over the last few generations.

By now this counter tradition of respect for kids' minds has accumulated an impressive record with all sorts of children on many continents. The tradition tends to be most at home with young children and the early years of school—Jeanette Amidon's work is classic. And it is true that the most widespread practice in the 1960s and 1970s was in the elementary schools. (Although there is a history of superb high school and college work that is slowly getting forgotten, too.) One unfortunate by-product of recent reform movements from the point of view of those of us interested in kids' creativity is that reformers have pressured the elementary schools to become more boring. Environments that were once good for little children become as deadly and sterile as the high school up the street.

This may be the reason why I am tempted now to write the word "reform" in quotation marks. If school reform means no more recess for children, then I am no reformer. The reign of quantitative testing continues, even as the scientific foundation propping up the tests has eroded. Thoughtful people are exploring alternative means of assessment. Some "policy" groups are almost beginning to catch up to the lifetime wisdom of Miss Jones, a British school principal I met years ago. "Children," she once assured a group of American visitors, "do not get any heavier for being weighed."

Jeanette Amidon, like the Armingtons, is in part a product of open education and its earlier British cousins. Much U.S. reform of the 1960s and 1970s—inspired by teachers and parents, or projects like the federal Follow Through program, or the early years of Head Start—reflected vital and creative work in U.S. education. Their example could offer important clues for genuine school reform today. Ms. Amidon might be said to speak for several generations of school veterans who have struggled to advance a vision of children's imaginations on into times when children count for less and less in the nation's concerns.

Of course there are always problems in moving an approach that began with young learners up into classrooms with older kids. Open education often floundered when it came to making the intellectual connections necessary to the curriculum in the later years of school. Still, there has been enough success with the later years of schooling to build on. In some lucky places, teachers have succeeded. The real problems remain matters of value—fundamental views of how children best learn. David Armington speaks of some of the difficulties of promoting active learning with older kids. He points to a pretty common attitude: It may be okay for little kids to learn through play, but the idea that all students require serious play—that such play is the essence of intellectual life—is a hard sell in an anti-intellectual nation where the Puritan hangover keeps hanging over. The fear of big kids and their energy in this culture is one of its least attractive features.

Still, many of us see small, hopeful signs. There is a lot of ferment in schools these days, and a great deal of fresh interest in children's thinking. Kids' writing has been undergoing a renaissance for some time now. Jeanette Amidon's approach is not as rare as it once was. Real books are making inroads, where pinched school budgets allow. The idea that math should be a conversation about ideas has gotten a huge impetus from new math standards, which in turn reflect some very creative classroom practice. A host of today's efforts reflect another new round of a good old idea: that children can construct intelligent meanings.

Evaluation is getting another look. Some are starting to see the sense in Pat Carini's long-standing contention that the root of the word "evaluation" is "value." The question of what values we wish to enact is central to assessment. If you want to test splinter skills instead of real reading and real writing, then you are placing a value on splinters and slices instead of the whole, live hog. Parents and activists in poor communities are mutinying, as they should, and many are looking for alternatives. Many middle-class parents constitute a potential clientele for progressive practice. Some systems are scurrying to provide options for students within a responsible public framework, as many of the charter schools do. You hear the sound of some new fiddles playing old tunes. The long worldwide quest for alternatives to lockstep teaching may be resuming its hesitant U.S. march.

I agree with David Armington that rigid U.S. school systems need an American version of *perestroika*, although I am deeply worried about recent calls for privatizing education and turning public schools over to the mercies of the free market. In the free market the rich get richer and the poor poorer. With education, as with health care, we need a common system. Whether we will get one in a nation more and more divided by what Jonathan Kozol calls "savage inequalities" is, alas, an open question. Armington is right to point to experiments with parental choice within public systems as a promising development.

I connect many promising stirrings in education today to a wider uprising against Mr. Gradgrind, who has hogged the microphone in this country for far longer than his turn. Charles Dickens created him in the 19th century in his novel *Hard Times*, but he is now alive and well in America, where his investments in human greed have prospered mightily. Mr. Gradgrind is the arch bean counter of all time. He is suspicious of appeals to children's imaginations. He does not want children to have ideas, or think for themselves, or have fun. He would call Jeanette Amidon's class a circus and an anarchy. He is out to destroy public education, partly because he is an ideologue promoting private enterprise and unchecked competition, but mostly because he fears strong, free minds.

In each generation, Gradgrind's one best system of education done on the cheap is actually a huge, costly failure. The developmental ideas captured so well in Jeanette Amidon's work—whatever their considerable difficulties—have the merit of conforming to children's nature. They are complex and subtle ideas, but they are more practical and realistic in the long run than Mr. Gradgrind's sentimental illusions of control.

If there is one thread linking some of the hopeful educational developments in our often bleak landscape, it's the belief that an education suited to children's nature is in fact possible and that classrooms can provide opportunities for—above all—intelligent reflection on experiences that matter. Children's thinking—the serious play of all truly intellectual work—is the watchword of much of the best current practice, as well as the academic theory that is limping as it tries to catch up to practitioners like Jeanette Amidon. It's time to revise the reigning cliches again.

Lastly, a simple point that gets lost in the rivers of anxious words. Hundreds of thousands of children are bored stiff in our schools. This would be a crisis if it weren't somehow normal. Jeanette Amidon's children love what they are doing. How, as someone says in these pages, did learning to read ever get to be such a grim business? Pin up this sentence on the wall: "Enjoyment seems to be the key."

Vivian Paley

V IVIAN PALEY is famous for using narrative to document classroom
life, and stories as a technique in her own writing and teaching, so,
a story:

Our fourth child, Miranda, was an articulate 3-year-old. Though we
were very veteran parents—her older sisters were 11 and 17—we all acted
as though Miranda made sense in our terms and thought the way we mostly
did. If she said the butter knife needed the butter, we took this as a metaphor or a way of talking. We saw a language mistake rather than someone starting with a small stock of knowledge who was observing the knife
come to the table first and conjecturing that the knife needed the butter
to in some sense to confirm its identity as a butter knife. My wife Helen
bought and read *Molly Is Three*, and her mind was blown (as we still said
in those days) by the surreal and wondrous and funny and serious world
of the 3-year-old. It dramatized to all of us the habit of deeper listening
and the power and rewards of genuine curiosity; it was also a warning
to those of us who work with and think we understand children to keep
digging. Our middle daughter, Caitlin, has continued to be taken with
this wonderful book and the author she first encountered at the age of
11. In college, she wrote Paley asking if she could spend 2 weeks of a
winter break in her classroom. Paley said she could, and Caitlin did—an
enormously formative experience for her. She is now a preschool teacher
in Manhattan, having graduated from Bank Street, where in her portfo-
lio session she showed us all the amazing and sophisticated and masterly
work in storytelling and drama she and her 4-year-olds are doing—much
of this work modeled on Paley's approach to drama and literacy in the early
years. To round out this family snapshot our good friend Aki Sakuma
translated *Molly Is Three* into Japanese.

So each of us in our family portrait was changed by a Paley book. We
learned to listen to young children more carefully and to become more
curious about how their minds work—to make curiosity a renewable
resource in teaching practice, to take thinking more seriously, to be ever
more fascinated by the intellectual power and wit and imagination of the
child. Every one of us has learned from Paley that the more we look and

listen the more there is to see and that looking and listening are moral as well as intellectual disciplines. She has taught all of us a practice of living with kids that goes beyond teaching and beyond the realm of ideas. Her writings have touched our lives. She has helped us improve not only our practice of teaching but our practice of living.

We are only a tiny part of an old and growing Paley fan club. She is one of a few teachers awarded a MacArthur grant—the so-called genius grant. Paley retired not so long ago from the University of Chicago Lab School. She first made a splash in the late 1970s with *White Teacher*, a brilliant chronicle of children's thinking about race relations in one classroom—and a White teacher's voyage of self-discovery around the seas of her own mind and identity. It is a classic, widely read, in undergraduate courses as well as graduate seminars. If I say the sentence "What we value we talk about," many will feel the weight of that infinitely profound and much-discussed sentence from *White Teacher*. Paley's books are turning into standards of both teaching and the study of children's thinking.

Paley is a model of how to do careful classroom inquiry. She is a model for thinking about teaching and curriculum. Her writings provide some of the best examples I know of of how teaching itself can become a continuous line of inquiry and child study. Paley does her part to restore the teacher's voice to educational debate and discourse—and that voice is a radical one.

Studying children and their thinking, Paley models careful classroom inquiry. She is also a model of how to present such data. Her spare, pointed storytelling—she is an admirer of Jane Austen, and thinks of classroom life as a center of human drama—has not had nearly enough influence on academic research. Nor have many scholarly researchers tried for her broad audience. She and Karen Gallas have along with Michael Armstrong added to a small but wonderfully promising turn toward practitioner research. They are leading the way to a kind of research closely tuned to the rhythms and realities of life in classrooms, able to grapple with the kinds of problems that teachers, parents, and kids face, not the demands of university disciplinary specialties. Despite much good research on classrooms, especially in the subject matter areas, a good deal of university research remains narrow and dull, and lacks genuine curiosity about kids' thinking—lacks life. Like Eleanor Duckworth, Paley takes Jean Piaget's basic technique—talking to children—and makes it into a principle of research and practice—divorced from any Piagetian orthodoxy. Paley's work refocuses us on children and teachers learning together—the two-way influence of mind on mind—which ought to be a fundamental educational topic. In a country and field beset by success stories and claims of instant results, Paley's research reflects the ongoing dilemmas of practice, failures and sorrows and pratfalls, as well as successes. In a field increasingly distorted by the shrinking lenses of scholarly specializations, she writes in a human voice for a wider audience than specialists.

Paley provides an example of a teacher reflecting on teaching and on her curriculum. *White Teacher, Kwanzaa and Me,* and *You Can't Say You Can't Play* are handbooks for the social curriculum. Her books exploring superheroes and the play of girls and boys and kids at distinct early ages all add profound insight into children's struggle to make sense of the world and to interpret it. *The Girl With the Brown Crayon* can be read as a kind of toolkit for ambitious work in early literacy. These books show one teacher rescuing literacy and drama from small technique—though accounts of good technique abound—to recapture the point of stories and books—imagination, and the interpretation of life. In a practical fashion, Paley shows how a teacher makes literature a humane encounter with texts, passions, and ideas—with life itself. She should be read by teachers in high schools and colleges, though few would see the relevance. Her work illustrates the truth of Deborah Meier's great dictum: that the ideal education from first grade through college would be a blend of good preschool practice and the approach of our best graduate seminars. These are the places where students are encouraged to have ideas and to pursue their own passions and interests—two essential aspects of any good education. Teachers at all levels have a lot to learn from Paley, if only they have ears to hear.

For teacher education programs like my own at Michigan State, Paley illustrates how teaching itself can be a continuous line of inquiry—how you can arrange to study children as you teach them subject matter. She demonstrates that the old polarity that says we have to choose between teaching the subject and teaching the child is profoundly false. I teach a course for entering juniors in the MSU program; it involves, among other things, a semester-long study of one child. Along with children's literature and other topics, we read *White Teacher* and *Girl With a Brown Crayon* as some of our examples of teaching with inquiry. Of all the teachers who are cases in that course, Paley is by far the favorite; she is the teacher my students really want to grow up to be. When my students become interns—nearly full-time for a year in a classroom with a veteran teacher—their inquiry projects reflect this thread. In many cases, the habit of child study is formed, and becomes an integral part of students' picture of teaching practice. My students learn the profound truth that curiosity and listening are renewable resources, and that most children respond to being paid attention to by flourishing and working hard—and learning.

We are living through an era when too many reformers are trying to change the schools by means of reforms that bypass teachers. Too many politicians and others are trying to change schools from the outside, trying (vainly) to script teachers and restrict their responses to kids. In the middle of all this, Paley stands as a beacon of sanity, saying, in effect, that there will be no real change in schools without the active support of teachers and more support *for* teachers, in both money and time. Paley reminds current reformers, bent on controlling classrooms though high-stakes testing, of the need for unpredictable human encounters. She shows that conversation on the wing lies at the heart of all good teaching. She shows that teaching is an uncertain art, and will always remain so—at the same time that she shows how a teacher can make her moves with intelligence and real authority and big intellectual ambitions for the children she teaches. Paley dramatizes and demonstrates the responsibility of teachers to lead groups of children, and in doing so she shows us the nature of legitimate adult authority in a convincing way. To a culture somewhat confused about legitimate adult authority in classrooms and other settings this is a real contribution.

Paley's portrait of her own authority includes grappling with the central issues of the time. The classroom, to use one of her favorite metaphors, is a stage for small dramas that enact the human condition in a particular time and place. *White Teacher* is a window on kids exploring race in the post-civil-rights era. *Kwanza and Me* and *The Girl With the Brown Crayon* reflect the hopes of our society at the same time that they illuminate teaching and learning. *Boys and Girls: Superheroes in the Doll Corner* shows how children mirror and make sense of the changing relations between men and women. Paley listens at the play corner—the place, as she says, where kids do the most sophisticated thinking—and tells us that children are always exploring who is powerful and who is less so—that growing up involves politics in a broad sense. Paley knows that education is always bigger than the topics of classrooms and schooling. In writing about her classroom, Paley is telling us about America and about life itself—her classroom is a stage for all the dramas of our times as well as the dramas of childhood.

Paley's books dramatize a woman's life in teaching—these vivid stories restore the teacher's voice to educational debate and discourse. Her own feelings about growing up Jewish become part of the story about why a teacher is concerned with African-American outsiders in *White Teacher*. This autobiography runs through all the books. Paley is part of a relatively fresh tradition—a movement in literature—that includes such classics as Elwyn Richardson's *In the Early World* and Herbert Kohl's *36 Children*. This movement brings the dramas and passions of live children and living teachers and the practice of teaching into literature. Molly with her wit and radiant intelligence is one of the great literary characters of the last 30 years. So is Reeny, the girl with the brown crayon. So is Paley, for surely one of Paley's finest creations is herself. This is the biggest favor she has done for those of us introducing a new generation to teaching. Paley is a genuine hero to students in our program: Her books humanize and dramatize teaching and remind us that teaching is an affair of passion and tears and laughter. Bloodless talk of teacher knowledge and dry university lectures on pedagogy badly need this more human and insistent voice that does justice to the true romance and drama of teaching. It is, for example, terribly moving in *The Girl With the Brown Crayon* that Paley is retiring—wondering what will come next. Paley paints herself as a hero who is fallible and often wrong. She doubts and reflects and worries about what to do next—unlike the John Wayne teachers in Hollywood films, who always know just what to do. She is often the straight man in a comic routine in which the children and life outstrip her ability to control and predict the next turn of events. By Paley's own accounts she is bowled over by the variety and intelligence of the children. Their creativity and experience surprise her into change. How refreshing in this solemn time of national educational reform to see Paley slipping and falling on her banana peel. All of course is not laughter. The real sadness and despair of real children—the fatalism of Clara and Angelo, their knowledge that they will always be rejected—have a message for us. For the most part Paley makes the moves that help children and herself pull together. In the end all her work is a celebration of the enormous power of groups of children led by thoughtful teachers to heal and teach each other. The sleeping giant in every classroom is this potential of groups to educate each other and help each other grow as a community. But without a teacher's conversation and curiosity, the group itself won't become a real community of learners.

The last quality I want to praise is less obvious because Paley writes so modestly and looks so much like someone's favorite grandmother. This is her radicalism, which is both an intellectual and a political quality. Paley has long been a deeply Socratic voice in education, insisting that you can't really teach people something they don't already know. This is the skeptical liberal spirit of Socrates, increasingly rare on the utilitarian and philistine U.S. campus. So many of her books are radical in another sense—she shows how a teacher can work modestly for a society very different from the racist and unequal society we now have.

In her quiet and thoughtful way, she is one of the strongest and most powerful critics of the complacency of our schools in relation to fairness and justice. *You Can't Say You Can't Play* is a prophecy about the costs to Clara and Angelo of business as usual in our schools. After Columbine and many other warnings, it's time to heed Paley's warning that our schools need to move against the grain of a society ruled by bosses and unequals. In the magnificent passages where she finally decides to enact the rule "you can't say you can't play," Paley is showing us how, in the compass of one school and one classroom, a teacher can do her bit and throw her weight against the deep unfairness that corrodes American life and threatens our hopes for a real democracy. "By kindergarten," she writes, "a structure begins to be revealed and will soon be carved in stone. Certain children will have the right to limit the social experiences of their classmates. Henceforth a ruling class will notify others of their acceptability and the outsiders will learn to anticipate the sting of rejection. Long after hitting and namecalling have been outlawed, a more damaging phenomenon is allowed to take root." There might be another way, she suggests. It might take its text from Leviticus:

> The stranger that sojourneth with you shall be unto you as the homeborn among you and thou shalt love him as thyself; for you were strangers in the land of Egypt.

Vivian Paley has taught my students the true romance of teaching. In a teacher education program in a big bureaucratic university, she speaks in a human voice about the intimacy of a lifetime with kids. In a time when teachers and kids are getting scripted curricula and high-stakes testing and narrow philistine and utilitarian visions of school, she vindicates the power of one teacher to help open children's minds and imaginations. She shows all of us, but best of all the rising generation of new teachers, that the agenda of kids' intellect and imagination and the agenda of social justice for kids are deeply connected—and that everything flows from respect and curiosity. "Leave no child behind" is a worthy motto even if the Bush administration has kidnapped it. Paley demonstrates a kind of teaching that could make this possible. This is the same message we hear from our other wise and grandmotherly teacher, Deborah Meier. Standing against shriveled visions of school reform that ignore teachers and the nature of children, these two women—significantly they are women—are prophets of education for a more equal and democratic America. They tell us that teaching will triumph when we learn to be more passionately curious about Molly— and that a deep curiosity about one child's mind is the richest and most practical way of signaling real respect. They say that nothing in education matters more than the question of respect for teachers and children.

Letter to a Young Teacher

January 1995

D EAR JOSIE,
You asked me for some advice about starting out as a teacher and what popped into my head first is an image of my grandmother. I never met her, but she remains a strong presence. She was the principal of a small, mostly immigrant elementary school in the Pennsylvania coal country. The stories of her teaching got buried with her, as so many teachers' stories do. She was one of many urban Irish Catholics who took part in the progressive educational and political movements of her day. I know that she was ambitious about kids' learning. The immigrant coal miners' children, whose families were often out of work, were to read high-class literature and poetry—she had a weakness for the English poet Robert Browning. She also checked to see that kids brushed their teeth. She was a force in local and state politics, fighting for labor rights, pioneering in women's rights, and leading the movement to end child labor. She was the first woman elected to the state Democratic committee in Pennsylvania. I think she saw a direct link between politics and her practice in education. Both had as their aim the general progress of ordinary people. She was on the people's side, creating an expansive democratic vision of education based on the idea of a country that would work for everybody, not just for the rich.

This seems to me a perspective—a tradition, really—worth reminding ourselves about in a confused political time. Fewer teachers now put matters in terms of politics, although it seems to me that teaching in the United States today more than ever involves a political commitment. I would argue that, like my grandmother, you should think of yourself as a recruit on the people's side, working to build a democracy that doesn't yet exist but is part of the American promise. My grandmother would surely point out that there is important work to be done both in and out of classrooms, and that sometimes school matters get framed by wider social issues. I'm sure that my grandmother would say that teachers today have a vital stake in a national health care system, for she always saw the connection between kids' learning and good health. Brushing your teeth and Browning were inseparable.

163

Thinking of her reminds me that society and its schools are both battlegrounds, on which different sides fight for rival visions of America and its possibilities. The real basics in education, she would argue, flow from the kind of country you want the kids to make when they grow up. She was voting for a real, rather than a paper, democracy. And she thought that teachers had a role to play in helping the people become more powerful.

New teachers often don't realize that there are sides to take, and that they are called upon to choose. The old idea that education is above politics is a useful half-truth—it helps keep the schools from being politicized. But it conceals the essentially political character of choices we make for kids. Do we see the children we teach today as low-paid workers for the global economy, or as the reserve army of the unemployed? If so, why be ambitious for their hearts and minds? Alternatively, we can frame fundamental aims: that we are creating a first-rate education for everybody's kids, so that as grown-ups they can make a democracy happen. My grandmother and many in her generation would say that schools should offer what students need to take part in a democratic society and its culture—a complex package for everybody's children that would equip them for full participation in work, culture, and liberty.

This is clearly an ambitious goal, rarely achieved in world history, let alone in America. Schools alone can never accomplish it. Still, our sense of the purpose of education matters, and for a long while too many of our schools have not believed in educating all of the people. The old Greeks said that some were born gold and others brass, and they designed education accordingly. A slave or a woman would not get a free man's education. Over the centuries around the planet, a lot of the human race has agreed, establishing separate educations for rulers and ruled. Hewers of wood and drawers of water would not read Jane Austen in advanced placement English classes. In a democracy, however, the people are supposed to rule. They are, the old phrase has it, the equal of kings. So the people need an education commensurate with their potential political, economic, and cultural power. To give the children of ordinary people the kind of education once reserved for the children of the elites—to do this for the first time in history—is the dream of the builders of U.S. education like Horace Mann and my grandmother and thousands of others who triumphed and struggled and died in obscurity.

You are a newcomer to a historic struggle. Some of this you may have learned already, just by keeping your eyes open. You probably know that the United States has always been a deeply flawed democracy and that education has always mirrored the systematic inequality of society. There was no golden age when the United States did right by everybody's kids.

This society still has vastly different expectations for well-off and poor kids. The gap seems to be growing, not shrinking. We are two educational nations. The schools for poor kids that you may visit and teach in will often look like schools in a desperately poor nation, not in the world's most powerful country. Textbooks are old, the roof leaks, and there is a shortage of paper. People of color and women and immigrants had to fight their way into the educational feast and are still kept at the margins in many schools. But you also need to know that in each generation, strong teachers like my grandmother have worked with parents and communities to make democracy happen. Her ghost is silently cheering you on.

My grandmother was not alone in thinking that schools have a special responsibility for the progress of the people's culture. In taking a large, ambitious, ample—democratic—view of education's aims, she was opposing minimalist views that reduce children to tiny gears in the nation's great economic machine. She was opposing the oldest human superstition of all, the belief in fundamental inequality. She was also laying rude hands on the second oldest superstition, the belief that because there is never enough to go around, existing unfairness must be endured. My grandparents' generation had a healthy respect for policies that generate jobs for the people, but they never made the mistake of thinking that all of life is embraced by the equations of economists or the maxims of bankers and investors. The economy should serve human life and its needs, not the other way around. There is, the old progressives argued, no real wealth but life. Making a living ought to be a means to a wider end: making a life. And in fact, students educated to fit narrow economic grooves—management's view of what will suffice for today's workforce —will never be equipped to take part in debates and movements to change society and build a democratic economy in which everybody has a fair share and basic security.

The capacity to participate—in work, in politics, in the thought of the times—is really in the end a matter of cultural development. The key to the people's success will be the quality of their characters and their minds— the quality of their culture. It is this hardheaded grasp of the radical importance of culture that makes the progressives of my grandmother's generation worth listening to again today. Symbols and ideas and understanding have to become the property of the people if they are to ever gain any control over their lives and the lives of their children. Symbols and ideas and words and culture are no replacement for jobs or political power, but without them, people will easily lose their way. Many in my grandmother's generation admired Eugene Debs, who once said that he would not lead the people to the promised land, because if he could take them there, some other leader could convince them to leave.

In a democracy, people should be educated to be powerful, to tell their stories, to make their own voices heard, and to act together to defend and expand their rights. Culture might be said to be a shorthand word for all the ways that people and their imaginations and identities grow—how we construct the world and make ourselves at home in it, and then reinvent it fresh.

Schoolteachers of my grandmother's era had an almost mystical reverence for the word *growth*. This is how you can tell that, for all their toughness (my aunt Mary had my grandmother in the fourth grade and said that she was really strict), they were Romantics under the skin. In tough times, against heavy odds, with huge polyglot classes, they kept alive an idea of democratic education itself as a romance. This language doesn't fit our current skeptical mood and circumstance. It has an extravagant and sentimental sound—it's the language of possibility, democratic hope. The old progressives believed in a version of true romance. Some got these ideas from politics, some from religion, and some from poetry, believe it or not. My grandmother mixed her poetry and her politics into a potent brew. One of her favorite Romantic poets, John Keats, put the argument for a Romantic, democratic view of culture this way: Now the human race looks like low bushes with here and there a big tree; spin from imaginative experience an "airy citadel" like the spider's web, "filling the air with beautiful circuiting," and every human might become great; in the right educational and cultural environment, everybody would grow to the full height, and humanity "instead of being a wide heath of furze and briars with here and there a remote pine or oak, would become a grand democracy of forest trees."

A forest of oak trees: This democratic and Romantic view of a people's culture—articulated in the nineteenth century by poets like Keats and Walt Whitman and 19th dreamers like Margaret Fuller, Elizabeth Cady Stanton, Margaret Haley, Jane Addams, W. E. B. Du Bois, Eugene Debs, and John Dewey—insists that the goal for which we struggle is a democratic culture in which everyone can grow to full height and take part in the world of ideas, books, art, and music as well as work and politics. To hardheaded teachers like my grandmother, this was a version of true romance—true, because they knew that no kid grows on a diet of dry academic splinters and stunted expectations. If you teach kids just minimalist stuff—isolated skills, for example—they never get to practice and enact the real thing, culture itself. They get slices of the animal but not the whole live hog. They lose what Emily Dickinson called the thing with feathers—hope. In today's hard times, ruled by bastard pragmatism, it is important to insist that beauty is a human necessity, like water and food and love and work. The multiplication tables need memorizing. So do the French verbs. Not all learning is fun. My grandmother and her husband knew all about the virtues and necessities of hard work. But an idea of learning that leaves out grace and poetry and laughter will never take root in kids' hearts and souls. Education is in the end a movement of the spirit. This is the realism behind the old vision of education as true romance. Children require, finally, things that cannot be bought and sold, accomplishments that last a lifetime. They are asking for bread. Too many of our schools are giving them stones instead. From our point of view today, the school culture of my grandmother's generation may have been too genteel—a White schoolmarm culture that often ignored or disdained the experience of immigrants, women, and people of color. It was a monochromatic culture, tied into the many weaknesses of gentility. But what is impressive today about it is the depth of its democratic aspirations: the assumption that everyone will rise up on the wings of hope.

As today, Americans in the past argued over whose version of culture to teach. The tug-of-war over today's (quite recent) canons of literature and history is an inevitable aspect of being what Whitman called a people of peoples. I believe—though my grandmother might disagree—that such tugging and pulling is a sign of cultural vitality, part of a process of democratic change that Whitman described as "lawless as snowflakes." The arguments over whose version of culture to teach will properly go on until the republic closes shop. A democracy educates itself by arguing over what to teach the next generation. But as grown-up groups struggle for each generation's balance of pride and recognition and representation and inclusion, we need to keep in mind how important it is for kids to be allowed to make and do culture, to participate in enacting live meanings and symbols. Opening up the school curriculum to the world's rainbows of cultures is a necessary step toward becoming a people of peoples, a real democracy—creating an education that helps kids become good citizens not only of their own country, but of the world. But it will not be much of a gain to substitute a new multicultural and multiracial orthodoxy for an older cultural orthodoxy. Nobody's version of the canon will matter if kids don't start reading real books sometime. Unless kids get a chance to make cultural meaning, and not passively absorb it, nothing will come alive. Anybody's version of culture can be delivered secondhand and dead. The real challenge is to help kids make cultural meanings come alive here and now, to act as creators and critics of culture, armed with the skills and discipline to—as Emerson put it—marry form and power. And what holds for kids surely holds for teachers too.

A Romantic and democratic vision of human possibility may in the end be a practical thing for teachers—as real as radium, and more valuable. Teaching is, after all, more like taking part in a religion or a political movement than anything else—the whole thing rests on what the old theologians called the virtue of hope. Its loss kills more kids than guns and drugs. The technocratic lingo of the educational managers and the boredom of today's colleges of education do no service to a profession that in the end requires true romance, the stuff that lights up the soul. Who would rise up on a cold, dark morning and go out to teach if the only goal were to raise the SAT scores? A democratic vision helps you not only in rethinking your purposes, in choosing the curriculum, for example, but also in making it through those February days when the radiators are banging and teaching school feels like the dark night of the soul. It says on the Liberty Bell, across the crack, that the people without vision shall perish. This should be a warning to us in an educational era dominated by dull experts, squinty-eyed economists, and frightened politicians. You will never survive your years as a teacher by listening to what passes for vision now in the United States.

Teachers and the rest of us need to start reimagining an expansive and democratic vision of education as true romance—not the romance of sentimentality and fakery and escape (the media have stuffed us all with too many such lies) but the true romance that knows that the heart is the toughest human muscle, the romance of respect for the people and what their children's minds are capable of.

To enact this true romance, we need to do many things. We need a democratic version of the humanities and the liberal arts from kindergarten through the university. At the university level, as in the schools, the older traditions of the "liberal arts" and the "humanities" and elite science and math are often preserves for privilege, crusted over with the practices and superstitions of human inequality. But the people's children deserve the best, and such subjects and traditions need to be rescued for them. Culture needs to be democratized, not abandoned. The people have a right to claim their heritage and take possession of what generations of leisure have given the privileged. Poor kids deserve the kind of education rich kids get.

Underlying the daily work in schools, then, is the task of creating a democratic culture, a task that may take generations. Of course, a genuine people's culture, when it emerges, will look very different from the oily "people's cultures" concocted by the commissars in totalitarian regimes. To begin such work, teachers need to be able to see "culture" in its several meanings: what used to be called the "high" culture, the traditional symbols of academic learning, the great books and works of art and music; newcomers to the canon; and also the local webs of meaning and tradition arising out of the lives of students and communities. Today we want to interrogate the old "high" culture and ask whom it included and whom it left out. But in the end, we also want our kids to get access, to break into the old vaults as well as savor new treasures.

Instead of thinking of culture as a separate realm of "high" experience, an elite commodity, we want to show our kids the common continuum of human experience that reaches from the great works of art of all times and cultures to children's talk and imagining right now, to help students move back and forth from their experience to the experiences embodied in poems, artworks, and textbooks. Skills matter, but they need to connect to a vision. Unlike my grandmother's generation, we want the visions of culture offered in our schools to be true rainbow bridges that the children crisscross daily in both directions—the home and neighborhood cultures on one end, and the wider worlds of culture on the other.

My grandmother had a vision of a teacher going forth to bring culture to the people. What we might add to that today is the image of the people and their children giving something back in a true exchange of gifts. Today we might be in a better position to see that culture-making in the schools has to be a two-way street. The idea of culture embraced by the school must also reach out to embrace the cultures of the students and their families.

As a teacher on the side of the people, you need to make yourself a careful student of the care and feeding of small, provisional human communities, for these are where people learn to make cultural meaning together, to practice and create the people's culture. This is why John Dewey called schools "embryonic democracies" and why some of the old reformers called them "little commonwealths." Classroom communities require certain elements: learning to talk the talk, learning to listen respectfully, finding a voice, learning to make and criticize knowledge in a group, giving and taking, finding the blend of intellectual and emotional support that a good classroom group can provide, valuing the habits and skills of reading and writing that arise when speakers and writers and artists get responses from audiences and listeners and readers. The discipline that lasts comes from participation, and it is the discipline of freedom.

In practice, then, helping the people progress in cultural terms means the ongoing creation of provisional forms of community. In good schools, students are learning not only skills but how to use them to make culture—the kind of broad, powerful, and purposeful meanings we associate with intellectual, artistic, scientific, and democratic communities—and to forge links between the kind of culture they are enacting in school and the cultures of their communities. In school subjects, they learn the discourse of many of the smaller worlds that make up the large world of culture, literacy, and the languages of math and science and the arts, as well as the logic of action required to go on making, remaking, and criticizing different kinds of community over a lifetime.

With her union background, my grandmother would warn you about of the need for solidarity as an educational ideal. The elites who manage today's schools want you to stay isolated and to think of education and politics as mainly a matter of competition between individuals. My grandmother would tell you something different: that we are brothers and sisters, that we learn from one another, and that we will have to work out a common fate on a troubled and threatened planet. Not only that, but to the extent that we remain isolated, the Gradgrinds will prevail. Look at the way they used the racial issue to divide the forces of American democracy throughout the 20th century.

Although individual students make the meanings, the business of taking part in culture always means participation in some kind of community, real or imagined. You are part of a music community, even when you play the guitar alone. Math skills and ideas have as their aim participation in the community of those who make, who "do," math. The old Greeks emphasized the communal side of math when they called it a performance art and—to our astonishment today—linked it with such communal arts as theater and dancing. They would be amazed to hear that we make kids study math solo, rather than reasoning together as a group.

I emphasize the community angle not to slight the individual—all education has to balance individual and social aims—but to stress the way that the individuality we prize so deeply in our students emerges from what they learn through community encounters with others, their families, peers, and teachers. But students who haven't learned to listen won't have much of a chance of finding their distinctive voices; nor will students who have never spoken in class about something that really matters to them or made some significant choices at some important points about their own learning.

My grandmother's generation was in love with the idea of growth. It's easy to see the importance of growth for students, but how about for you? When you start teaching, you do not know enough, but you are also not culturally developed enough to be a model for your students. This might be particularly true if you come from a family that never had much access to "high" culture. Even if you got a lot of "culture," is it really yours, or is it a ragbag of secondhand experiences and unexplained views? How do you help your kids build the rainbow bridges back and forth? How can you sell them on literacy if you yourself don't read much and don't enjoy books? What about your identity as a teacher? What about the struggle for democracy? You might like the picture of the teacher going out to meet the people, but what do you really have to offer? This is a harsh question, but you have a big responsibility if you are signing up as a teacher. How do you start the lifetime work of becoming a practical intellectual who can help the people progress culturally?

The question of your own cultural development may in the end be the big question about your future as a teacher. With some attention, I think that you can begin to see how democracy is the underlying issue in our society today, and how education reflects a wider, worldwide struggle. It may be more difficult to see the democratic cultural challenge; to see that a lively discussion of *Frog and Toad* in the second grade is one step toward a people's culture. A vision helps, but it needs to come alive daily in your teaching practice. How can you start to become a practical intellectual who is able to bring culture to the people's children and able to accept their gifts back? This will never be easy. But don't despair, you aren't dead yet. There are lots of ways to begin expanding your own possession of culture, ranging from exploring your roots to developing your own literacies and your acquaintance with ideas, traditions, and symbols in a host of realms. My grandmother, with her message of solidarity, would urge you not to go it alone, to join up with other teachers and reach out to people in your community. Your own ability to nourish a learning community in your classrooms will be helped immeasurably if you yourself inhabit—and help create—genuine learning communities outside of class. The things you want for your students—the development of skills, culture, interests, identities, and a voice—are all things that you need as a teacher. One or two genuine interests to share with kids are worth their weight in gold. Finding one or two ways to link your teaching to the wider struggle for democracy will show you the meaning of your work. Read Herbert Kohl's great essay "The Good Old Days . . ." in his collection *Should We Burn Babar* to begin to get a sense that history and democratic tradition are resources to draw on in the work of teaching. Learn something about your own history, because that can give you an important angle on where you stand in relation to culture making.

Culture is like—is another name for—growth and development and education itself. Like history, it has no end. Generations of thoughtful teachers have taken part in the long struggle. Now, just your luck, it's your turn. All the best.

Joseph Featherstone

P. S. I call you "Josie" because that's what W. E. B. Du Bois calls his student in his sketch of himself as a teacher in the rural South in *The Souls of Black Folk*. Josie represents all the life and vitality of the people and craves a formal education, which she never gets, dying young. Du Bois was the young teacher going out to meet the people, and Josie was the people meeting the teacher. Both had something to offer in the exchange. The result for Du Bois was the complex educational agenda embodied in *The Souls of Black Folk*[1]: to learn the ways and the powers of the wider culture represented by school learning and the classics, but to keep your soul and know your roots. Du Bois was the spiritual granddaddy of the civil rights generation—he died in exile just as the 1963 March on Washington was taking place—but his vision of a democratic culture awaits our work. I know that the dreadful premature harvest of young Josies has not stopped, but I like to think that some are making their way into teaching, like you.

NOTE

1. This passage was quoted, significantly, by that Romantic John Dewey (1934) in *Art as Experience*, his great argument for a democratic approach to art and culture.

References

Aries, Philippe (1962). *Centuries of childhood*, New York: Vintage.

Blackie, John (1971). *Inside the primary school*, New York: Schocken Books.

Bourne, Randolph (1916). *The Gary schools*, Boston: Houghton Mifflin.

Bourne, Randolph (September 1917). "Conscience and intelligence in war," *The Dial*.

Bourne, Randolph (October 1917). "Twilight of idols," *Seven Arts*.

Boyer, Ernest, and the Carnegie Foundation for the Advancement of Teaching (1983). *High school: A report on secondary education in America*, New York: Harper & Row.

Buber, Martin (1949). *Paths in Utopia*, London: Routledge & K. Paul.

Chase, Richard (1957). *The American novel and its tradition*, New York: Doubleday.

Coleman, James S. (1961). *The adolescent society: The social life of the teenager and its impact on education*, New York: The Free Press.

Coleman, James S., with the assistance of John W. C. Johnston and Kurt Jonassohn (1966). *Equality of educational opportunity*, Washington, DC: U.S. Government Printing Office.

Dennison, George (1969). *The lives of children*, New York: Random House.

Dewey, John (1902). *The child and the curriculum and the school and society*, Chicago: University of Chicago Press.

Dewey, John (1907). *The school and society*, Chicago: University of Chicago Press.

Dewey, John (1916). *Democracy and education*, New York: Macmillan.

Dewey, John (1925). *Experience and nature*, Chicago: Open Court Publishing.

Dewey, John (1933). *Art as experience*, New York: Minton, Balch.

Dickens, Charles (1854). *Hard times*, New York: T. L. McElrath.

Du Bois, W. E. B. (1903). *The souls of black folk: Essays and sketches*, Chicago: A. C. McClurg.

Featherstone, Joseph (2000). *Brace's cove*, Kalamazoo, MI: New Issues.

Goffman, Erving (1959). *The presentation of self in everyday life*, New York: Anchor Press.

Goodlad, John (1984). *A place called school: Prospects for the future*, New York: McGraw-Hill.

Goodman, Paul (1960). *Growing up absurd: Problems of youth in the organized system*, New York: Random House.

Goodman, Paul and Percival (1947). *Communitas: Means of livelihood and ways of life*, Chicago: University of Chicago Press.

Goodwin, Richard (January 4, 1969). "Sources of public unhappiness," *The New Yorker*.

Glazer, Nathan (July 1969). "Student politics and the university," *The Atlantic Monthly*.

Hawkins, David (1974). *The informed vision: Essays on learning and human nature*, New York: Agathon Press.

Hebrews, 13:14. New Testament.

Hirsch, E. D. (1987). *Cultural literacy: What every American needs to know*, Boston: Houghton Mifflin.

Hofstadter, Richard (1963). *Anti-intellectualism in American life*, New York: Knopf.

James, Henry (1886). *The Bostonians*, New York: Macmillan.

James, William (1977). *A pluralistic universe*, Cambridge, MA: Harvard University Press. (original work published 1909)

Jencks, Christopher (1972). *Inequality: A reassessment of the effect of family and schooling in America*, New York: Basic Books.

Keniston, Kenneth, and Carnegie Council on Children (1978). *All our children : The American family under pressure*, New York: Harcourt Brace Jovanovich.

Kessen, William (1965). *The child*, New York: Wiley.

Keynes, John Maynard (1924). *Monetary reform*, New York: Harcourt Brace.

Kundera, Milan (1980). *The book of laughter and forgetting*, New York: A. A. Knopf.

Lasch, Christopher (1977). *Haven in a heartless world: The family besieged*, New York: Basic Books.

Lawrence-Lightfoot, Sara (1983). *The good high school: Portraits of character and culture*, New York: Basic Books.

Lazerson, Marvin (1985). *An education of value: The purposes and practices of schools*, New York: Cambridge University Press.

Lynd, Robert S., and Lynd, Helen Merrell (1929). *Middletown: A study in modern American culture*, New York: Harcourt Brace Jovanovich.

Meier, Deborah (1995). *The power of their ideas: Lessons for America from a small school in Harlem*, Boston: Beacon Press.

Moynihan, Daniel Patrick (1965). *The Negro family: The case for national action*, Washington, DC: Office of Policy Planning and Research.

Moynihan, Daniel Patrick (1969). *Maximum feasible misunderstanding: Community action in the war on poverty*, New York: Macmillan.

Mumford, Lewis (1926). *The golden day: A study in American experience and culture*, New York: Boni and Liveright.

O'Neill, Eugene (1956). *Long day's journey into night*, New Haven, CT: Yale University Press.

Orwell, George (1940). "Inside the whale," from *Inside the whale and other essays*, London: Victor Gollancz.

Perrone, Vito (1998). *Teacher with a heart: Reflections on Leonard Covello and community*, New York: Teacher's College Press.

Péguy, Charles (1958). Alexander Dru, trans., Pierre Manent, foreword, *Temporal and eternal*, Liberty Fund. (The "mysticism" quote is from the 1910 essay *Notre jeunesse*, which appears in this volume in an edited and abbreviated form.)

Ravitch, Diane (2000). *Left back: A century of failed school reforms*, New York: Simon & Schuster.

Riesman, David, with Reuel Denney and Nathan Glazer (1950). *The lonely crowd: A study of the changing American character*, New Haven: Yale University Press.

Rousseau, Jean-Jacques (1933). *Emile*. New York: E. P. Dutton. (Original work published in 1762)

Sen, Amartya (2001). *Development as freedom*, New York: Oxford University Press.

Silberman, Charles E. (1970). *Crisis in the classroom: The remaking of American education*, New York: Random House.

Sizer, Theodore (1984). *Horace's compromise: The dilemma of the American high school*, Boston: Houghton Mifflin.

Thernstrom, Stephan (1964). *Poverty & progress: Social mobility in a nineteenth-century city*, Cambridge, MA: Harvard University Press.

Twain, Mark (1883). *Life on the Mississippi*, Boston: J. R. Osgood.

Twain, Mark (1889). *A Connecticut yankee in King Arthur's court*, New York: Charles L. Webster.

Tyack, David (1974). *The one best system: A history of American urban education*, Cambridge, MA: Harvard University Press.

U.S. Department of Labor, Office of Policy Planning and Research (1981). *The Negro family: The case for national action*, Westport, CT: Greenwood Press.

Veblen, Thorstein (1914). *The instinct of workmanship and the state of the industrial arts*, New York: Macmillan.

White, Morton (1947). *Social thought in America: The revolt against formalism*, Boston: Beacon.

White, Morton (1972). *Science and sentiment in America*, New York: Oxford University Press.

Whitman, Walt (1881). "Calamus," from *Leaves of Grass*, Boston: J. R. Osgood. (original work published in 1860)

Wordsworth, William (1888). "My Heart Leaps Up," from *The complete poetical works*, London: Macmillan. (original work published in 1802)

Index

Education Week listed **Joseph Featherstone** as one of 100 notables who have influenced U.S. education in the last century. He is one of the founders and faculty leaders of an acclaimed teacher education program at Michigan State University. He has taught at Harvard and Brown Universities, served as principal of the Commonwealth School in Boston, and was for many years an editor of the *New Republic*, where he wrote on education, politics, and literature. He is the author of two books on education and school reform (*Schools Where Children Learn*, Liveright, 1971; and *What Schools Can Do*, Liveright, 1976), and a poet whose recent collection is *Brace's Cove* (New Issues, 2000).

Caitlin Featherstone teaches 3- and 4-year-olds in New York City. She earned a Master's in Education at Bank Street College.

Liza Featherstone is an author, journalist, and critic. She lives in New York City.

DATE DUE